CONTENTS *Part Two: Stitch 'n Bitch Patterns*

stitch 'n bitch
part one

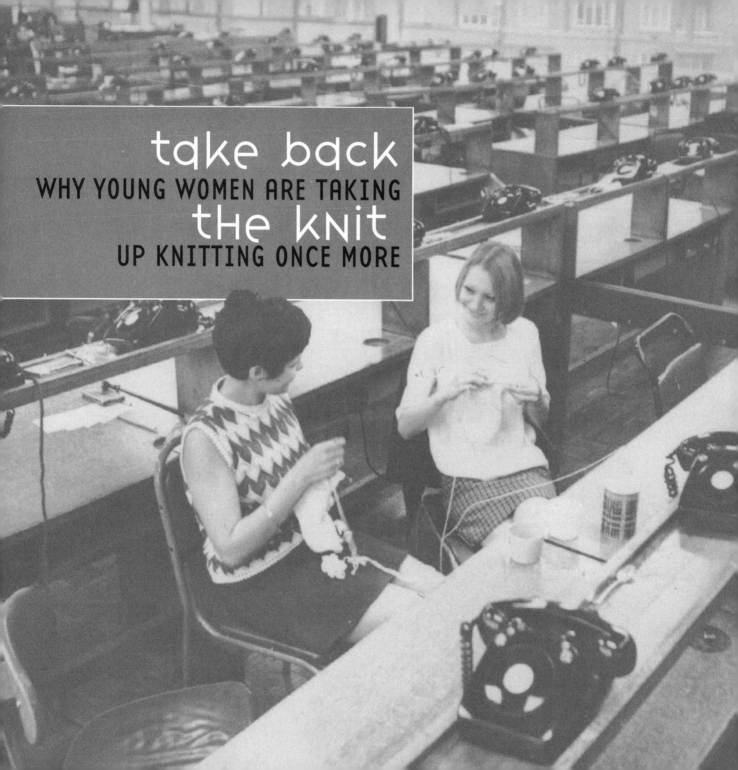

take back
WHY YOUNG WOMEN ARE TAKING
the knit
UP KNITTING ONCE MORE

my crafty family

My grandmother sits, straight-backed, in the living-room chair, her feet planted firmly on the floor in front of her. As always, her hands are in motion—constantly in motion—as her knitting needles go back and forth, yarn feeding through her hands from a ball that unwinds slowly at her side. My grandmother's hands are old and so smooth they seem to have had the fingerprints worn off them. Her sister, my great-aunt Jo, sits beside her, tatting lace onto the edge of a handkerchief. My mother and Aunt Hetty work on their own embroidery projects, and, along with the other aunts and uncles who are visiting, all of the adults are engaged in a lively conversation, punctuated by rounds of hearty laughter. Too young to join in the grown-ups' discussion, I sit on a small stool, quietly eating cake. After all, this is a birthday party.

My mother met my dad and moved to America when she was twenty-four, but for most of my childhood we spent our summers back in Holland with her relatives. Between my grandmother and her eight sisters, and my mom and her two sisters, there were always aunts and great-aunts around. Women filled every room. And whenever the relatives were gathered together, the women's hands were always working. With very few exceptions, and with barely any attention paid to what was going on below their elbows, the women would be busy knitting or sewing, darning or tatting. It didn't so much matter what they were making—after all, what purpose is served by hand-tatted lace sewn on the edge of a handkerchief?—as long as their hands remained in motion, for, as my grandmother used to say, "Idle hands are the devil's workshop."

But there was something else behind all this activity as well. The handwork of my grandmother and great-aunts seemed to provide comfort and serenity. Seated at these family gatherings, their purposeful motions gave them a focused air of self-containment, an earthy solidity. They were, after all, women who had learned their crafts as children, and who had practiced these skills throughout their lives—before and after the birth of children, the loss of husbands, and through two world wars. Their knitting was as regular and rhythmic as their breathing, as familiar as the feel of their own skin, and just as much a part of them.

My grandmother and her sisters were too humble to consider their work "expressions of their creativity." They were craftspeople, plain and simple, who were capable of taking on the most complex of knitting projects but who, for the most part, were content to keep themselves working on functional items whose patterns they knew by heart. From the time she first learned to knit, at age six, my grandmother was responsible for knitting socks to cover each of the thirty feet in her family. "In the evenings, the boys were free to do anything they liked," she once told me, with a lingering tinge of resentment, "but all the girls had to sit and knit." Later on in her life she made more extravagant items, including a fanciful knit suit in a beautiful, dusty-rose-colored nubby yarn, which my aunt still talks about to this day. But my grandmother always returned to her sock knitting. Even in her nineties, when her eyesight began to fail, she could still turn out perfect pairs of socks—the memory of their creation so well worn into her hands that she could knit

Clockwise, from lower left: *My first, unsuccessful, knitting attempts; My grandmother, age twenty-one, poses with her parents, eight sisters, and four brothers, 1920. A knitter since the age of six, she was responsible for knitting socks to cover the thirty feet in her family; My grandmother shows me (age twenty) the ropes once more.*

them practically by feel alone. My grandmother's hand-knit socks are still the only thing my father ever wears on his feet.

In my grandmother's time, knitting was not just a way to keep one's hands busy—it was also a way to save money. When my mother was small, it was standard practice to buy yarn and knit a sweater for a child, then, a year or so later, unravel and reknit it, with a bit more yarn, when the child had outgrown the original. Then there was the time, during the Second World War, that my grandmother had to unravel an old cotton bedspread—which her own mother had knit—to make underwear for her children. My mother still remembers sitting on uncomfortably hard wooden school benches, the bumpy side of the knit underwear leaving marks on her behind.

In America my mother carried on the frugal family tradition and made almost all of the clothes my brother and I wore. "Those girls are handy with a needle and thread," my grandmother would often say, proudly, about her daughters. The sight of my mother's heavy gray sewing machine set up at the end of the dining table was so familiar to me that it almost seemed like another sibling, and when she wasn't sewing, she was knitting, or embroidering. Walking through a department store, my mother would often finger the material on an item of clothing, then check the price tag and sniff, "I could make that myself." A few weeks later, I'd be presented with a hand-knit sweater or dress that was virtually indistinguishable from the store-bought variety.

Spending summers at Aunt Hetty's house in Holland as a child, I was in awe of the beautiful tapestries she had made using a combination of appliqué and embroidery, and, of course, she also sewed and knit. And then there was her homemade jewelry—long strands of pink and purple glass beads that hung around her neck and dangled from her ears. On rainy days, when Aunt Hetty would set me up at her kitchen table with scraps of yarn, colorful beads, and embroidery floss left over from her projects, I'd feel like Hansel and Gretel arriving at a house made of candy. Only in my fairy tale, there was no witch and nothing to fear.

i knit, therefore i am

My earliest attempts at knitting were a disaster. At the age of five, I remember fumbling with a pair of aluminum needles and the squeaky pink acrylic yarn my mother had given me to practice with. My sweaty, dirty child hands made the needles sticky and slowly turned the yarn from light pink to gray. No matter how hard I tried to get the loops to appear in nice, orderly rows the way my mother had shown me, I couldn't do it. My yarn would get tangled up, my stitches would fall off the needles, and I'd give up in frustration. That's when my mother would take the work from me— "These needles are so *sticky*"—gently put the fallen stitches back on the needles, straighten up the few stray loops I had managed to make, and hand the mini torture device back to me. But I never got any better at it, and the needles and yarn would be put away until the next time.

I wasn't a clumsy child—I had learned to do cross-stitch, and I could even sew dresses for my Barbie dolls on a mini sewing machine—but I just never seemed to be able to get the hang of knitting.

But unlike my grandmother, I didn't *need* to know how to knit. And soon the world began telling me that I'd be better off not knowing how. I was only ten years old when I first became aware of "women's libbers," but as Helen Reddy's "I Am Woman" blared from my transistor radio, I became completely swept up in the ideas of the women's movement. Taking their cue from Betty Friedan's influential book *The Feminine Mystique*, feminists were claiming that anyone who spent her days cooking and cleaning and her nights knitting and sewing, all in an effort to please her husband and her children, was frittering her life away. Women were made for greater things, they argued, so why, in a world of dishwashers and ready-to-wear, hadn't their time been freed up to pursue loftier goals?

I quickly became convinced that being a housewife was a dead end. After all, wouldn't my mother, with her careful attention to detail and great storytelling ability, have made a wonderful writer? Wouldn't Aunt Hetty, with her exceptional visual sense, have made a great decorator or graphic designer? I saw the limitations of their lives as a great tragedy, one that would never befall women in the future, least of all me. So my needlework and crafts went the way of my pink frilly dresses.

Yet, every time I'd return to Holland, my fingers would get itchy to do something crafty, and I'd pick up a cross-stitch project to work on in secret. When I lived in Holland for a year in my twenties, I had a particularly talented roommate who inspired me to give knitting another try. With a strange mix of excitement and trepidation, I asked my grandmother to reintroduce me to the ways of wool.

Under her skilled and patient guidance, I succeeded at making loops of yarn the way they were intended to be made, although my knitting progressed slowly—very slowly. By the time I finished the project I had started that winter—a Yohji Yamamoto–inspired boxy black number

with punky holes purposefully sprinkled all across it—the damn thing was no longer in fashion. Besides, it looked terrible on me. I didn't wear it even once.

Knitting just took too long. It required patience and an almost painful attention to detail. I tried another sweater a few years later and didn't get past the first sleeve. That unfinished sweater and the remaining balls of wool stayed in my closet for years, mocking me and reminding me of my failure. I'd take the piece out and bring it with me when I'd go on long vacations—to the beach, to the country—hoping that, with some time and a change of scenery, I might have the patience to get it finished. But each time, I would only manage to knit another few rows before giving up.

Finally, in 1999, I was scheduled to go on a cross-country book tour. Since flying is not one of my favorite things, I had arranged to do a good part of my travel by train—including a three-day trip from New York to Portland, Oregon. Afraid that I'd be bored out of my gourd with that much time on my hands, I packed my bags full of things to keep me occupied: books on tape, a laptop loaded with computer games, cards, books, and, yes, that long-suffering half-made sweater.

On the second day of my trip, I took the sweater out of my bag. As I stared at the needles and yarn, I tried desperately to remember how to cast on that first row of stitches. With a bit of fumbling and a few glances at the knitting primer I had brought for backup, it started coming back to me. Then slowly, like some sort of sense memory, my hands began casting on stitches with a deftness and agility I didn't even know they had. I took the needles in my hands and instinctively tucked the right needle under my right arm. I wrapped the yarn around my hand and started making tentative knit stitches. After a little while, the yarn was flowing from my finger comfortably, and I found myself making perfect little rows of stitches in time with the rhythm of the swaying train carriage. I looked through the window at the passing pastures outside and felt a sense of exhilaration. It had finally clicked! My hands and my body and my brain and my eyes had finally gotten into sync, and knitting felt comfortable, pleasurable—relaxing, even. I couldn't stop knitting. And each time I'd come to a difficult point in my work—when I'd have to increase or decrease stitches, for instance—I'd just walk up and down the length of the train until I saw another woman knitting in her cabin, and ask her to help me over the hump. By the time I arrived on the West Coast, my sweater was done.

After I returned home from the tour, I sought out my local knitting store and bought yarn and a pattern to make another sweater, which I completed on my next train trip a few weeks later. I couldn't get enough of my newfound love—I would borrow every book I could find on the craft from my local library, then lie awake in bed late at night reading them. I found my eyes opening up to details I had never noticed before: the way that sweaters are constructed, the way that different fibers produce different knit textures, and the huge variety of objects that could be made from simple knit and purl stitches. I was hooked.

When I'd tell people about my latest obsession, I'd invariably get one of two responses. The first, "Can you teach me, too?" was a common and very welcome reply. But other friends responded with "Really?" or "How interesting," both spoken with an air of disbelief, even a touch of disdain. After all, I had gotten a Ph.D. in the psychology of women and had started *BUST,* a feminist magazine—what was I doing knitting? Soon it occurred to me that if I had told these folks I'd been playing soccer, or learning karate, or taken up carpentry, they most likely would have said, "Cool," because a girl doing a traditionally male activity—now, that's feminist, right? But a girl doing a traditionally female activity—let alone one as frivolous and time-wasting as knitting—well, what were they to make of that?

It made me rethink my original feminist position. After all, it had been thirty years since the feminist revolution of the 1970s and housewives as we knew them had pretty much gone the way of the dinosaur, so why, dammit, wasn't knitting receiving as much respect as any other hobby? Why was it still so looked down on? It seemed to me that the main difference between knitting and, say, fishing or woodworking or basketball, was that knitting had traditionally been done by women. As far as I could tell, that was the only reason it had gotten such a bad rap. And that's when it dawned on me: All those people who looked down on knitting—and housework, and housewives—were not being feminist at all. In fact, they were being anti-feminist, since they seemed to think that only those things that men did, or had done, were worthwhile. Sure, feminism had changed the world, and young girls all across the country had formed soccer leagues, and were growing up to become doctors and astronauts and senators. But why weren't boys learning to knit and sew? Why couldn't we all—women and men alike—take the same kind of pride in the work our mothers had always done as we did in the work of our fathers?

FAMOUS KNITTERS, REAL AND FICTIONAL

Angela Bassett

Audrey Hepburn

Aunt Bea, *The Andy Griffith Show*

Bette Davis

Betty Rubble, *The Flintstones*

Betty White

Bob Mackie

Brooke Shields

Cameron Diaz

Carol Duvall

Carole Lombard

Caroline Rhea

Charlotte York, *Sex and the City*

Courtney Thorne-Smith

Daryl Hannah

Debra Messing

Dorothy Parker

Dr. Laura Schlessinger

Eartha Kitt

Edith Piaf

Eleanor Roosevelt

Elke Sommer

Frances McDormand

Goldie Hawn

Gromit, *Wallace and Gromit*

Harriet Nelson, *Ozzie and Harriet*

Hawkeye Pierce, *M★A★S★H*

Hilary Swank

Iman

Ingrid Bergman

Isaac Mizrahi

Jane Jetson, *The Jetsons*

Joan Blondell

Joan Crawford

Joanne Woodward

JoBeth March, *Little Women*

Joey Tribbiani, *Friends*

Julia Roberts

Julianna Margulies

Julianne Moore

Kate Moss

Katharine Hepburn

Laura Ingalls Wilder

Laurence Fishburne

Laurie Metcalf

Lucille Ball

Madame Defarge, *A Tale of Two Cities*

Madeleine Albright

Madonna

Margaret "Hot Lips" Houlihan, *M★A★S★H"*

Marilyn Monroe

Martha Washington

Mary, mother of Christ

Mary-Louise Parker

Megan Mullally

Monica Geller Bing, *Friends*

Monica Lewinsky

Phoebe Buffay, *Friends*

Queen Elizabeth II

Rita Hayworth

Rose McGowan

Russell Crowe
Okay, there is some debate about whether this one is true or not, but there are some fetching photos of Russell holding knitting needles.

Sandra Bullock

Sarah Jessica Parker

Scarlett O'Hara, *Gone with the Wind*

Tiffani Amber Thiessen

Tyne Daly

Tyra Banks

Uma Thurman

Whoopi Goldberg

Wilma Flintstone, *The Flintstones*

Winona Ryder

YOU AIN'T SHIT
IF YOU DON'T KNIT

I had a mission. It was time to "take back the knit." Not only was I determined to improve my own knitting skills, but I also wanted to do everything in my power to raise knitting's visibility and value in the culture. I began to knit in public. I organized the first New York City Stitch 'n Bitch group as an open forum where women or men interested in learning to knit could mingle and share their knowledge. I told anyone who'd listen how wonderfully relaxing and satisfying the craft was. I wrote about it, with no shame or ironic edge, in *BUST*. I firmly believed that knitting—a centuries-old craft that women had perfected—deserved to be as respected and honored as any other craft, and I wanted to make sure that it got its props.

I had my work cut out for me. Knitting had become such an arcane activity that doing it in public always elicited a response. It sent older men into fits of nostalgia ("My mother used to knit all the time," they'd say with an air of melancholy). Older women would look at me with a knowing smile, as if we were both part of some long-forgotten secret society. And some young men and women would stare at me with openmouthed curiosity; as far as they were concerned, I might as well have been churning butter on the crosstown bus.

The fact that knitting was so gendered an activity also put people off. It was such a girly thing to do, in fact, that even a few of the flamboyantly gay men I knew—men who would have no qualms about, say, walking down the street dressed as Carmen Miranda—admitted to me that they were too embarrassed to knit in public.

"Oh no, I would never knit on a plane," one said. "I'd get too many stares."

But it was exactly the gendered nature of the craft that drew me to it. Whenever I would take up the needles I would feel myself connected not only to my own mother, grandmother, and great-grandmother, but also to the women who lived centuries before me, the women who had developed the craft, the women who had known, as I did, the incredible satisfaction and sense of serenity that could come from the steady, rhythmic *click-click-click* of one's knitting needles. These women had experienced the meditative and peaceful quality that overcomes one's mind while knitting; they understood the way that one's thoughts get worked right into one's knitting, discovering, as I did, that whatever I was thinking about when I last worked on a piece would immediately spring back into my mind when I picked up the work again later on, as though knitting were a sort of mental tape recorder. Betty Friedan and other like-minded feminists had overlooked an important aspect of knitting when they viewed it simply as part of women's societal obligation to serve everyone around them—they had forgotten that knitting served the knitter as well.

I wasn't the only one rediscovering the joys of knitting. I began seeing other women—young women—knitting on the subway. Soon, they were everywhere: at coffee shops, on lunch lines, at the movies, even in bars. Some of these women were pierced, dyed, and tattooed. Others were fashion-forward, trendy types. Still others were of the crunchy-granola variety. And plenty of them could not be categorized at all. The only thing we all had in common was our new hobby. And it wasn't just a New York phenomenon. Other Stitch 'n Bitches began popping up all over the country and beyond. People were knitting in San Francisco, in Chicago, in London, even in

Tokyo. Magazines started covering the phenomenon. So did newspapers. And after years of watching knitting stores go out of business, we suddenly saw new, lively ones begin cropping up.

Today, there are over 38 million knitters in the United States, with 4 million newcomers to knitting in the last few years. According to a 2000 survey by the Craft Yarn Council, nearly one in three women knits. Younger women especially are taking up the craft; the percentage of women under forty-five who knit or crochet has doubled since 1996. These new knitters are college students, indie rockers, middle-aged Brooklynites, theater people, and sissy girls proudly asserting their sissiness. They are single and married, bohemians and professionals, introverts and extroverts. Why do they knit? It's a strange mix of pragmatism, politics, and the desire to be fashionable.

Some "crafty" feminists, like myself, are reclaiming what have been called the "lost domestic arts," realizing the importance of giving women's crafts their due. Others are more interested in freeing themselves from a dependence on what they see to be an exploitative corporate culture. Still others, such as those with Emporio Armani tastes but Salvation Army budgets, figure that they can learn to make fashionable items more cheaply than they can buy them.

Knitting is part of the same do-it-yourself ethos that spawned zines and mix tapes. By loudly reclaiming old-fashioned skills, women are rebelling against a culture that seems to reward only the sleek, the mass-produced, the male. But every generation puts its own spin on the craft, and for today's knitters the emphasis has been on using chunky yarn and fat needles for

quickly completed projects; experimenting with exotic fibers sheared from alpaca, silk recycled from Indian saris, and yarn spun from hemp plants; and creating funky, colorful sweaters, bags, and scarves.

Knitting makes for a great urban hobby because a ball of yarn and a knitting project are light and portable, they're easy to carry from home to work, and they don't take up much space in small, cramped apartments. In an age when so many of us sit in front of computers all day long, we may feel the desire to create, to touch, to make something tactile with our hands. And in these uncertain, anxious times, warm handmade scarves and cozy sweaters feel protective and comforting. Of course, this last discovery we can't claim for ourselves—it's something our grandmothers have always known.

bringing it all back Home

A month ago, my mother and I went to Holland for a week. We were going to say good-bye to my grandmother, who, after 103½ years of living, was finally, slowly, dying. Every day, my mother, my aunt Hetty, and I would travel to visit my grandmother at the hospice where she lay, quietly, in a strange half-slumber. Her vision was almost completely gone, as was her hearing. She was like a baby again, depending on everyone around her to feed her, clean her, pat her head, kiss her. We'd sit her up in her bed and feed her spoonfuls of food, her mouth opening hungrily after each bite. "Do you want more, Oma?" we'd ask, close enough to her ear so she could hear us. From somewhere inside there'd be a glimmer of recognition. "Yes," she'd mumble. "How's the food?" we'd say, loudly. There would be a pause, and then, a slow spark. "Good." We couldn't tell whether she was aware of who we were, but it was good just to be with her, hold her hands, give her whatever comfort we could. I always brought my knitting along with me on those daily visits—a colorful, simple sock I was working on for a friend—and would sometimes find my mother and my aunt staring at my work with a certain longing. "Can I knit a row or two?" my aunt would ask, her hands hungry for the soothing ritual of sock knitting, something to calm her soul during the stressful and uncomfortable moments spent watching a parent die. "I want to, also," my mother would say, and the sock would be passed to her.

Maybe my grandmother felt left out. One day, we entered her room to find her strangely agitated, her hands restlessly moving in the air above her bed. Perhaps she was dreaming, or perhaps the present and the past had melded together in her mind, but after days of silence, suddenly she was chattering, talking aloud to herself in the room. "I already knit one sock," I heard her say, anxiously, as I came closer to her bed. "But now I still have to knit the other one." My aunt gasped; it was difficult for her to see her mother all wound up about an imaginary sock that she thought needed to be knit. I grasped my grandmother's hands in mine. "That's a beautiful sock you made," I told her, calmly. "Knitting is nice and relaxing, isn't it?" "Yes," she murmured, becoming a bit more restful. I put a cool towel on her head and kissed her cheek, but soon she began to grow anxious again. "It's over there, it's drying," she repeated, gravely, "but now I have to knit the other one." I squeezed her hands tightly. "Rest, Oma, don't worry," I said, as I felt her hands slowly unclench. "I'll knit the other one for you."

A Stitch in Time: A Brief History of Knitting

No one really knows when knitting began. Unfortunately, that secret likely died with the craft's inventor. And we have very few samples of ancient knitting, because fabric disintegrates quickly. However, a few fragments have survived, including bits of blue-and-white cotton socks that seem to have been made in Egypt somewhere between A.D. 1000 and 1300. Historians have concluded that knitting's roots most likely lie in this ancient land.

Anonymous 13th-century painting of the Virgin Mary knitting

In the mid-1300s and 1400s, a number of paintings were made in Italy and other areas of Europe showing the Virgin Mary, with little baby Jesus at her feet, knitting away on some sort of round garment. They suggest that, by the late Middle Ages, knitting had arrived in various parts of Europe. Working with four needles—no slouch, she!—the knitting Mary in these paintings tells us that even Jesus Christ wore sweaters made by his mom.

Both men and women knit in those days, but the men belonged to fancy, exclusive guilds where they would spend six years training to become master knitters, the pièce de résistance of their studies being a vast knit carpet they would complete at the end of their schooling. For most of its history, however, knitting has been a women's craft, perhaps because it is so portable and can be done in small stretches of time, which makes it perfectly compatible with child rearing. Knit one, purl two, nurse the baby, knit another row.

Knitting also served as an important source of income for many poor and rural women—that is, until 1589, when a British clergyman named William Lee, upset that his wife was spending more time with her knitting needles than with him, invented the first knitting machine. Eventually, the machines put most home knitters out of work, as hand knitting lost its profitability.

Still, before the widespread availability of cheap, manmade clothing, hand knitting was one of a woman's, and a girl's, basic chores. It was also a leisure-time hobby among Victorian ladies. In fact, knitting became so fashionable that new methods of holding the needles were introduced to make the craft appear more ladylike to the casual observer. Today, many women still knit holding their needles like pencils as the Victorian ladies did, which is much slower than

A knitting bee, circa 1916

holding the needles under the palms of the hands, but apparently much more attractive to potential suitors.

Although women of all ages have always knit, it has been associated with grandmothers for at least the past hundred years and has gone through alternating cycles of falling in and out of favor with younger women. In the

Red Cross poster from World War I

1890s (the era of the "New Woman"), women had taken to wearing the then-shocking bloomers (pants, basically) and gave up spinning wheels for bicycle wheels, as knitting became associated with "old-fashioned" womanhood—on both sides of the Atlantic. But by 1906, a London magazine for girls reported that "the art we were wont to associate with grandmothers and quaint, lavender-perfumed old ladies is to-day a favorite pastime." In the 1920s, knitting was once again rejected as "silly domestic work" by young American women who had just achieved the right to vote. Yet during the Depression, a tight economy dictated that women take up the needles once more, and the craft became popular again, a trend that lasted through the next several decades.

During times of war, knitting's popularity has soared. Although we've often heard of Rosie the Riveter, we've overlooked someone whom I'll call Ned the Knitter—the men at home recovering from war injuries, the veterans too old to serve, and the young Boy Scouts, who, during the last two world wars, were enlisted to help knit socks and blankets for the soldiers, right beside the womenfolk. Apparently, in times of war the false limitations of gender fall away. Of course, we've always known there's no reason men can't knit just as well as women can.

With the resurgent women's movement of the 1960s and 1970s, knitting came to be seen, once again, as a symbol of women's entrapment in the home. But while some women were rejecting the hobby, others got into it as part of their hippy-dippy, back-to-nature thing.

Today's knitting phenomenon is just the most recent upswing in the history of a craft that has cycled in and out of fashion with the younger generation for the past two centuries. With legions of young knitters "taking back the knit" (and more and more girls picking up sticks every day), the popularity of knitting is at an all-time high. Major media have embraced the craft, touting knitting as the "new yoga" and "not for grannies anymore."

Chicks with sticks. New York Stitch 'n Bitch, 2003

f you want to knit, the first thing you'll have to do is get yourself some yarn. This can be more complicated than you might expect—choosing a color isn't even the half of it. Step into any knitting store these days and you'll see that not only does yarn come in every color from fresh-off-the-sheep brown to not-found-in-nature acid-green, but it also ranges in texture from bumpy to silky smooth; and in thicknesses from as thin as thread to as thick as rope. To a new knitter, it may come as a surprise to learn that knitting needles, too, are made in all shapes and sizes and in a variety of materials, from aluminum to plastic to bamboo to milk (yes, really). With all these choices, how will you know what to get? Don't worry: I'm about to tell you everything you ever wanted to know about yarn and needles but were afraid to ask.

Material girl
Getting to Know Yarn

ome folks like to call all yarn "wool," which is as silly as calling all shoes "Birkenstocks." While it's true that plenty of the stuff out there comes from sheep, don't let anyone pull the wool over your eyes: Yarn is made of fibers derived from sheep, rabbits, goats, hemp, flax, cotton, chemicals, and more.

Animal-based fibers are what Mother Nature has come up with, after thousands of years of research, to be the best body covering for warm-blooded creatures. And she knows what she's doing. Fabric made from animal fibers has practically magical properties: It insulates, keeping you toasty warm when it's cold outside and cool when it's hot. And it is super-absorbent: A wool sweater

or hat can absorb up to one-third its weight in water before it—and you—start to feel wet. (Which may explain why you've never seen a sheep wearing a raincoat.) Some animal fibers are warmer than others (the fiber from alpaca, a llama-like animal, is exceptionally warm), but even seemingly weightless fibers, like mohair, can knit up into an airy sweater that's as warm as a heavy down coat.

Plant fibers are not as insulating as animal fibers, but one thing they do especially well is absorb moisture. They're also strong and very breathable, which is why cotton or linen yarn makes great summer clothes. Also, all plant fibers are hypo-allergenic, so they are a natural choice for anyone allergic to wool.

Man-made fibers, such as acrylic, are petroleum-based—meaning they're essentially plastic. While that may sound pretty unappealing, acrylic yarn does have a couple of advantages over natural-fiber yarns: It's cheap and it's easy to wash. (Fabrics made of animal and plant fibers often require all kinds of tsuris to clean.) Still, while clothes made of acrylic fibers can be thrown in the washer and dryer, they won't be very warm, and unlike wool or cotton, they won't be very absorbent. And, truth be told, some acrylic yarn is made so cheaply that it downright squeaks.

Nevertheless, there are very soft acrylic yarns to be had, as well as some popular acrylic-wool and acrylic-cotton blends. And for sock knitting, wool with a small percentage of nylon will wear much better than wool alone. Still, if you can afford it, go for the animal- or plant-based yarns. If you're used to wearing acrylic-blend store-bought clothing (which most of us are), experiencing the way your first 100 percent wool sweater keeps you warm without overheating you will come as a revelation—you might swear there were little electric heaters in there. In the end, you'll probably agree that if it's good enough for sheep, llamas, and other critters, it's good enough for you.

Here are some of the most popular yarn fibers to knit with, and what makes 'em special:

WOOL Of course you know that wool comes from sheep. What you might not know is that different breeds of sheep yield different kinds of wool. Wool from Icelandic sheep, which grow long shaggy coats, for instance, is rough and can be scratchy, but it is as strong as nails. Merino wool is at the other extreme; it's made from the superfine fleece of Merino sheep, and it's as soft as cotton but has a tendency to "pill" (create little balls of fuzz). Merino is one of my favorite yarns to knit with—it's not too expensive, and it feels great against your body.

MOHAIR This fuzzy, glamorous wool comes from the fleece of a goat—one that is confusingly called an Angora goat. But beware: Mohair can be itchy when it's worn right next to the skin, so a mohair scarf might not be the best idea. On the other hand, a mohair tunic or cardigan would be right on.

CASHMERE Cashmere is the most luxuriously soft and fluffy yarn of all, and it's combed from the bellies of cashmere goats (now there's a job I'd like to try). Cashmere is expensive, so, to make a sexy sweater that won't break your bank, try a yarn that has cashmere blended together with something else, such as wool.

ALPACA Alpaca comes from a llama-like animal and it is exceedingly—some might say excessively—warm. That's great for hats and scarves and mittens, but it could be overkill on a sweater, when you might be better off using an alpaca and wool blend.

ANGORA Sweater girls of the '50s based their reputations on this stuff, which comes from bunnies—bunnies!—and is wonderfully fine and fluffy, like yarn made out of a baby's hair. Unfortunately, angora yarn can also shed like a rabbit, so save it for accents like collars and cuffs, or try making one of those figure-flaunting sweaters using an angora-wool blend.

SILK Silk comes from the long fibers of unraveled silkworm cocoons. It's an extremely strong fiber—those silkworms are pretty clever—and yarn made from it is lustrous and shiny. Silk is also expensive, but its lightness makes it a great choice for a special summer item, such as a tank top or a shawl.

COTTON Lovely, light, and absorbent, cotton is not as stretchy as wool, which means it can be a little harder to knit with. It also shows irregularities in your knitting more than wool does, so save it for when you've gotten pretty comfortable with the craft, then use it for a summer project, such as a bikini or light sweater.

LINEN Making cloth from linen goes back—and I'm talkin' *way* back—to around 8000 B.C. Linen yarn is spun from the long fibers of the flax plant, and it's superstrong and cool. Stuff knit with linen yarn can be a bit stiff and will wrinkle easily, but I like this fiber just because it's so ancient. It's frequently blended with cotton, which makes it much easier to knit with. Use it for a simple project, such as a boxy tunic, and get in touch with your inner hunter-gatherer.

ACRYLIC Because it washes so well, acrylic yarn can be a great choice for projects intended for babies or pets. The fact that it's inexpensive makes it a good choice for beginners or for anyone on a tight knitting budget. But try to buy a brand that has at least some wool blended in—it will be much nicer to knit with and to wear. And most of the coolest and weirdest new yarns—such as something called "eyelash" yarn, which has little bits of hair sticking out of it, or fuzzy, fake-fur types of yarn, or yarn with cool little bits of flotsam and jetsam mixed in—are made using acrylic. When it comes to having fun with these "novelty" yarns, I say put away your fiber snobbery and dive right in—the water's fine.

in the thick of it
Yarn Weights

to make things more interesting, yarn also comes in a variety of thicknesses, called "weights." To complicate matters further, there are American and British names for each of these weights. Also, grouping yarns by weight is somewhat less than exact—there can be a lot of variety within one category. Still, knowing a yarn's weight is important because if you ever want to use a different yarn than the one called for by your knitting pattern, you'll want to look for yarn of the same weight. (For best results, though, always check your gauge, see page 51.) Here are five of the most common yarn weights (alternative names are given in parentheses):

Fingering (or baby or 4-ply) weight: This very thin weight of yarn is good for making light, fine garments such as baby sweaters, socks, or a lacy shawl.

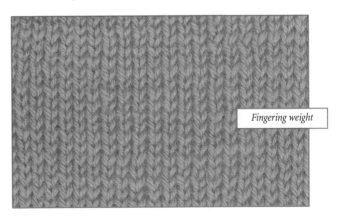

Fingering weight

Sport (or double-knitting or DK) weight: Now here's a very curiously named yarn weight. I mean, just what kind of sports item would you make out of this stuff? A knit jock strap? Sport weight yarn is roughly twice as thick as fingering yarn, so at least "double-knitting" makes sense. It is a good weight for socks and also works well for baby or children's items. Many adult sweaters are also made out of it, albeit thin ones.

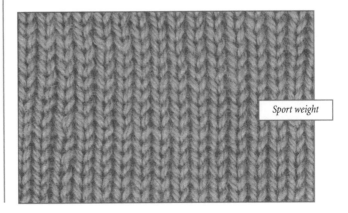

Sport weight

Worsted (or Aran) weight: Despite its name, "worsted" might very well be considered the *best* yarn out there—it's certainly the most common weight, and there are more kinds of worsted-weight yarn on the market than anything else. Worsted is about twice the thickness of sport yarn (Aran is just a tad heavier), and it's great for making scarves, hats, sweaters, gloves, afghans, or just about anything else you want. It's a great choice for beginners. Get to know worsted-weight yarn: It is your friend.

Chunky (or bulky) weight: The plot thickens. Chunky and bulky yarns are around twice as thick as worsted, and they knit up quickly on larger needles, making them great for heavy sweaters, such as Icelandic yoked sweaters, or thick gloves or scarves.

Extra-bulky (or super-bulky) weight: When it's time to bring in the big guns, use extra-bulky yarn. This fat, almost ropy stuff is thicker even than chunky, and that's why I recommend it for knitters with attention deficit disorder: Its bulk makes it possible to knit up a sweater in a weekend. A word of caution: If you're the type of gal who is more likely to be described as "full-figured" than "willowy," stay away from these yarns for anything other than accessories. A form-fitting sweater in extra-bulky yarn worn on a zaftig figure is the next best thing to wearing a fat suit. You'll end up looking like a barrel, and you will not like it. Trust me—I'm speaking from experience here.

Worsted weight

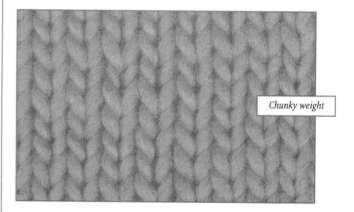

Chunky weight

Extra-bulky weight

Knitting Takes Balls . . . and Skeins, and Hanks

Usually yarn comes in **balls** (relatively round) or **skeins** (oblong), and if you're lucky, you will have what's called a center-pull ball or skein: The yarn will all come out of one end, and the ball won't bounce and roll around so much when you're knitting. Finding this end, however, can be tricky; often it is hidden under the yarn label. You might need to go poking around inside the left or right end of the ball to find it. If all else fails, just knit with whatever loose end you can find.

ball

If the yarn comes in a **hank**, which is essentially a big coil of yarn wrapped up in a twist, you can ask the friendly folks at your yarn store to wind it into a ball for you—they usually have a machine for doing just that. Alternately, you can wind it into a ball yourself. The easiest way to do this is to pop the untwisted hank over a friend's outstretched hands, then wind away (you've seen this done in cartoons hundreds of times). In the absence of a set of helping hands, just place your feet about a foot apart (hah!) and hang the hank over them to keep your yarn from getting all tangled up as you wind your ball.

skein

hank

HOW TO MAKE A CENTER-PULL BALL

Open your hand so that it faces you, then lay the end of the yarn across your palm, leaving about a 6-inch-long tail hanging free. Wind the yarn in a figure eight around your thumb and pointer about fifteen to twenty times.

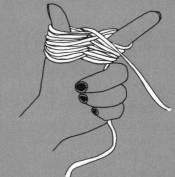

Remove the wrapped yarn from your fingers and fold it in half. Place your thumb over the part where the long tail enters the yarn wad and begin winding the yarn into a ball. Keep winding this way and that until all your yarn is wound, always holding your thumb over the spot where the yarn tail enters the ball.

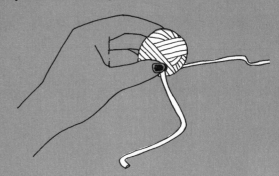

How to Read a Yarn Label

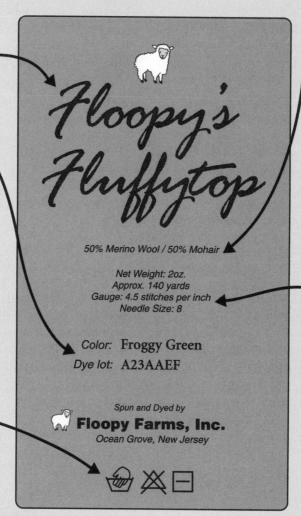

The yarn brand and name:
If this is Floopy's Fluffytop, it will say it here.

Yarn color and dye lot:
If the yarn color is "Froggy Green," it will say it here. But more important is the dye lot number, written in some sort of nonsensical gibberish like "A23AAEF." It's very important that you buy all your yarn from the same dye lot. Otherwise, your sweater might be one shade of green in the front, and a slightly different shade in the sleeves. (Most yarn stores will allow you to return unused balls of yarn, so buy extra.)

Washing instructions:
You may not be able to decode the washing hieroglyphics on yarn labels, but, well, at least they try. These say that the yarn should be hand-washed, never ironed, and dried flat.

Fiber content:
What the heck is this stuff made of, anyway? Possum fur? Dog hair? Pieces of lint? Probably the first thing you'll read on a label, the fiber content will tell you what the yarn is made of, and the percentage of each fiber. A common blend for socks, for instance, is 80 percent wool and 20 percent nylon.

Suggested needle size and gauge:
Yarn labels usually tell you how many stitches and rows you will get per 4-inch piece of fabric while knitting with the suggested size of needle. This info is particularly useful when you are trying to use a different yarn than what a given pattern calls for. If the yarn has the same recommended needle size and gauge listed on the label, it's a safe bet that you can use it in place of the pattern's yarn.

Floopy's Fluffytop

50% Merino Wool / 50% Mohair

Net Weight: 2oz.
Approx. 140 yards
Gauge: 4.5 stitches per inch
Needle Size: 8

Color: Froggy Green
Dye lot: A23AAEF

Spun and Dyed by
Floopy Farms, Inc.
Ocean Grove, New Jersey

GETTING THE GOOD STUFF: HOW TO BUY THE BEST YARN FOR LESS

Among knitters, there are people known as "yarn snobs." These are the folks who won't knit using anything that has even been in the same room with synthetic yarn, let alone buy their yarn from the local Everymart. They do all their yarn shopping at their LYS (local yarn store) and prefer to knit only with expensive, fancy yarns. If Barney's ever started a yarn store, they would be there on opening day.

But you don't have to be loaded to get the very best yarn for your projects. Here are some ways to find great yarn at bargain-basement prices:

BARGAIN BINS: Every local yarn store will have a bargain bin containing yarns that are out of season, are left over from a larger dye lot, or have been discontinued by their manufacturer. Check out this bin each and every time you visit your LYS, as its contents will turn over quickly. I've gotten amazing deals out of bargain bins, where even the highest-quality yarns can be found marked down by 50 percent or more.

eBAY: Although you can't rely on online auctions to find a particular brand of yarn in a specific color or quantity, searching for "yarn" on eBay will bring up hundreds of yarn choices at less-than-retail prices. Of course it's best if you are familiar with the brand and make of yarn—like if it's something you've already touched in person—otherwise, you might be disappointed when that fluffy-looking ball of hot pink yarn turns out to be as rough as steel wool when it arrives. Another caveat: Buy yarn only from "smoke-free" environments, or your hand-knit sweater may end up smelling like old Uncle Irving.

ONLINE STORES: There are many online stores that specialize in discounted yarn, and a simple Internet search for "discount yarn" will bring up the most current listings. Be sure to factor in the price of shipping and handling before placing your order to know if you are actually saving money.

tools of the trade

Scissors When patterns say "break yarn," they really mean cut it with sharp scissors. Tiny little folding scissors or scissors that come on a clip for attaching to your shirt are perfect for this purpose. In a pinch, even nail clippers will work.

Safety pins These can be used to pin knit pieces of fabric together before sewing up seams, and to help you keep track of things like where increases and decreases have been made. Get the kind without coils, if you can, as they're less likely to get tangled up in your yarn.

Stitch holders Sometimes you'll need to set a few stitches aside for a time. To keep them from unraveling, you put those stitches on a stitch holder. There are all sorts of holders, some of which resemble giant diaper pins. My favorite looks like a little plastic double-pointed knitting needle with a pair of point protectors connected by a rubber band.

Yarn needles Also called a "tapestry" or "darning" needle, this blunt-end needle looks like a giant sewing needle with an eyehole that's large enough to pass yarn through. Yarn needles are a necessity for knitters; you'll need one to sew your pieces of fabric together, and it's what you'll use to darn away yarn ends.

Stitch markers You place these small, colored rings in between stitches on your needle to serve as little landmarks. They don't do anything—just slip them off one needle and onto the other as you knit—they're just there to remind you, "Hey, jerky, don't forget to increase a stitch when you get to me."

Needle gauge This cute little metal or plastic device lets you know what size your needles are after you've lost their packaging and the numbers have rubbed off. They've got a hole for every needle size—just poke your needle through until you find the one that fits. Some also have a little slot to help you measure your gauge—that is, how many stitches you get to the inch.

Row counters Stick these at the end of your needles to help you remember what row you're on—so when your pattern tells you to knit 12 rows, you can use the counter to keep track. (Remember, if you put a counter on only one needle, you should increase it by 2 rows each time you get back to it.) If you are using circular needles, thread a piece of yarn through a row counter and hang it on your circular needle where your round begins.

Cable needles These fancy numbers are used to make cables, and they come in two basic types: straight and curved. I like the U-shaped curved ones best—they hang nicely from your cable while the stitches are not being used and the stitches are less likely to fall off.

Crochet hook Like a scalpel to a doctor, a crochet hook is the most important tool for performing quick surgery on your knitted work, such as picking up a dropped stitch or fixing a backward stitch. Of course, some knitted items require a bit of crocheting, and you'll need a hook for that as well. Don't leave home without one.

Point protectors These are little rubber caps to put at the end of your knitting needles before you put your work away. I'm not sure your points really need protecting, but these little guys will keep your stitches from coming off the needles when you're not knitting.

Tape measure A tape measure is an absolute necessity for knitters, as you will constantly need to measure things once you get going. Get one, pop it in your bag, and guard it with your life.

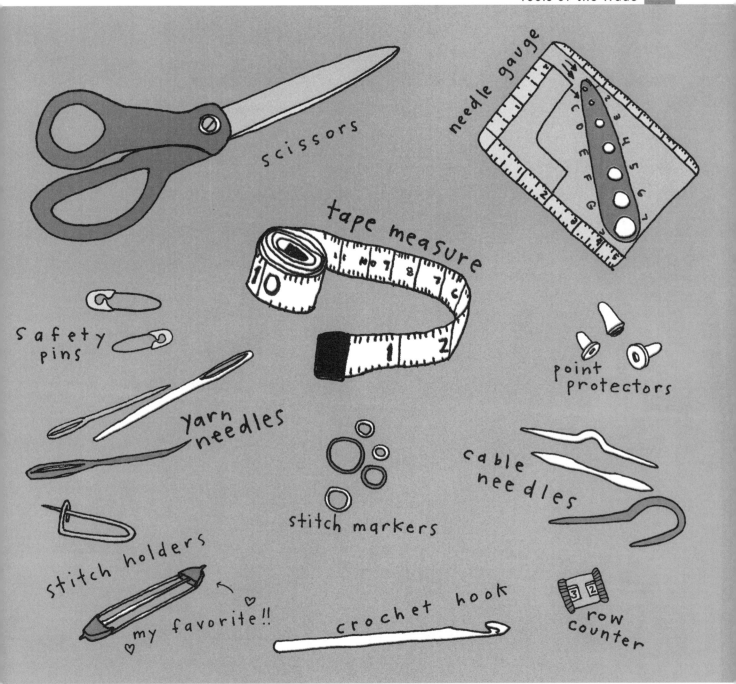

scissors

needle gauge

tape measure

safety pins

yarn needles

point protectors

stitch markers

cable needles

stitch holders

my favorite!!

crochet hook

row counter

pointers
What You Need to Know About Needles

besides yarn, needles are the only other absolute must for any knitter. Knitting needles of yore were made of steel, but today's needles come in a whole assortment of materials, each with its own special qualities. Aluminum needles are the cheapest and most common, and they're nice and smooth for sliding yarn across. Bamboo needles are less slippery, but they're also prettier to look at, become warm with handling, and are flexible and easy on the hands; they're my fave by far. Wooden needles are chic but expensive, and casein needles, which are made of milk protein, are cool-looking and flexible, but they taste weird, so try not to lick them.

Like yarn, knitting needles come in varying thicknesses, and, as I'll explain below, the thickness (or diameter) of your needle can make a big difference in your knitting. They also come in different styles—straight and circular—and different lengths. In this next section, I'll try to help you answer the pointed question: Which needle should I use?

size Matters
The Importance of Needle Width

the diameter of your needles (along with the thickness of your yarn) will determine the look and feel of the fabric you knit. Large, thick needles will create more open, lacy fabric, while smaller needles are used to make a tighter, closer cloth. In general, however, you'll use thinner needles when you're knitting with thinner yarn, and thicker needles when knitting with thicker yarn.

Here in the United States, knitting needles go from size 0000 all the way up to 19, 35, and 50, with the majority of needles falling between 0 (very delicate) to 15 (for

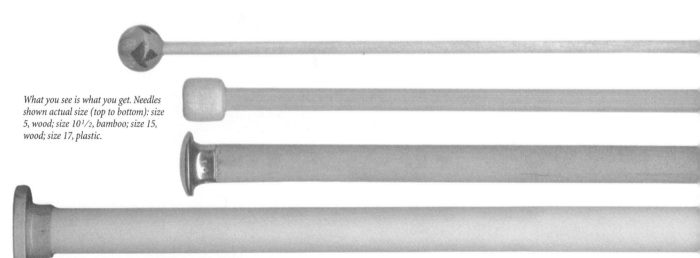

What you see is what you get. Needles shown actual size (top to bottom): size 5, wood; size 10½, bamboo; size 15, wood; size 17, plastic.

bulkier pieces). The basic, middle-of-the-road-size needle is a size 8, and it's a good choice for a beginner. So what do these numbers represent? Absolutely nothing. In Europe they use a different numbering scheme—one that actually corresponds to the diameter, in millimeters, of the needle itself. Thus, a size 6 needle in Europe is 6mm in diameter. Over here, that same needle is a size 10. But ours is not to wonder why; ours is but to knit or die.

The thickness of your knitting needles makes a big difference in the gauge (see page 51) of your knitting—meaning the number of stitches you have to knit in order to create an inch of fabric. If you're a tight knitter, you'll squeeze more stitches into that inch than would a loose knitter, and using thicker or thinner needles is one way to adjust for that personal difference. Although knitting patterns always suggest a particular size needle, the size you'll end up using will depend on your personal gauge.

Once you get into knitting, you'll probably want to build up a needle collection. That way, you won't have to buy new needles every time you start a project. To keep track of what needles you already have in your collection, make a copy of the needle tracker below, fill it out, and keep it in your wallet. And if you ever come across a large collection of knitting needles at a yard sale or a thrift store—and this happens quite often—snatch them all up. Chances are they'll be super-cheap (new knitting needles can cost anywhere from three to fifteen dollars a pair), and you'll get a good start on your collection.

My Needles

Metric	2.0	2.25	3.0	3.25	3.5	4.0	4.5	5.0	5.5	6.0	6.5	8.0	9.0	10.0	
US	0	1	3	4	5	6	7	8	9	10	10.5	11	13	15	
Straight	☐	☐	☐	☐	☐	☐	☐	☐	☐	☐	☐	☐	☐	☐	
Double PT	☐	☐	☐	☐	☐	☐	☐	☐	☐	☐	☐	☐	☐	☐	
Circular 16	☐	☐	☐	☐	☐	☐	☐	☐	☐	☐	☐	☐	☐	☐	
Circular 24	☐	☐	☐	☐	☐	☐	☐	☐	☐	☐	☐	☐	☐	☐	
Circular 32	☐	☐	☐	☐	☐	☐	☐	☐	☐	☐	☐	☐	☐	☐	
Crochet	B	C	D	E	F	G	\	H	I	J	K	L	M	N	P

the Long and Short of it

Needle Length

Needles also come in different styles and lengths, each of which has its own use:

Single-pointed straight needles are the ones that usually come to mind when you think of a knitting needle: a stick with a point on one side and a knob on the other. Straight needles generally come in two lengths: 10-inch and 14-inch. I recommend getting the 14-inch length—with knitting needles, as with other things, longer is better. Not only can you knit wider fabric on longer needles, but the 14-inch length fits nicely under your arm when you knit, and, as I'll explain in the next chapter, this can be very helpful.

Double-pointed needles look a bit like the sticks in the game of Pick Up Sticks and usually come in sets of four or five. These straight needles have points at both ends, which means you can knit stitches off of either end, and *that* means you can knit "in the round" as it's called. Double-pointed needles are shorter than single-pointed needles and usually come in lengths of 6 or 8 inches. Four or five of them are used at the same time to knit tubular-shaped objects such as socks and hats. Although some people say that knitting with double-pointed needles is like wrestling with an octopus, once you get in the groove, it can be quite fun, and fast.

Circular needles are two short, straight needles connected with a flexible plastic cord. Circular needles are all the rage these days. They are used to knit in the round, but also to knit flat pieces. The annoying thing about circular needles, however, is that the lengths vary widely—from 12 inches, used for cuffs or collars, to 16, 24, and 36 inches, for other pieces. Oftentimes, you will need many different needles for a single project.

Nevertheless, lots of Stitch 'n Bitch knitters love them to death. It also seems that circular needles, with their short, stubby needle ends, are particularly good for those knitters who prefer the Continental style of knitting, in which the needles tend to fly around a lot. I, however, who prefer to knit English style and even like to hold the needle end in my right armpit—impossible to do with circular needles—much prefer the old-school straight needles. In any case, you should try both types and go with whichever feels best to you. And remember that you can knit straight pieces of fabric on circular needles by just knitting back and forth (you can't knit tubular fabric on straight needles, however).

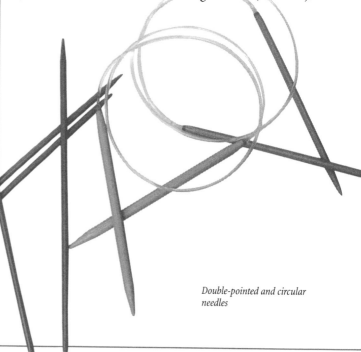

Double-pointed and circular needles

PACK UP YOUR YARN BALLS IN AN OLD KNIT BAG: MANAGING YOUR STASH

Straight needles can be kept in decorative buckets or pencil cups on bookshelves. Needles, like socks, have a habit of getting separated, so put a rubber band around matching pairs. You can also make a nice fabric needle holder (see the pattern on page 234) that you can fold up and store in a drawer.

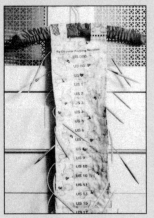

CIRCULAR NEEDLES can quickly become a nasty tangle, so make your own circular needle holder (see the pattern on page 236), or keep circular needles in Ziploc bags, writing their sizes in permanent marker on the outside of the bags.

BALLS OF YARN are best kept in large plastic containers. You don't want moths—or worse yet, mice—getting in there. Keeping them in the basement is a one-way ticket to musty-smelling balls, which you most definitely want to avoid. Keep them in a hallway closet instead, and toss a bar of nicely scented soap in with the yarn to keep it fresh-smelling.

KNITTING PROJECTS are well stored in canvas or cotton tote bags (see the pattern on page 231). Be sure to include a copy of the pattern slipped into a plastic sheet protector. If you have more than one project going at a time, store each one in a separate tote bag.

THE KNIT KIT: A BASIC TOOLBAG

Get yourself a funky-looking makeup case, toss the following items inside, and throw it in your knitting bag:

Small pair of scissors

Tiny bottle of hand lotion

Tape measure

Stitch markers, yarn needles, and safety pins, kept in an empty mint tin or film canister

Row counter

Cable needle

Crochet hook

the knitty-
LEARNING TO CAST ON,
gritty
BIND OFF, AND KNIT

gather 'round, chillins, I'm gonna teach you to knit. The act of knitting is really nothing more than pulling one loop of yarn through another loop of yarn; it's not unlike what you do every day when you tie your shoes. But first you have to learn how to put those loops of yarn onto a knitting needle (cast on), knit those loops row by row, and then get those loops off the needle (bind off) so that you have—what else? A length of fabric! Or, as it is known in some circles: a scarf. (Or the front of a sweater or a baby blanket—whatever.)

But first, I want to let you in on a little secret: Knitting is probably not as easy as you think, so be prepared to do a lot more bitching than stitching before you're really in the loop. I've seen it happen more than once: A beginner comes to our Stitch 'n Bitch group with a freshly purchased pair of needles, a ball of yarn, and the best of intentions and plans to leave with a sweater, or at least a scarf. Unfortunately, it doesn't happen that way. I mean, you wouldn't go to your first guitar lesson expecting to leave with a demo tape, would you?

The good news is that just about anyone can learn to knit. In fact, it wasn't all that long ago that knitting was taught to every eight-year-old girl in elementary school. And if they could do it, so can you. Unlike guitar playing—or swing dancing or painting—knitting doesn't require any special talent. It just takes time and patience, like learning to drive. At first it's totally awkward and takes all of your concentration, but eventually you can do it while thinking about other things or even carrying on a conversation (but not while drinking; please, never drink and knit).

Knitting is a simple process, yet it's so damn clever that I bet you'll develop a newfound appreciation for whoever invented the technique thousands of years ago. Here's the basic idea: You put a number of loops of yarn on a knitting needle. Then, you pull a loop of yarn through each of those loops with another needle. And that's the part that makes knitting so tricky: You use a pointed stick to pull those loops through rather than a hook, which seems so much more logical. It will feel awkward and difficult at first, but it's a bit like learning to use chopsticks: At first it seems like using a fork is so much easier, but with some practice, you can pick up everything from a huge tempura shrimp to the tiniest grain of rice with finesse. So pick up your sticks and let's get started.

casting call
How to Cast On Stitches

putting the first row of yarn loops on your knitting needle is called casting on, and there are a couple of ways to do it. Besides being easier or harder to do, some cast-on methods will give you a loose bottom edge, while others give you a firm edge. I'm going to teach you my favorite method here: the double cast-on. It's versatile enough to use for most projects because it leaves a nice, sturdy-but-stretchy edge at the bottom of your work.

Every cast-on method starts with a slip knot. Making a slip knot is a lot easier to do than to explain, but I'll try.

Making a Slip Knot

1 Unwind a strand of yarn at least 8 inches long from the ball and hold it in your left hand between your thumb and forefinger. (The ball end of the yarn should be on the right, and the "tail" to the left.) With your right hand, wrap the ball end of the yarn clockwise around your forefinger and middle finger, with your fingers spread approximately 1 inch apart.

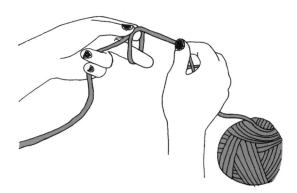

2 Pull a loop of the ball end of the yarn through the loop of yarn around your fingers.

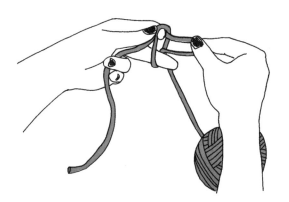

3 Drop the yarn off the fingers of your left hand while still holding on to the loop with your right hand, and gently pull the tail end until a knot forms at the bottom of the base of the loop. Voilà! Le slip knot!

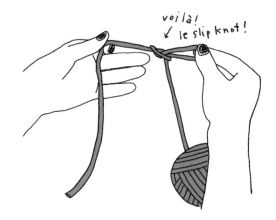

voilà!
↙ le slip knot!

4 Slide that slip knot onto a knitting needle, and pull on the tail and ball ends to tighten it around the needle. (You get it? The knot slips!) As you do, think of the knot as a warm scarf hugging the needle rather than a noose choking off its air supply. You want this stitch to have a snug hug, not a yoke choke.

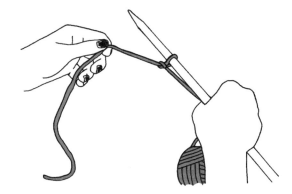

THE RIGHT SITCH FOR LEARNING TO STITCH

Just like skinning a cat, there's more than one way to learn to knit.

ME, MYSELF, AND I: Teach yourself from a book (this one, I hope). If you find it difficult to read and wield needles at the same time, try reading the instructions into a tape recorder, then listen to it while you practice making the stitch. A good number of the Stitch 'n Bitchers I know taught themselves from a book.

WITH A LITTLE HELP FROM YOUR FRIENDS: Even if none of your friends knows how to knit, it's fun to learn together from a book. That way, one person can read the instructions while the others get busy with their needles and yarn.

BRINGING IN THE BIG GUNS: This is the time to call on Grandma, Great-Aunt Bess, or that chick in accounting who's always knitting. Offer to bring over some cookies, then plan to spend the entire afternoon (or several) with her. Besides the chance for a little family or office bonding, learning from an old-timer means you'll pick up some great time-tested advice and techniques. I still think of Great-Aunt Jo whenever I make a certain edge stitch that she taught me more than twenty years ago.

Double Cast-on

this cast-on method may seem a bit confusing at first, like cat's cradle, but practice it a couple of times and soon you'll be casting on stitches like nobody's business. Plus, it looks kinda cool—like you're holding a slingshot.

Make a slip knot, leaving a tail that's at least three times the width of the piece you want to knit. So, for a 10-inch-wide scarf, you'd leave about a 30-inch tail of yarn. Hold that needle with your right hand, with the long tail end hanging to the left and the ball end hanging to the right. Place your right pointer finger over the slip knot to hold it in place. Close the bottom three fingers of your left hand around the yarn, about 4 inches down from the needle. Now, with your thumb and forefinger, spread apart the two strands of yarn like you were opening a tiny little curtain. Bring your fingers through these strands from behind, making sure that the tail end is over your thumb and the ball end is over your forefinger. Your left hand should be in a stick-'em-up position, like you're holding a gun.

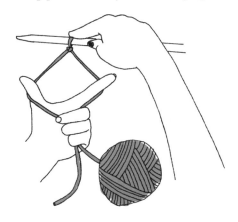

2 With the needle in your right hand, scoop up the strand of yarn that runs across your palm to the bottom of your thumb.

3 Wrap the yarn on your left forefinger around the front of your knitting needle, counterclockwise.

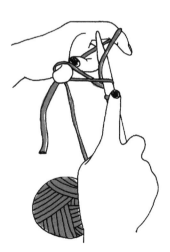

4 Bring the loop of yarn that's on your left thumb up and over the tip of your knitting needle.

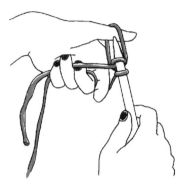

5 Pull your thumb outta there and tighten the cast-on stitch.

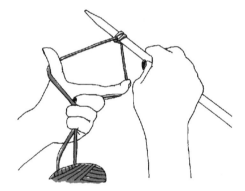

Continue steps 2–5 until you've cast on the desired number of stitches, leaving you with several loops of yarn on your needle, each with a cute, snug little butt at the bottom.

TIP: If you find that you cast on stitches too tightly, you can make like the Europeans do, and cast on over two needles held together. When you are done, just pull one of the needles out and there you go—nice loose stitches remain on the other needle!

knit Happens
How to Make a Knit Stitch

Okay, you've got stitches on your needle; say amen, somebody. It's time to try your hand at some real knitting.

There are two basic ways to make the knit stitch: English and Continental. I don't know why the two methods are called this, because while the Brits may very well knit English style over their tea and crumpets, my Dutch relatives on the other side of the pond are downing cookies and coffee and knitting English style too, thank you very much. Most Americans knit English style, and it's my preferred method, but most Germans knit Continental. Ja, wool!

The difference in the two methods has to do with whether you hold the ball end of the yarn in your left or right hand. You might try learning the more popular English style first, because it's always nice to be down with the popular crowd. Later, especially if you're the trendsetting type, you can come back and try Continental, which is starting to win more and more American fans. Or try both and see which one feels more comfortable to you. Me, I'm a stodgy diehard, and I'll never switch my stitch, even if they do claim that the Continental method is faster. I just remember my grandma, who never knit a Continental stitch in her life, yet churned out enough socks to cover the feet of a small army.

NOTE TO LEFTIES: Some folks will tell you that lefties should do everything explained here in the reverse, but others simply advise lefties to start with the Continental method, since you hold the yarn in your left hand, and knit right along with righties. That's what I'd suggest too. It will definitely be easier than trying to learn how to knit while holding this book up to a mirror!

KNITTY DITTIES: RHYMES TO KNIT TO

Rhymes were used to teach little children to knit, but they are really helpful to grown-ups, too, because they can remind you that there are basically four moves to every knit stitch. I've modified one of them, and like to use it when I'm teaching knitting:

GO IN YOUR FRONT DOOR (insert right needle up into the center of the loop on your left needle)

AND GRAB YOUR SCARF (wrap the yarn counterclockwise around the tip of the right needle)

THEN TAKE IT OUTSIDE (draw the right needle back out through the loop on the left needle, taking the new loop with it)

BEFORE THE CAT BARFS (push the old loop off the tip of the left needle)

tHrow AwAy
The English (Right-Hand) Method

1 Take the needle with the stitches on it in your left hand. Hold it the way you would a set of keys when unlocking a door: with your thumb and forefinger resting just behind the first stitch on the needle, and your bottom three fingers supporting the needle. With your right hand, hold the yarn using one of the methods shown on page 38, then pick up your second knitting needle. Hold it the same way you do your left needle, but with your pointer finger pointing up in the air. Your thumb should be resting about an inch from the tip, and your other three fingers are holding up the needle. If you are using long (14-inch) needles, you can tuck the end under your arm or in your armpit to hold it up. This is the way that I knit, and although it can result in smelly knitting needles, I like it.

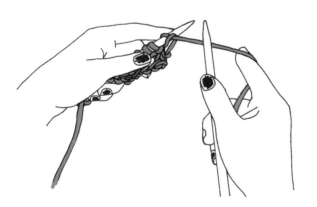

2 Slide the point of the right needle through the first loop on the left needle from front to back (and from left to right) so that the two make an X. The left needle is on the top of the X (closest to you), and the right needle is on the bottom (away from you).

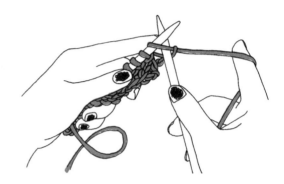

3 If you aren't holding the needle under your arm, hold the X part of the needles (the point where they cross) with the thumb and forefinger of your left hand. (You should be able to let go of the right needle without it dropping to the ground.) Pick up the ball end of the yarn and wrap it around the tip of the right needle counterclockwise (from back to front). In English-style knitting, this is called "throwing" the yarn, and by doing it, you've created a new loop. Yay!

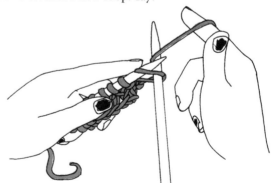

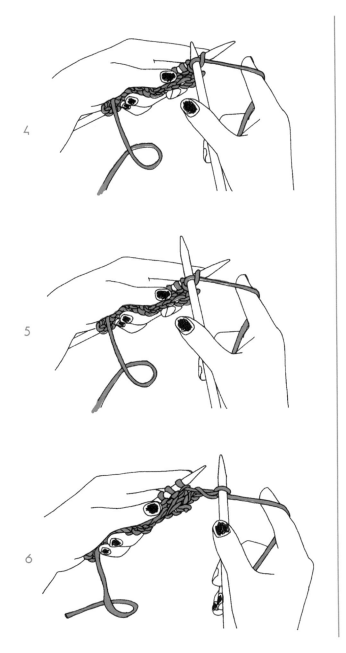

4 Now here's the tricky part: Take hold of the right needle with your right hand again. Pull the yarn taut (not tight!) with your forefinger. Then, slide the point of your right needle down and back out of the loop the opposite of the way you came in: *from the back to the front.* Make sure you bring the new loop along!

5 Once you're back out, slide the right needle up again so that the new loop is about 1½ inches from the tip and the needles are in an X shape again.

6 Slide the right needle to the right, thereby pushing the old loop off the tip of the left needle.

Hey, you did it! You made a knit stitch! Sucked, right? Doesn't seem like it will ever get easier? It will.

knit picking
The Continental (Left-Hand) Method

1 With your left hand, wrap the yarn using one of the methods described in Holding Your Own (page 38), then pick up the needle with the stitches on it. Keep your pointer finger, with the yarn wrapped around it, pointing in the air, and place your thumb and middle finger just behind the first stitch on the needle. Use your bottom two fingers to hold the needle up. Pick up your second knitting needle with your right hand, and hold it the way you would a set of keys, getting ready to open a door: with your thumb and forefinger resting about an inch from the tip, your forefinger resting on top, and your other three fingers supporting the needle.

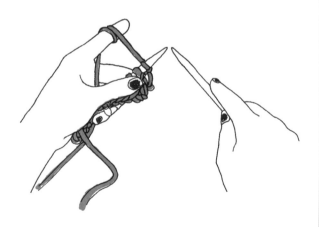

2 Slide the point of the right needle through the first loop on the left needle from front to back (and from right to left). Stick the point through about 1½ inches. Your needles should be making an X, with the left needle on the top of the X (closest to you), and the right needle on the bottom (away from you).

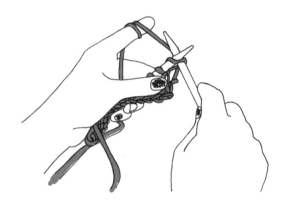

3 Okay, here's the tricky part in Continental knitting: With the tip of the right needle, grab that strand of yarn that's coming from your forefinger so that it wraps counterclockwise around the right needle.

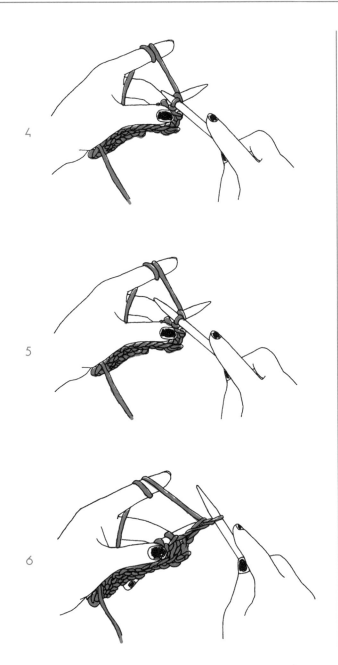

4

5

6

4 Pull this new loop back out the loop you came in from. (It sometimes helps to twist your hands so that your palms face you.) With Continental knitting, you're doing all the work with your right needle rather than your fingers, and you are "picking" stitches from the strand. And guess what? You've just created a new loop. Wunderbar!

5 Once you're back out, slide the right needle up again so that the new loop is about 1½ inches from the tip. Your needles should be back in an X shape.

6 Push the old loop off the left needle.

Hey, you did it! You made a knit stitch, Continental-wise. Now go get yourself a Continental breakfast and celebrate!

Keep It Comin', Love

Just keep knitting each stitch from the left needle onto the right needle until there are no stitches left. Then, switch hands: Place the needle with stitches in your left hand, and take the empty, naked needle in your right. Make sure your yarn is hanging straight down and in front of the needle (see Caution, page 38), and go back the other way. Then, just like a little human typewriter (you've seen one of those ancient machines, right?), work each row, switch hands, and knit back again until your piece of knitting is as long as you want it to be.

CAUTION: A super-easy and common mistake to make at this point is to have the yarn hanging down but to the *back* of your needle, making it look like you have two stitches at the end of your left needle instead of one (**figure 1**). Lots of beginners then actually knit both of these stitches, adding a stitch to each end of their knitting and creating a weirdly shaped shawl-like object instead of a scarf or other straight piece of knitting. So make sure your yarn is hanging down correctly (in front of the needle) before you head back (**figure 2**).

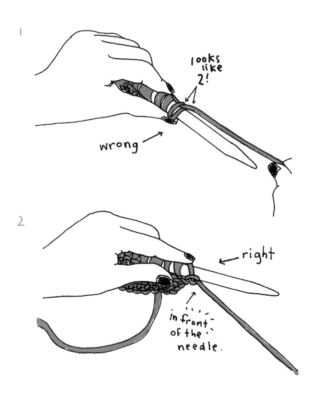

Holding Your Own

Whether you're knitting with the yarn in your left hand or your right hand, "you gotta know how to hold 'em," to borrow from Kenny Rogers. There are plenty of beginning knitters out there who pick up the yarn between thumb and forefinger every time they need to make a stitch, then drop it until they need it again. Now, I'm not going to say that you can't knit this way, just like no one would argue that you can't floss using only one finger. The thing is, you'll be limiting yourself to never getting as good as you could be if you did it with the yarn wrapped around your fingers.

The goal is to find a way to wrap that yarn (around your right hand, for English method, or your left hand, for Continental) so that it feeds smoothly off your finger with just the right amount of tension—not too tight and not too loose. Once you get it right, the yarn will feed off your finger like fishing line off the end of a fishing pole. Here are a couple of holds to try:

Two Right-Hand Holds for English Knitting

1 Weave the yarn under your pinky, over your ring finger, under your middle finger, and over your pointer. The yarn should run just between the nail and first knuckle of your pointer, and you can fold your last two or three fingers around it.

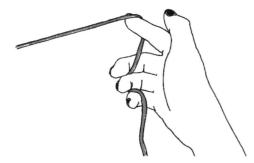

2 Wrap the yarn counterclockwise around your pinky, then under your ring and middle fingers, and back over the top of your pointer finger. Lightly close your pinky, ring, and middle fingers around the yarn and let it run across the top of your pointer, between the first and second knuckle. This is my favorite method.

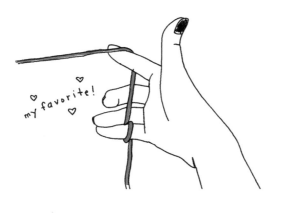

♡ ♡
♡ favorite!
my ♡ ♡

Two Left-Hand Holds for Continental Knitting

1 Wrap the yarn clockwise one-and-a-half times around your pointer finger, so that the wraps are between the first and second joint of your finger. The ball end of the yarn hangs down, and your pinky, ring, and middle fingers lightly close around it, to help with the tension. This is a very popular method and is particularly well suited to the Continental way of knitting.

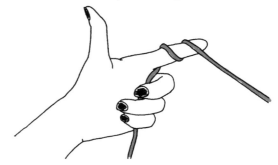

2 If you crochet, this hold will be easy. Wrap the yarn clockwise around your pinky, then under your ring and middle fingers, and back over the top of your pointer finger. Lightly close your pinky, ring, and middle fingers around the yarn and let it run across the top of your pointer, between the first and second knuckle.

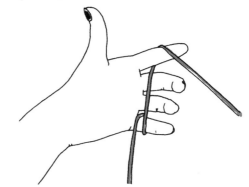

THE ANATOMY OF A STITCH

You already know that a knit stitch is a loop that hangs off your needle, but it's also important to know exactly *how* it hangs off the needle—since there's a right way and a wrong way. I like to think of the loop as a little gymnast straddling a balance beam, with one leg in front and the other in back. Your knitting needle is the beam, and the leg in front is the side of the loop that's hanging closer to you, the leg in back is the one that's farther way.

The thing to know is that the leg that's in front should be the leg that's on the right side of the loop, and the leg in back should be the one on the left side of the loop. If you're knitting and a stitch falls off the needle, it's super-important that you put that gymnast back on the balance beam that way: with the leg on the right side in front, and the leg on the left side in back. Another way to think of it is that the leg in front should be the one closer to the tip of the needle.

bound for glory
How to Bind Off Your Work

there's one last thing you need to know, and that's how to get the darn thing off the needles when you're done. Otherwise, you'd be walking around with a scarf that had a big pointed stick at one end. Okay, maybe you'd like to rock a stick-in-the-mud look this season, but it's still a good idea to know how to get those stitches off the needle and how to secure them so they don't unravel. It's called **binding off,** and it's easy. Really. Here's how:

Starting at the beginning of a row, knit a stitch. Let's call it Sally. Knit another stitch and call it Harry.

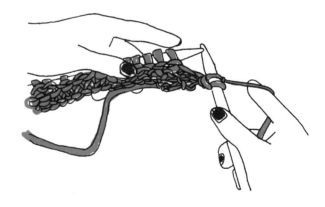

2 Slide the tip of the left needle under Sally's front leg (the first stitch you knit).

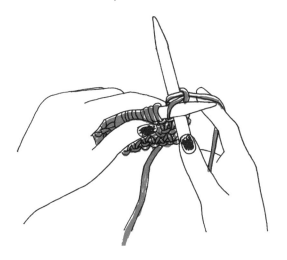

3 Then let Sally play leapfrog with Harry (the second stitch), by lifting Sally up and over Harry and then letting her drop off the tip of the right needle.

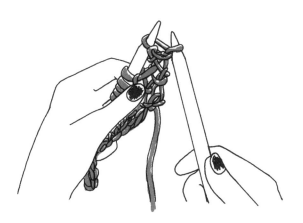

4 Only Harry is left on the right needle.

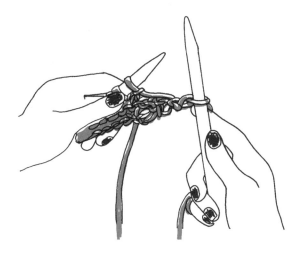

5 Repeat steps 2 and 3 over and over again, knitting a stitch, then leapfrogging the previous stitch over it, until all of your stitches have been bound off, and you're left with only one stitch. Cut the yarn about 6 inches from the end and pull it through that last stitch, tightening gently.

OUT WITH THE OLD: HOW TO START A NEW BALL

You can knit for a good long time with one ball of yarn, but eventually you'll run out. The best place to start a new ball of yarn is at the beginning of a row, so you don't have a big ol' ugly knot right in the middle of your scarf. How do you know if you have enough yarn left to finish a row? If you have about three times the width of your piece remaining, go ahead and knit the row. If you don't, get ready to start a new ball.

Cut the old yarn, leaving about a 6-inch-long tail. Hold this tail and the beginning 6 inches of the new yarn together with your left hand. Now just start knitting with the yarn. Don't worry that the very first stitch is a little loose, you can fix that later. **(figure 1)** Knit about 6 stitches, stop, and tie the ends of the yarns together in a nice, neat little square knot. Later when it's time to work away the ends, you can untie that knot. **(figure 2)**

Another way to secure that new yarn is to knit the first one or two stitches using the old and new yarn together. This method only works well if you aren't using yarn that is very bulky, and you should be careful, on the next row, to knit the two yarns together as one stitch, and not two.

Finally, there's the cheater's way out: Make a slip knot in the new yarn, pass the old yarn through it, and slide the new yarn up to the base of the first stitch, then knit away. This can make for a sloppy beginning of a row, but try it, you might like it. **(figure 3)**

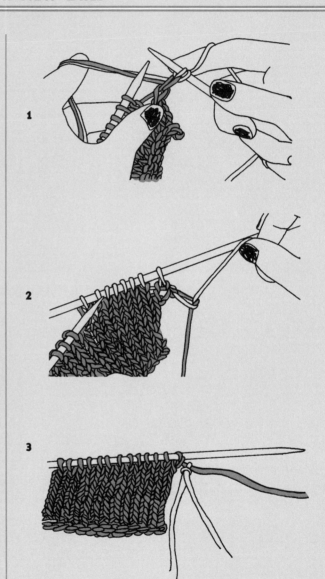

1

2

3

coLor my world
Learning to Make Stripes

Okay, so you know how to add a new ball of yarn when you're knitting. Now what if that new ball is a different color? Know what you'd have then? Stripes, my friend. And stripes are one of the easiest ways to make your knitting colorful and more fun. Add stripes by ending the old yarn, starting the next color of yarn, knitting for a few rows until your stripe is as wide as you want it to be, then adding the next color. Of course, you will always want to start your stripes at the *beginning* of a row. (Because you've been paying attention and you'd never dare add new yarn in the middle of a row, right?)

If your stripes are only a few rows wide, you'll get pretty tired of starting new yarn over and over again. Instead, just let the yarn you aren't using hang along the side of your piece. Then, every time you get to the side where this yarn is hanging, just twist it once with the yarn you are using to knit. When you are ready for it, start knitting with the other yarn again.

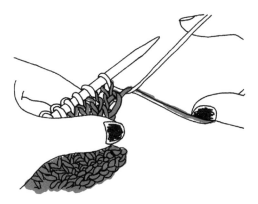

the end of the Line
How to Weave in Yarn Ends

When you've finished knitting a piece of fabric, you'll have a couple of yarn tails hanging along the side. You might want to pass these off as some kind of really weird fringe, but you'd be better off to hide them by weaving them in. Here's how:

Thread the yarn end through a yarn needle (see page 22). Bring the yarn in and out through the bumps along the edge or the back of your piece until you've tucked in about 4 inches of your yarn tail. Snip the yarn close to the end.

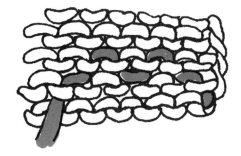

Baby's First Swatch

Before you start knitting any real projects, you should practice by making a little square of knit fabric. This little test square is called a swatch, and even experienced knitters make them, to see how their yarn knits up with a certain size of needle. You'll learn more about that in the next chapter, but for now, get ready to make a cute little test swatch in garter stitch, which is what you get if you knit every row.

Start with a pair of size 8 needles and some worsted-weight yarn, such as Brown Sheep Company Lamb's Pride Worsted. Size 8 needles are the middle size of needles, and worsted-weight yarn is the middle weight of yarn, so this combo is a good one to start with.

It may not look like much, but it's all yours.

Using the slingshot, double cast-on method, cast on 20 stitches.

Knit 30 rows.

As you're going along, stop every now and then and count the stitches you have on the needle after you've finished a row. Make sure you only have 20 stitches. If you end up with more than 20 stitches, check to see if you are hanging your yarn in front every time you begin a new row (see Caution, page 38). If you have holes in your knitting, make sure you are leaving your yarn in the back between every stitch, and not accidentally crossing it over the top of your needles and adding new stitches (and holes). If you do end up with extra stitches, don't worry. Just continue knitting with the new number of stitches. Your goal is to be able to knit at least 10 rows without adding or subtracting stitches.

Bind off. Cut the yarn, leaving a 6-inch tail hanging. Work away your yarn ends.

Hooray! Save your garter-stitch swatch. It is the very first thing you knit, and you'll want to cherish it. Toss it in your bag with your sunglasses; it will make a great lens cleaner.

beginner's basic 1
Go-Go Garter Stitch Scarf

Here's a nice, chunky scarf that can be made in a few evenings and will help you to practice some basic skills: casting on, knitting, adding a new color of yarn, and binding off. Best of all, by the time you're done with it, you will really be comfortable making the knit stitch.

Use an extra-bulky yarn. We used some really beautiful 50% alpaca/50% wool yarn from Blue Sky Alpaca (100 grams, 45 yards), 1 skein of each of the following three colors: green, purple, and teal. Other yarns you could use would be Brown Sheep Burly spun, Rowan Big Wool, or GGH Marakko in three colors that you like.

You'll also need a pair of size 17 straight needles—these are humungo and usually come only in plastic.

Start by casting on 10 stitches using the green yarn. Knit 14 rows. Cut the green yarn, leaving a 6" tail. Add in the purple yarn, and knit 14 rows. Cut the purple yarn, leaving a 6" tail. Add in the teal yarn, knit 14 rows. Cut the teal yarn, leaving a 6" tail. Repeat this striping pattern (the green yarn is next) 3 more times—so you have 4 repeats altogether. Bind off. Work all the yarn ends away with a yarn needle.

Using such fat yarn on such big needles means you will need to knit only 2 stitches to make an entire inch wide of fabric. And since this scarf starts with 10 stitches, that means it will come out to be 5" wide. After the striping repeats, it will be about 69" long. You can make this basic garter stitch scarf over and over again. Use a thinner yarn and you'll end up with something lacier. Or use a thinner yarn (like a worsted weight yarn) on thinner needles (like size 10) and start by casting on 20 stitches instead of 10, if you want something a little less bulky.

See page 123

purl, too

LEARNING TO PURL AND MAKE SIMPLE STITCH PATTERNS

Poor little purl stitch. Long the underdog of the knitting world, the purl stitch is destined to be always a bridesmaid, never the bride. Some people despise purling so much that they knit in the round just to avoid it; others, like certain friends of mine, claim to prefer it, simply because of its status as the unloved, black-sheep sibling of the more popular knit stitch.

So how did the purl stitch get such a bad rap? After all, *a purl stitch is nothing more than a knit stitch facing backward.* In fact, both stitches are just loops; the only difference is that when you knit, you *pull* the loop from the back to the front of the old loop—like pulling a tissue out of a box. When you purl, you *push* the loop through the front to the back of the old loop—like pushing that tissue back into the box. And that difference alone makes purling a stitch more difficult than knitting a stitch.

Still, if you're going to knit things on two needles, back and forth, you're going to need to learn to purl. Why, you ask? Allow me to explain.

Whether knitting or purling, the loop you make looks like a droplet, only upside down, with the point at the bottom and the curved part at the top. When you make a knit stitch, the bottom of the loop (the "V") lands on the front of your work, while the rounded part of the loop (the little bump) lands on the back of your work. When you purl, the reverse happens: The bump winds up in the front, and the little V winds up in the back. Once you can both knit and purl, you can control whether your Vs land on the front of your fabric or on the back, no matter which side of the fabric you're working on. Knowing how to purl means you can create fabric that has *all* the little Vs on one side and *all* the little bumps on the other—and that makes a very nice fabric indeed.

But the purl stitch will let you do more than just hide all those unsightly stitch bumps in the back. Some folks like to use the bumps and Vs to make designs in their fabric—for instance, they might make a heart shape out of purl bumps on a flat background of knit Vs. In any case, once you know both knit and purl, you know all of the knitting stitches there are. Really, it's all based on those two little stitches. And even they are just two ways of making the same stitch.

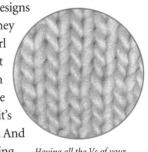

Having all the Vs of your stitches on the front makes a nice flat fabric.

Okay, so let's purl already. But fasten your seat belts; it's going to be a bumpy (get it?) ride.

right on
Purling with Yarn in the Right Hand (English)

Hold your yarn and needles the same way you would to make a knit stitch, with the yarn in your right hand, but before you begin, bring the yarn between the tips of your needles so that it is *in front* of your right needle.

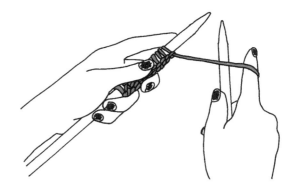

2 Insert the right needle from back to front (and from right to left) through the first stitch on the left needle. It's like your needle is playing a game of limbo by going under the front leg of that first stitch. Your needles are now in an X shape.

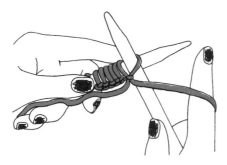

3 Hold the center of the X with the thumb and fore-finger of your left hand so that the needles don't fall, take the yarn in your right hand, and loop it around the point of your right needle counterclockwise (from back to front).

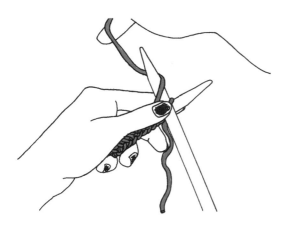

4 Holding the yarn down below the center of the X with your right forefinger, carefully slide your right needle down along the base of the left needle, pushing the point of the right needle—and your new loop—out through the back of the stitch you came in through.

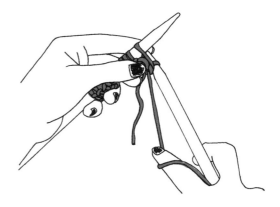

5 Push the right needle back up again (it should now be behind the left needle). You have an X once more.

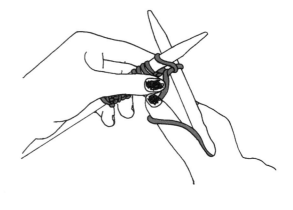

6 Slide the old loop up and off the left needle.

Admire your new stitch. You did it, Purly McPurlsalot!

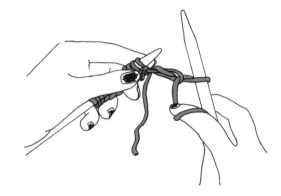

Left out
Purling with Yarn in the Left Hand (Continental)

1 Hold your yarn and needles the same way you would to make a knit stitch, holding the yarn in your left hand, but before you begin, bring the yarn between the tips of your needles so that it is *in front* of your left needle.

2 Insert your right needle from back to front (and from right to left), through the loop on the first stitch on the left needle, passing the right needle *underneath* the front leg of that stitch. The ends of your needles are now in an X shape.

3 Bring the yarn in your left hand around the point of your right needle counterclockwise, then bring your left pointer finger (the one with the yarn around it), down below the center of the X.

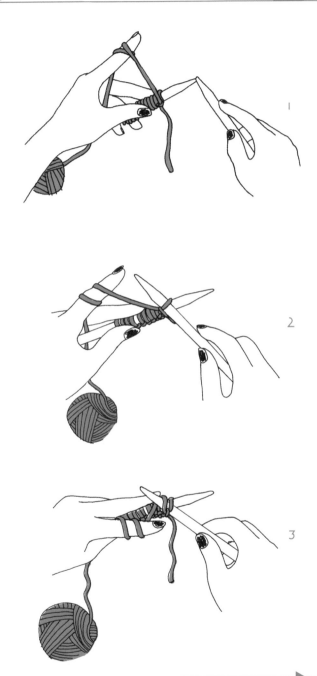

4 Continue to hold the yarn in this position while you carefully slide your right needle down along the base of the left needle, pushing the point of the right needle out through the back of the stitch you came in through. Be careful not to let the new loop you created fall off!

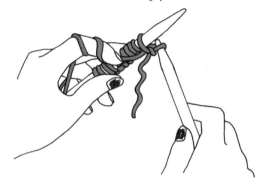

5 Push the right needle back up again (it should now be behind the left needle). You have an X once more.

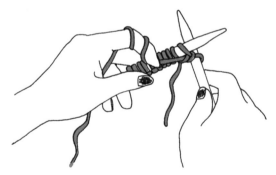

6 Push the old loop up and off the left needle.

Take a bow, Purlana Purlstein! Keep on keepin' on until you've purled each stitch on the needle.

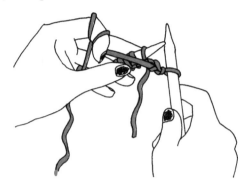

Look Who's Stocking
How to Make Stockinette Stitch

Now that you've learned to purl, you should really give yourself a pat on the back, because you now know how to make all the stitches there are in knitting. When you knit across one entire row, and then turn around and purl your way back across the next row, then knit the third row, and purl the fourth row, and on and on—you create what's known as stockinette stitch. Basically, you're making fabric with all the V parts of the stitches on one side (the front, or "right" side of your fabric) and all the bump parts of the stitches on the other side (the back, or "wrong" side), which makes the front

THE RAGE FOR GAUGE

To make a swatch in stockinette, cast on 20 stitches, knit a row, then purl the next row, and continue alternating this way for 30 rows. Then bind off, knitwise.

Take a look at your swatch. It's as smooth as a baby's butt on one side, and as bumpy as a teenager's forehead on the other. But there's something else that can be learned from this swatch, and that's called **gauge**. Gauge is the number of stitches per inch that you get with a particular size of needles, a particular thickness of yarn, and your particular pair of hands.

To calculate your gauge: Lay your swatch flat and measure how wide it is. Try to make your measurement exact—at least to the nearest quarter-inch. Now take the number of stitches you have—in this case, 20—and divide it by the width of your swatch, in inches. So, if your swatch measured 4 inches wide, your gauge would be 20 divided by 4, or 5 stitches per inch. On the other hand, if your swatch measured 5 inches wide, your gauge would be 4 stitches per inch. Different knitters get different gauges even when they are using the exact same yarn and needles; a tighter knitter will squeeze more stitches into an inch than will a looser knitter.

Most patterns will give you a gauge, such as "16 stitches per 4 inches using size 8 needles." That means you should make a swatch using those size 8 needles and the yarn the pattern recommends. And no, don't gauge your gauge by casting on 4 stitches, knitting a couple of rows, and seeing if your swatch measures an inch wide. Instead, cast on 16 stitches, knit at least an inch or two of fabric, and see how close that comes to being 4 inches wide. Better yet, cast on something like 24 or 30 stitches, knit up a square, and measure over the center 16 stitches.

What do you do if it doesn't come out the right size? Do you have to start knitting tighter or looser to get your stitches to fit the pattern's gauge? No, you don't have to change anything about the way you knit. Instead, use smaller or larger needles and reknit the swatch. Keep on sizing down or sizing up until the swatch measures what it should. Use that needle size to knit your entire piece.

Making a gauge swatch before you begin any project is super-important. Nevertheless, I'm sure that at some point in your knitting life you're going to knit a project without making a gauge swatch. And I'm just as sure that some day, after spending months knitting what was to have been a nice, comfortable sweater you end up with a belly-baring nightmare. And when that day comes, don't say I didn't warn you.

Small gauge

Medium gauge

Large gauge

These three swatches were all knit using the same yarn, but with different size needles. The small one (top) was knit with size 5; middle with size 8; and bottom with size 10 1/2.

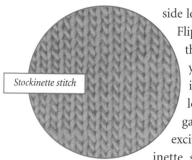

Stockinette stitch

side look really nice and smooth. Flip it over to the side where all the purl bumps are, and you've got reverse stockinette. Stockinette stitch looks quite different from garter stitch. It can be pretty exciting to knit your first stockinette stitch swatch, because the fabric looks so purty·and professional. In fact, stockinette stitch is by far the most popular stitch pattern out there.

REMINDER: Bring the yarn to the back of your needles when you begin a knit row, and bring the yarn to the front of your needles when you are purling. Otherwise, you'll end up with all kinds of craziness on your needles.

prime ribbing
How to Make Rib Stitch

Stockinette stitch fabric is very good at being stretchy and smooth, but not so good at lying flat. Fabric knit in stockinette stitch likes to curl at the edges, which makes it great for covering tube-shaped body parts, like torsos, arms, and legs. But if you knit yourself a scarf in stockinette stitch, you'll end up with something that looks more like a tube; the edges will roll in. So for things like a blanket or a scarf—or the bottom edges of sweaters and sleeves that you don't want rolling up— you'll need something that lies flat.

That's where the rib stitch comes in. Fabric made in rib stitch—or **ribbing**—is much stretchier than stockinette

---

CLOSE TO THE EDGE: MAKING NICE EDGE STITCHES

Sometimes the stitches at the very edge of your work get all loose and wacky. That's why some folks like to use a special stitch at the beginning and ends of their rows, called an edge stitch. One way to do this is to knit the last stitch of every row, always. Another way is always to slip the first stitch from one needle to the other without knitting it. But the method I like best is one I learned from my favorite knitting author, Maggie Righetti (see page 119), and it's the one I teach to all the Stitch 'n Bitchers I meet:

1. Knit (or purl) the first stitch of the row the usual way.

2. Put your needle into the next stitch like you're getting ready to knit (or purl) it, but don't do anything else. Stop and pull the yarn tight. Then go on knitting like there's no tomorrow.

Do this at the beginning of every row, and you'll have the most beautiful edges you ever did see. Plus, you'll get one edge stitch for every row (rather than one edge stitch for every two rows, which you'll get if you slip stitches at the ends of rows), and that's nicer to have when it comes time to sew two knit edges together.

2 x 2 rib stitch

it's important that the stitches are in the right places. This first row will be a bit slow going, but that's okay; in time you'll pick up speed with this maneuver.

Row 2: You purled the last 2 stitches of that first row. Now, going back, you are going to knit those same 2 stitches. By doing this, you are lining up the Vs of the knit stitches with the Vs on the back of the purl stitches on the row below. So, start by knitting the first 2 stitches. Then, bring the yarn between the needle points to the front, and purl the next 2 stitches. Carry on till the end of the row. You should end with 2 purl stitches.

stitch fabric—almost like an accordion—and it lies very nice and flat. Like stockinette, ribbing is made using knit and purl stitches, but instead of placing all the Vs and the bumps on just one side of the fabric, you align them vertically, to form long columns, or "ribs," of V stitches with valleys of purl bumps in between.

To make what's called a **2 x 2 rib**, here's what you do: Cast on some stitches in a number that is evenly divisible by 4 (that simply means to cast on 16 stitches, or 24, or 40), and then do the following:

Row 1: Knit 2 stitches the usual way. Now, bring your yarn between the tips of your needles to the front. You are in purl position! So go ahead, purl 2 stitches. Then, bring yarn to the back between the points of your needle, and you're all ready to knit once more. Go ahead and knit the next 2 stitches, then purl 2 more. Keep alternating 2 knit stitches and 2 purl stitches this way. Always remember to take that extra step of bringing the yarn to the back before knitting or to the front before purling, and always carry it between the needle points when you do so. Repeat knitting 2 stitches and purling 2 stitches, till you get to the end of the row. You should end with 2 purl stitches. If you don't, unravel and try again, because

purl, interrupted
How to Tell When to Knit or Purl

When making ribbed fabric, you could chant "knit, knit, purl, purl" across every row to keep track of which stitch to make next. But that can be risky, because it's easy to lose track or get interrupted. Besides, it can be annoying to the Stitch 'n Bitcher sitting next to you. Luckily, there's a better way. In fact, you can learn to let the stitches *themselves* tell you whether they need to be knit or purled. Here's how: Look at the base of the next stitch on your needle. If you see a little V hanging around its neck—as if the stitch is wearing a scarf—it means that, in order to stack another V on top of it, you will need to knit it. However, if you see a little rounded bump at the base of the stitch—as if the stitch on your needle has a little noose around its neck—then in order to stack another bump on top of it, you will need to purl that stitch. This is what instructions for ribbing mean when they say "knit the knits and purl the purls."

Unlike stockinette stitch, ribbing looks exactly the same on the front and the back, which makes it perfect for scarves, because they're usually seen from both sides when wrapped around your neck. Its stretchiness also keeps the bottom edges and sleeve cuffs of sweaters close to your body and around your wrists, so you can stay nice and warm. And also, as I explained before, it keeps those edges from rolling up.

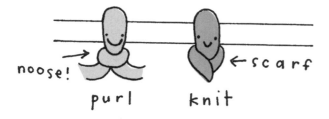

Ribbing does not have to be done with two knits and two purls; a **1 x 1 rib** is made by alternating only one knit stitch and one purl stitch across an entire row. Fabric made with 1×1 ribbing is not as stretchy as 2×2 ribbing, but, like its cousin, it is just as flat and reversible.

MIND YOUR P'S AND K'S

Having trouble remembering which stitch makes V shapes and which one makes bumps? One way is to think of the little bump as being kind of pearl-like (I actually think of it as pearl barley). You could also think of the middle of the letter K (in Knit) as having a V in it, and the top of the letter P (in Purl) as having a bump.

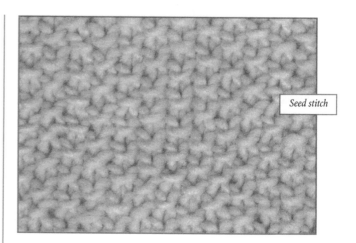

Seed stitch

gone to seed
Making the Seed Stitch

There is another very nice stitch pattern you can now make using knits and purls. It's called seed stitch by American designers, and moss stitch by the British. The two are exactly the same, though, so you can call it whatever you want, including Fred.

Anyway, making seed stitch is a little bit like what would happen if you were to do a 1×1 rib while you were drunk: Instead of knitting the knits and purling the purls, you will be *knitting the purls and purling the knits.*

To create the seed stitch, you will knit one stitch, then purl one stitch all the way across a row. (I don't have to remind you always to bring the yarn to the back before you make a knit stitch, and to the front before you purl, do I?)

On the second row, you are going to knit the purls, and purl the knits. If you are working across an even number of stitches, this means you will start with a knit and end with a purl; if you are working across an uneven number of stitches, you will start and end with a knit. Basically, every time you see a purl bump (a little noose on your next stitch), you will knit it. And every time you see a knit V hanging off your next stitch (a cute li'l scarf), you will purl that stitch. Do that all the way across the row. And on the next row.

Seed stitch makes a very interesting fabric. Like garter stitch, it is bumpy; like stockinette, it is flat; and like ribbing, it doesn't curl in at the edges. It is a very textured stitch that has kind of an earthy, organic look. It is also reversible, so it works well for scarves. And because it's less stretchy in the vertical direction than a garter stitch, it will take fewer rows to knit the same amount of fabric. Use it for whatever you'd like; it's fun to make, and now you know how to do it.

bump and grind
Making Designs with Knits and Purls

Since knit stitches make a smooth surface, and purl stitches make a bumpy surface, and since you now know how to do both, you can make fabric that has a raised design made of purl bumps on a smooth knit background. Instructions for making purl and knit patterns are often given on a graph or chart like the one on the right.

The chart represents how the fabric looks from the front; each box represents a stitch. Empty boxes represent knit Vs, and boxes with little dashes represent purl bumps. So, if you are knitting with the front side of the fabric facing you, you will knit the blank spaces and purl the dashes.

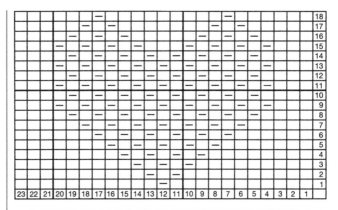

23	22	21	20	19	18	17	16	15	14	13	12	11	10	9	8	7	6	5	4	3	2	1	Row
							—								—								18
						—	—								—	—							17
					—	—	—								—	—	—						16
						—	—	—	—				—	—	—	—							15
					—	—	—	—		—	—	—		—	—	—	—						14
					—	—	—	—	—	—	—	—	—	—	—	—	—						13
						—	—	—	—	—	—	—	—	—	—	—							12
						—	—	—	—	—	—	—	—	—	—	—							11
							—	—	—	—	—	—	—	—	—								10
							—	—	—	—	—	—	—	—	—								9
								—	—	—	—	—	—	—									8
								—	—	—	—	—	—	—									7
									—	—	—	—	—										6
									—	—	—	—	—										5
										—	—	—											4
										—	—	—											3
											—												2
											—												1

Knit your heart out

But what happens when you turn around and knit back the other way? When you are knitting with the *wrong* side of the fabric facing you, you must do the *opposite* of what I just told you: That is, you must knit the dashes and purl the blanks. Think about it: From this side when you knit the dashes, you'll be putting the bump part of the stitch on the *front* of the fabric, which is where you want it, and when you purl the blanks, you'll be putting the flat, or V, part of the stitch on the front of the fabric, which is also what you want.

Try making the heart design above. Start by casting on 23 stitches, and knit a few rows in stockinette stitch.

Then, starting on the knit side, begin the chart. The row at the bottom of the graph is the first row you are going to make, and you will read it from right to left. In fact, when reading a graph like this, *you always read the odd-numbered rows from right to left.* So, according to this graph, you will knit 11 stitches, purl 1 stitch, then knit 11 more stitches.

For row 2, read the next row up on the graph from left to right. Yup: *You always read the even-numbered rows from left to right.* Remember, too, that this row is being knit with the wrong side of the work facing you, so you will do the opposite of the stitch shown on the chart: You will purl 10 stitches, knit 1, purl 1, knit 1, then purl 10.

Row 3 is an odd-numbered row, so you will read it from right to left, making knits for the blank boxes and purls for the dashes. It can be difficult to keep your place when you are knitting from a chart, so here are some techniques you can use to keep track of where you are:

1 Use a row counter on the end of your needles. Usually, people use one row counter at the end of one needle, but there's no rule saying you can't use two row counters, one on each needle. When you come to a new row, turn the counter *two numbers* (since you will always be knitting odd-numbered rows from one needle, and even-numbered rows from the other needle).

2 Make a photocopy of the pattern. Each time you complete a row, put a line through it with a highlighter (to show it's been done, but so you can still see it). By looking at the row you've just completed, you can use the stitches from it as pointers for the row you are working on (like, "On this next row, I have to start making my purl bumps one stitch earlier than in the last row, and I have to continue them for one stitch longer").

3 Make vertical lines through your graph every 5 or 10 stitches, and put matching stitch-counter rings on your needles at the same intervals.

BINDING OFF IN PATTERN

When binding off fabric that's made in ribbing or seed stitch, it's best to bind off in pattern. In the last chapter, you learned how to bind off knitwise. Now you are going to bind off in purl, which is no big shakes, really. To do it, just purl a stitch, then, while your yarn is still in front, stick the needle into the back of the previous stitch to lift it up and over your purl stitch, and off the needle.

To bind off in pattern, just bind off knitwise after making a knit stitch, and bind off purlwise after making a purl stitch.

She Gets Around: Knitting on Circular and Double-Pointed Needles

Now that you know how to make a purl stitch, you should know that there is a way to avoid having to make them very often, and that is by knitting stockinette stitch in the round—which involves making row after row of knit stitches.

To knit on circular needles, you will need to have a needle whose length is smaller than the circumference of the fabric you are knitting—you can't knit a hat that's only 22 inches around on a 26-inch circular needle, for instance. Your knitting pattern will tell you what size needle you need.

Start by casting on the requisite number of stitches. Then bring the ends of your circular needles together in front of you, with the first cast-on stitch at the end of the left-hand needle, and the last on the right-hand needle. Then, making sure that none of your stitches is twisted (in other words, all of their butts are hanging down), start knitting in the regular way. You'll find that your knitting is now joined in a round. Then just keep going, round and round and round. What you're really doing is more like knitting in a spiral than in the round, but it comes out to pretty much the same thing.

Knitting on double-pointed needles is a bit more complicated, but you don't need to worry so much about the size, as any sized tube can be knit on any sized needle (unless you're trying to make a really giant tube on really tiny needles). Begin by casting all the called-for stitches onto a single one of your double-pointed needles. Then, divide the stitches evenly onto three needles, slipping the stitches purlwise from one needle to the next.

Finally, bend the needles into a triangle shape with the open end facing you. Make sure that the first stitch you cast on is at the end of the left-hand needle in front of you, and the last stitch you cast on is on the right-hand needle, and also see to it that none of your stitches are twisted. Then, with the free needlepoints facing you, and the middle needle farther from you, take the fourth needle and begin knitting the stitches off of the left-hand needle. It's very easy to accidentally do this backwards, knitting with the tips of the needles farthest from you and the middle needle close to you. If you do that, however, you will actually be knitting your tube inside out! When you finish knitting all of the stitches on the left-hand needle onto the fourth needle, the left-hand needle will suddenly be free. Now you can use it to knit all the stitches off of the next needle, and so on and so forth all the way around.

beginner's basic 11
Ribbed-for-Her-Pleasure Scarf

Here's another great beginner's scarf. Done in a knit 2 purl 2 rib, it looks the same on both sides—which is just what you want in a scarf. Plus, making it will really help you learn your purls from your knits.

This scarf takes 2 skeins of Brown Sheep Company's Lamb's Pride Bulky yarn in color #M38, Lotus Pink, and a pair of size 10 (6mm) knitting needles. Cast on 32 stitches.

Row 1: Knit 2, purl 2, repeat to end of row. (Your row should end with purl 2).

Repeat that row until you've used up both skeins of yarn, then bind off your stitches *in pattern*. When you're done, your scarf will be about 5" wide and 64½" in length. As you're knitting, make sure that your ribs are lining up the right way. Remember to knit the knits and purl the purls, and, if you see mistakes, unravel your knitting back to the place where the error is, put all 32 of your stitches back on the needle (be sure to put them on the right way!), and continue on, correctly.

Once you've made one of these ribbed scarves, you can get a little fancy. One thing that works well and looks great is to make the scarf using two yarns held together—such as a wool yarn with a mohair yarn, or a sparkly yarn. It's a classic that you can make over and over again, and an always welcome gift that can be knit up in less than a week.

See page 123

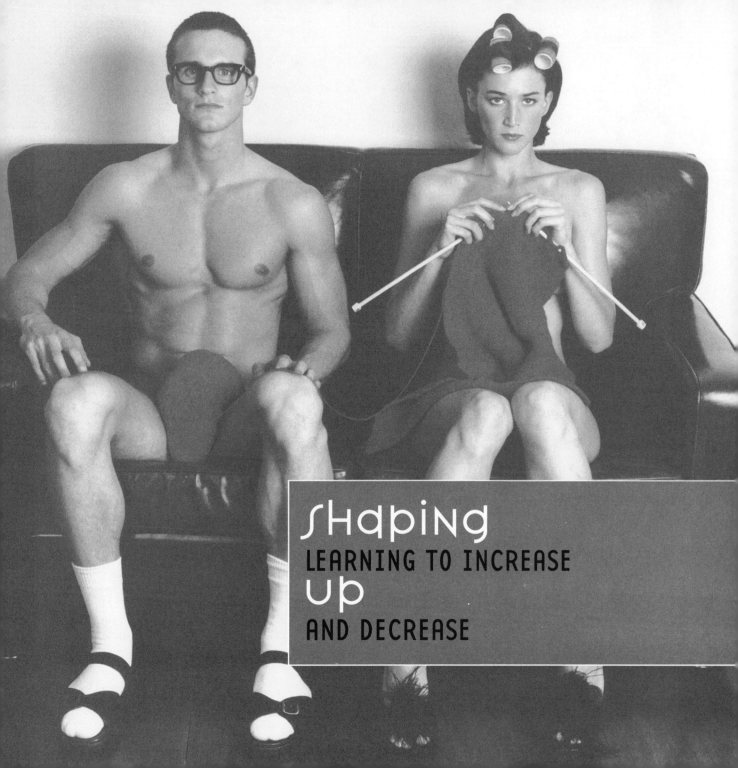

shaping

LEARNING TO INCREASE

up

AND DECREASE

Once you know how to cast on, bind off, knit, and purl, you can make lots and lots of pieces of knit fabric, but until you learn to increase and decrease, you'll be stuck making only squares and rectangles. And while that's great for pillows, blankets, and scarves, it's not so great for making fabric meant to cover the human body, which is not shaped like a box. For the most part, the human body is tapered and curvy: Your arms are wider at the shoulder than at the wrist, your torso narrows at the waist and gets wider at the chest, your head is bigger around the forehead and gets smaller at the crown (at least, I hope so).

In order to knit clothes to fit around these shapely body parts, you'll need to create fabric that gets narrower or wider accordingly. When you're sewing clothes from woven fabric, you simply cut the cloth into the pattern shapes, then sew them together. But can you imagine taking a pair of scissors and cutting into your knit fabric? Even if you've been knitting for just a short time, the thought should make you shiver in horror.

Instead, knit pieces are knit right into the shape they need to be. Whether simple or complex, these shapes are all made by increasing stitches at certain points to make the fabric wider, or decreasing stitches at other points to make the fabric narrower. Learning to increase and decrease stitches allows you to make everything from trapezoid-shaped pieces of fabric to be sewn together for sleeves, to scooped-out curves for necklines, to bell-shaped sleeve caps, to dome-shaped hats.

In fact, just knowing how to increase and decrease will allow you to make fabric in just about any shape you choose.

A walk on the wide side
How to Increase

There are a few different ways to increase. Increased stitches can be invisible (which is what you usually want) or visible (which can be used for decorative purposes, or because it fits in better with a given stitch pattern).

double dipping
The Bar Increase

The bar increase makes two stitches out of one, but it leaves a little "bar"—one that's similar to a purl bump—where the extra stitch was made. Some folks appreciate this fact, because it's easier to keep track of where they made their increases. Plus, it's kind of cute-looking. On the other hand, if you make this increase on ribbing or seed-stitch fabric, the bar will blend in with the rest of the purl bumps, and it won't be as visible. Here's how to do it:

1 Knit into the next stitch on the needle, *but don't drop it off the left needle.*

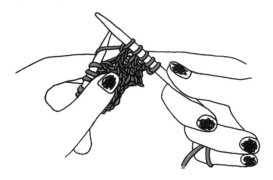

2 Now, knit into the *back leg* of that same stitch, inserting the right needle under it from front to back. This time lift it off the needle; you should now have an extra stitch on your right needle. Knitting twice into the same stitch might stretch that loop out some, but don't worry about it; it will get its regular shape back as you knit on.

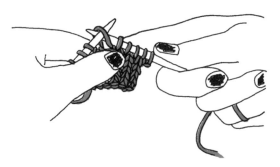

Can you do this on the purl side as well? You betcha. Just purl into the front and the back of the same stitch. Purling into the back leg of a stitch will require a good amount of finagling, and you may have to use your fingers to pull out the stitch so you can get your needle in there. But you can make it happen.

now you see it, now you don't
The Make One Increase (M1)

With this method, you will create a new knit stitch in between two already existing knit stitches, and, if you are doing it on stockinette fabric, it won't even show. This stitch must be done at least one stitch in from the edge. Here's how:

1 With the right needle, pick up the strand of yarn that lies between the stitch you just knit and the next stitch on the needle. Pick up this strand by inserting the needle under it *from front to back.*

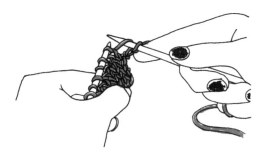

2 Lift this strand off the right needle and onto the left by inserting the left needle under it *from front to back* and dropping it off the right needle.

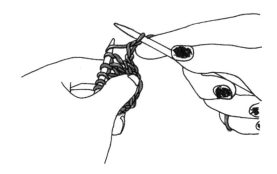

3 Knit into the back loop of this stitch. This is a little tough, and you may have to use the fingers of your left hand to pull this stitch down so that you can insert your right needle into that back leg from front to back. Knitting into the back loop causes the bottom of this new loop to twist, and it needs that twist to become invisible.

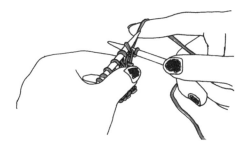

Caution: If you accidentally knit into the front of the loop (the way you usually make a knit stitch), you will create an extra stitch, but you will also create a gaping hole underneath it.

You can also make this increase on the purl side of the fabric; just purl into the back loop of the stitch that you pick up instead of knitting into it.

Hole-in-one
The Yarn Over (YO)

Y arn overs add stitches, but they also create big holes in your knitting—in fact, you probably made a lot of them, accidentally, when you were first learning to knit. Making a hole in your work on purpose can sometimes be a good thing—for instance, when you want to create a small buttonhole, or in lace knitting. But remember: While you can pretty much use the M1 and bar increases interchangeably, don't use a yarn over to add an extra stitch unless your pattern instructs you to.

To make a yarn over between two knit stitches:

1 Knit the first stitch, then bring your yarn to the front between the two points of your needles.

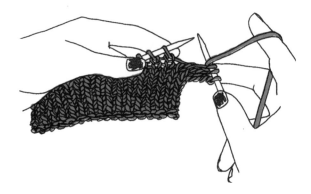

2 With the yarn still in front, instead of in back where it usually is while knitting, knit the next stitch. Knitting a stitch this way will leave an extra strand of yarn lying across your needle. When you come back to it on the next row, you just knit that strand as if it were a regular stitch.

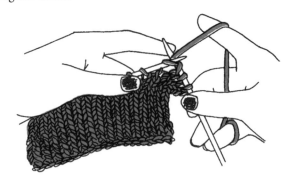

To make a yarn over between two purl stitches: Follow the same directions as above, but in reverse: Purl a stitch, then bring your yarn to the *back* of your work between the points of your needles before purling the next stitch.

INCREASING EVENLY ACROSS A ROW

Sometimes a pattern will tell you to "increase X number of stitches evenly across a row." It's often called for right above the ribbing at the bottom of a sweater, and it usually only happens once in a pattern. There is a formula for calculating where you should increase your stitches, and it's pretty simple: *Add 1 to the number of stitches you are supposed to increase, and divide the stitches on your needle by that number.*

So, let's say you have 20 stitches and you have to increase 4 stitches evenly spaced. First, you'd divide 20 by 5 (4+1) and come up with 4. If you increase once every 4 stitches, your first increase will come after your first 4 stitches, and your last increase will land 4 stitches *before* the end of your row. Ahhh . . . that's easy, isn't it?

Of course, I was sneaky in choosing an example that divided nicely by the number of increases; that won't always happen. Let's pretend I had 22 stitches on the needle to start with. When I divide that number by 5 (the number of increases I need to make plus the magical number 1), I get 4.4. How on earth are you supposed to increase every 4.4 stitches? Well, you can't. Instead, you gotta be a little fancy. You just increase every 4 stitches a couple of times, and then every 5 stitches a couple of times. And it's all good.

narrow-minded
Decreasing Stitches

Whereas increases are usually made the same way no matter where in a row you make them, decreases slant either to the left or to the right. Most often, you'll want to make a right-slanting decrease on the left side of your work, and a left-slanting decrease on the right side of your work, and the effect will look like the stitches on the left and right sides are doing a nice yoga stretch toward the center of your work. But sometimes you don't want a decorative edge— you want the fabric to get narrower, but you want the stitches on the sides to point straight up. In that case, you'd do the opposite: You'd use a right-slanting decrease on the right side of your work, and a left-slanting decrease on the left side. Luckily, you won't have to worry your pretty little head about this too much, since knitting patterns usually tell you which type of decrease to use at the beginnings and ends of rows.

Right-slanting decrease on right edge

Left-slanting decrease on right edge

wHeN two becomeſ oNe
Knit Two Together (k2tog)

this is the only right-slanting decrease you'll ever need, and it's as simple to make as it is lovely to behold. It's what you use when creating something that has multiple decreases that go around in a spiral, like the top of a hat, for instance.

1 Stick the right needle into the next two stitches on the left needle knitwise.

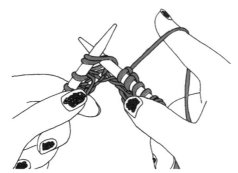

2 Knit these stitches together as one.

Piece of cake, right? And, just as you can knit two knit stitches together, you can also purl two purl stitches together.

ſLip ſLidiNg Awɑy
Slip, Slip, Knit (ssk)

My fave by far, slip, slip, knit makes a very nice left-slanting decrease. The technique is a little odd, but it's not hard, so hang in there.

1 Stick your right needle into the next stitch as if you were going to knit it, but then just slide it off the left needle and onto the right without actually doing anything else. This is called "slipping as if to knit" or "slipping knitwise."

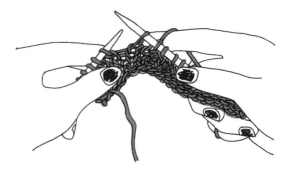

2 Slip the next stitch knitwise, too.

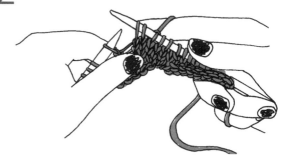

3 Take your left needle and slip it through the front legs of those two stitches, from left to right. Your left needle should be in front of your right needle.

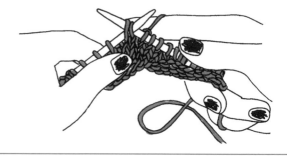

4 With the needles in that position, make a knit stitch by wrapping the yarn around, pulling the loop through to the front, then dropping the old loops off the left-hand needle.

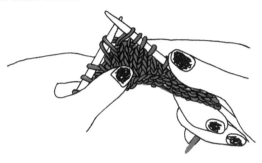

juſt paſſing through
Slip, Knit, Pass Slipped Stitch Over (skp)

this is a rather popular decrease that, like ssk, also slants to the left.

1 Slip one stitch knitwise.

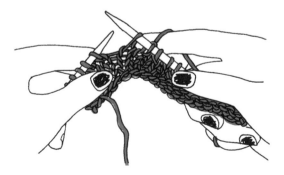

2 Knit the next stitch.

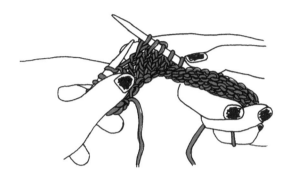

3 Insert the left needle into the front leg of the slipped stitch and lift it over the stitch you just knit, leapfrogging it over and off the needle—just like you do when you're binding off.

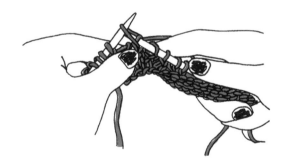

UNDER *WHERE*? PLACING INCREASES AND DECREASES IN YOUR KNITTING

Increases and decreases are usually made only on the right (front) side of the fabric. (Remember that when knitters talk about the right side of the fabric, they mean right as opposed to wrong, not right as opposed to left.) The right side of the fabric is the front side—the one shown to the world when the piece is worn. The wrong side of the fabric will be against the body, where the sun don't shine. So, if a pattern tells you to increase one stitch at each end of a row (increases are usually paired) on the following and every alternate row (and this is often how patterns are written), it means that when you are knitting on the right (front) side of the fabric, you will increase one stitch at the beginning of the row and increase another stitch at the end of the row. On the next row, the wrong side, you won't do anything except purl (or knit, or whatever) straight across.

To avoid raggedy edge stitches, make increases and decreases at least one, and sometimes two, stitches in from the edge, leaving the selvage (the edge that usually gets enclosed in a seam) all nice and smooth for sewing later on. This method also leaves a nice-looking band of sloping stitches at either end of your work. For a wider band, just make your increases or decreases even farther in from the edge.

For sloping edges, make a left-slanting decrease at the beginning of a row, and a right-slanting decrease at the end of a row. A decrease that slants to the left (ssk or skp) is a good one to use at the beginning of a row, since that side will slant toward the left as you narrow your fabric. When made one or two stitches in from the edge, a nice left-slanting band of stitches can look mighty purty on fabric that also slants to the left. A decrease that slants to the right, like k2tog, is best used at the end of the row, one or two stitches in from the end, to create a corresponding right-slanting band of stitches on that side. Here's how this is written in knitting instructions: "knit until you have 4 stitches left, k2tog, k2."

Decorative paired decreases

in a bind
Decreasing by Binding Off

When you need to decrease more than one stitch in a row, or you want to make an L-shaped angle in your knitting rather than a sloping edge, you will have to bind off those stitches, rather than use any of the decreases described above. *Stitches can be bound off at the beginning of rows or at the center of a row*—you should never try to bind off stitches at the end of a row (if you do, you won't be able to turn your work and knit back).

Binding off stitches is simple: Just knit two stitches and leapfrog the first stitch over the second stitch (see pages 40–41). Then knit another stitch, and leapfrog again. Repeat that for the required number of bound-off stitches, then knit the rest of the row in the regular way.

Most often, you'll bind off stitches at the beginning of a row, but sometimes you'll need to bind off stitches in the center of a row—for instance, when shaping a neckline. And this is where things can get a little hairy. It all starts innocently enough: You knit up to a certain point in your row, then you bind off a number of stitches in the center of your fabric (this is the bottom center of the neckline), and then you continue knitting to the end. On the next row, you knit until you get to the bound-off point—and that's when it hits you. The rest of your stitches are stuck on the other side of the needle, past the stitches you just bound off! So how do you get to them?

Well, what you do is you drop the yarn you are working with and knit the stitches on the other side of the gap with another ball of the same yarn. Genius! If you don't have another ball of the same yarn, just wind one up starting from the other end of the ball you are working with, and cut it off. From that point on, you will knit with this ball (let's call it Fred), till you get to the end of your row.

Then, turn and knit using Fred till you get to the gully. Drop Fred. Pick up Ethel (the original yarn) and knit the rest of the row. At the end, turn around and knit back with Ethel, till you reach the gully. Then just grab Fred again.

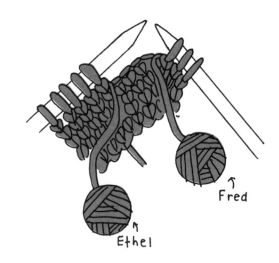

Fred

Ethel

increase the piece
Casting On Stitches

Just as binding off stitches makes a swift, slope-free right angle at the edge of your fabric, casting on stitches allows you to make a new bit of fabric jut out at a right angle from the piece you are knitting. And, unlike binding off, casting on can be done at the beginning or at the end of rows. Unfortunately, you can't use the double cast-on method because that requires having two strands of yarn, and you have only one (since you're already knitting). Instead, use one of the following cast-on methods:

Loop de Loop
The Single Cast-on

This is the easiest method to use when you need to add a few stitches to the beginning or end of your row.

At the beginning of a row:

1 Take the needle (with all the stitches on it) in your *right hand*, and close the bottom three fingers of your left hand around the ball end of the yarn. Then, let the yarn run across your palm and over your thumb, *clockwise.*

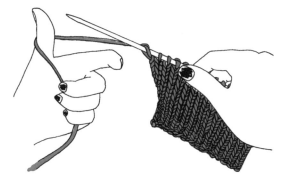

2 Bring the needle with the stitches on it, (now in your right hand) down and scoop up the yarn strand that runs from your three fingers to the base of your thumb from underneath.

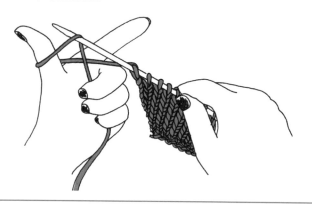

3 Drop that loop off of your thumb. You have created one cast-on stitch. To cast on another stitch, twirl your thumb clockwise to create another loop over your thumb. Scoop up the yarn strand again with the right needle.

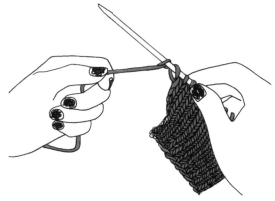

Once you've cast on the desired number of stitches, switch the needles around again and begin knitting. The first stitches you'll knit will be the ones you just cast on. Knitting these stitches will not be easy, so just be patient about getting your needle point into these loops. You may also get some crazy long strands in between these stitches as you start knitting, but don't let it get you down. Just knit away, trying to keep your stitches as regular as possible, and it will all even itself out.

At the end of a row: You will already have the needle with all the stitches in your right hand. Just follow the exact same instructions as above.

In the middle of a row: Knit to the point where you want to cast on stitches, then follow the same instructions as above. When you've cast on the desired number of stitches, just keep knitting the stitches off the left needle.

standing firm
The Cable Cast-on

to add stitches that are firmer and easier to work with, use the cable cast-on method. It's only a bit harder than the single cast-on you just learned.

At the beginning of a row:

1 Hold the needle with the stitches on it in the normal way, with the left hand. Knit a stitch, but do not drop the old stitch off the left needle.

2 Transfer the new stitch to the left-hand needle by inserting the left needle into the front leg of this loop from *right to left* (and from front to back) and pulling it off the right needle. You have cast on a single stitch. (Hint: You'll have to twist your left needle a bit and come at the front leg from underneath.)

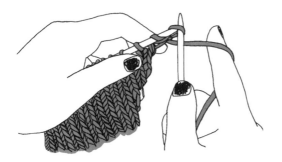

3 To continue casting on, stick your right needle *in between* the first two stitches on the left needle and knit a stitch (wrap the yarn around the needle, and pull it through to the front), but do not drop the old stitch off the left needle. Transfer the new stitch to the left needle in the same manner as you did in Step 2.

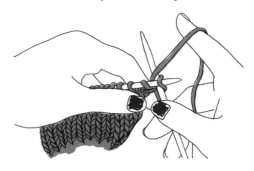

4 When you have finished casting on the desired number of stitches, begin knitting (starting with the new stitches) in the normal manner.

At the end of a row: Switch the needle with the stitches on it to your left hand, then follow the same directions as above.

In the middle of a row: First knit to the point where you want to create the additional stitches. Then switch hands, so that the needle with the stitches you have just knit is in your left hand. Follow the directions above to cast on the desired number of new stitches. Then switch hands again and continue knitting.

Once you've learned the cable cast-on, you can also use it to cast on the foundation stitches at the beginning of any piece. After making a slip knot, just follow the instructions above for the remaining stitches.

LEARNING TO MAKE A BUTTONHOLE

Now that you know how to add stitches and subtract stitches by casting on and binding off in the middle of rows, you can use this knowledge to do something else: make buttonholes!

It's easy: Just knit to the point where you need the buttonhole, bind off the number of stitches your pattern tells you to, then continue knitting to the end of the row.

On the next row, knit to the point where you bound off stitches in the previous row. Then switch the needles: Put the right needle in your left hand and vice versa. You can use the cable cast-on method to cast on the same number of stitches you bound off. There's a little trick here: *Before you transfer the last cast-on stitch to the left needle, bring the yarn to the front of your needles.* Switch your hands back and continue knitting the row. You may notice that the buttonhole looks a little sucky. Don't worry about it; knit buttonholes *always* look kind of sucky. But they do the job. And you can always neaten them up later with some blanket stitches (see page 89).

beginner's basic III
Kitschy Kerchief

this simple triangle-shaped scarf, knit in garter stitch, is a great way to test out your increasing skills. All you need is a ball of sport-weight yarn and a pair of size 8 straight knitting needles. We used Blue Sky Alpaca's lusciously soft 100% alpaca (2 oz, 134 yards) in color #307, Turquoise.

You will need to keep track of your rows with this project, since the increases are made only on every other row. Stick a row counter onto the end of one of your needles, or wrap a rubber band around the end of one needle so you know to increase every time you are knitting onto the needle with the rubber band.

Start by putting a slip knot on your knitting needle (the needle without the row counter or rubber band).

Row 1: Knit into front and back of the stitch. You have just increased one stitch.

Row 2: Knit across both of these stitches.

Row 3: Knit into the front and back of both stitches. You now have 4 stitches.

Row 4: Knit across.

Row 5: Knit the first stitch, knit into the front and back of the next stitch, knit into the front and back of the next stitch, knit the last stitch. You have 6 stitches.

Row 6: Knit across.

Row 7: Knit the first stitch, knit into the front and back of the next stitch, knit until there are only 2 stitches left on the needle, knit into the front and back of the next stitch, knit the last stitch.

Repeat rows 6 and 7 until your kerchief is about 7½" long, or the size you want it to be. You should have about 64 stitches on your needles at this point, but count the number of stitches you actually have, then bind them all off.

To make ties for your kerchief, cast on half as many stitches as

you ended up with, then just bind them all off. Make 2 ties this way. Put a knot in the end of each, and sew the other end to the corners of your kerchief.

See page 123

THE RULES OF ENGAGEMENT, OR WHAT NOT TO KNIT FOR YOUR BOYFRIEND

Here's a legend known to all knitters across the land: It is bad luck to knit a sweater for a boyfriend, as it guarantees that the relationship will end. Of course, if you're looking to rid yourself of said boyfriend, this might not be the most direct way of going about it. Like most myths, it holds a good amount of truth. If you've spent a month or two working long and hard on a sweater for your guy, only to have him not appreciate it enough or not wear it very often (and this happens all the time), you might catch a lingering resentment and wind up dumping the ungrateful lout. The theory, I suppose, is that if you're married to the guy and make him a sweater he never wears, you're still stuck with him.

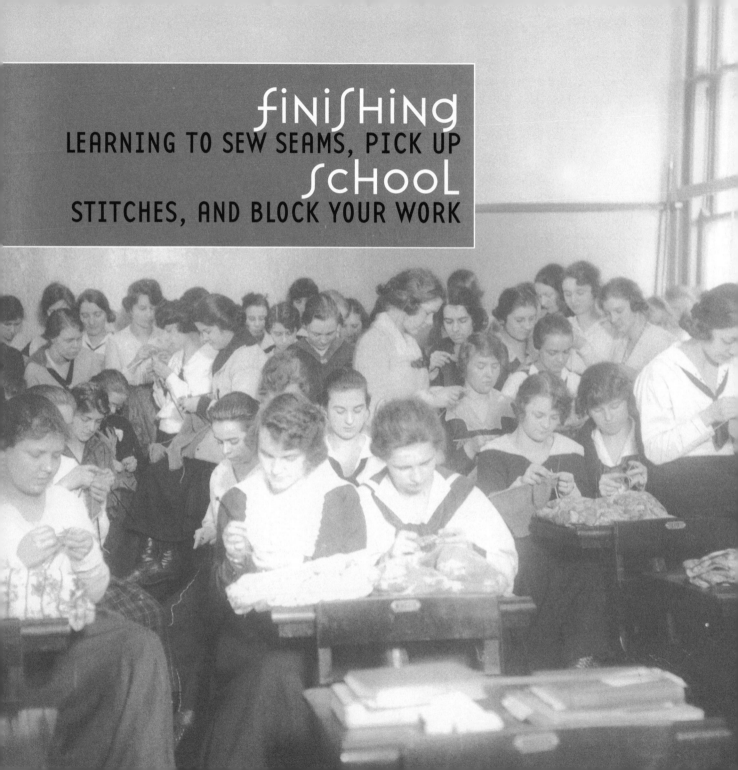

finishing school

LEARNING TO SEW SEAMS, PICK UP STITCHES, AND BLOCK YOUR WORK

Sewing your knit fabric together, knitting on collars, and working away your yarn ends is known as "finishing" in the knitting biz. That's because once you've done this part, you're finished! Unfortunately, it's also considered to be a tedious chore by most knitters. You've knit and knit and knit your heart out, and now you have to put away your beloved knitting needles, take out your yarn needle, and—dammit!—sew. The horror.

Some knitters hate this part so much they bring all their knitted pieces to their local yarn store and pay to have them stitched together. But don't let the naysayers get you down. I'm here to tell you that the finishing process doesn't have to finish you off. In fact, finishing can be pretty fun—exciting, even. For one thing, there's the thrill of sewing a seam, pulling your thread taut, and watching as the sides of your pieces fit together like Tetris blocks, the sewing yarn itself vanishing into a perfect, invisible seam. It's also immensely satisfying when you pick up your stitches in exactly the right place so that it looks like they grew directly out of the neckline, rather than having been added on at the end. And nothing beats the miracle of blocking your handmade sweater, which starts out looking lumpy and sweated over and irregular, only to emerge from the process looking like it had been knit by the steady, skilled hands of a mythical knitting goddess.

Finishing gives your projects nothing less than a fabulous makeover, better than the best "it's time to update your bad '80s look!" episode of your favorite trashy talk show. Once you learn the finishing techniques in this chapter, your knitting will be deserving of the *oohs* and *aahs* of a live studio audience.

pick up the pieces
Joining Knit Pieces Together

Your mission, should you choose to accept it, is to make the connections between your knitted pieces as flat and invisible as possible. There are three basic types of joins you will make in your knitting: connecting the sides of two knit pieces together, as for the sides of sweaters; joining the top edges together, as you do on shoulder seams; and attaching the top of one knit piece to the side of another, as you would when sewing a sleeve into the body of a sweater.

When sewing any knit fabrics together, you should place the pieces next to each other on a flat surface, with their right sides facing up. Use safety pins to loosely pin your fabric together (start by placing pins on the outermost corners of your pieces, then place a few in between to hold the pieces in place while you sew). Always sew your seams using the same yarn that you knit with (unless you're using a bulky or super-bulky yarn, in which case you should sew with a thinner yarn, but in the same color and fiber). You'll also need a yarn needle with an eyehole large enough to accommodate your yarn.

ſide to ſide
Sewing Side Seams

begin by threading a yarn needle with a length of yarn long enough to sew the entire seam, with at least another 12 inches left over. Then tack the yarn in place by pulling the needle up through the right-most corner stitch at the bottom of the left-hand piece. Secure the yarn by inserting the needle back up through the same hole. Now bring the needle up through the left-most corner stitch at the bottom of the right-hand piece, and then up through the same hole in the left-hand piece. Pull taut. You've made a little figure eight, and the two corners of your fabric should be right up close together.

Now, depending on what kind of join you're making, you'll follow one of these methods:

bar crawl
Using the Mattress Stitch on Stockinette Fabric

take a close look at the side edge of a piece of stockinette fabric. If you carefully pull apart the edge stitch—which is usually a bit weird looking—and the first real row of knit V stitches, you will see something like a ladder of yarn bars that runs between them. Some folks call these **running bars.** You'll be sewing the two sides together by stitching around these bars. Start by pinning your pieces together, right sides up, and tacking the yarn in place. Then do the following:

1 Pass the needle under the first two running bars of the right-hand piece of fabric, from the bottom to the top.

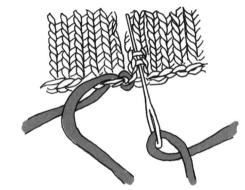

2 Now pass the needle under the first two running bars of the left-hand piece of fabric the same way.

3 Insert the needle down into the same point where it came out on the right-hand piece of fabric, carry it under the next two running bars, and come back up again.

4 Finally, insert the needle back into the same point where it came out on the left-hand piece of fabric, and come up two bars later.

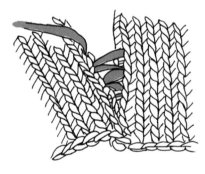

Keep repeating those last two steps until you have about two or three inches done. Then pull the yarn taut (not tight) and watch as the two pieces of fabric come together and the seam becomes almost invisible. Just like magic!

NOTE: The mattress stitch is intended to connect each row of knitting in one piece of fabric to each row of knitting in another piece of fabric. It will work out perfectly if

you have the exact same number of rows in both your pieces. However, since nobody's perfect, it is very likely that you *won't* have the exact same number of rows in each piece. Don't let it bother you. Just pick up some of the slack by sometimes taking only one running bar from one side and two running bars from the other side. That'll even things out, and nobody will be the wiser.

bumps in the night
Using the Mattress Stitch on Garter-Stitch Fabric

first, take a look at your reverse stockinette or garter fabric. Sure, it's wall-to-wall purl bumps, but look carefully and you'll see that half of the purl bumps are curving upward, like a smile, and the other half are curving downward, like an umbrella. The smiling bumps are called the **underbumps,** and the umbrella bumps are the **overbumps**. To sew two pieces of reverse stockinette or garter-stitch fabric together, you will pass your needle through an underbump from one side, and then through an overbump from the other side.

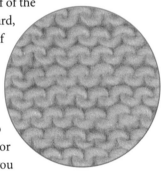

Let a smile be your umbrella

Start the same way as with stockinette fabric, by placing the pieces next to each other, right sides up, and tacking the yarn in place at the bottom corners of your fabric. Then:

1 Pass the needle under the bottom-most underbump on the left-hand piece of fabric.

2 Pass the needle under the bottom-most overbump on the right-hand piece of fabric.

3 Insert the needle underneath the next underbump on the left-hand piece of fabric.

4 Insert the needle under the next overbump on the right-hand piece of fabric.

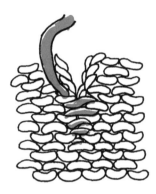

NOTE: When sewing garter-stitch fabric, try to grab the overbumps as close to the fabric edge as you can.

Carry on, my wayward son. When you have a few inches done, just pull the yarn taut and watch it get sucked up like a bug in a Venus's-flytrap. Cool, isn't it?

baby'ſ got bαckſtitcH
Using the Backstitch

Unlike most seaming methods used in knitting, the backstitch makes bulky, nonstretchy seams. Still, sometimes that's just what you're looking for when you want a strong, stabilizing seam on a project like a bag or a backpack. To make it, start by pinning your knit fabric right sides together. Tack your yarn at the right-most end as usual, then put your needle down through both layers of fabric, about ¼ inch from the top edges, and draw it back up about ½ inch to the left. Pull the yarn through (**figure 1**). Put your needle back down about ¼ inch to the right, and come up about ½ inch to the left. Now, just keep putting your needle down where you came up with your last stitch, and up about ½ inch to the left of that (**figure 2**).

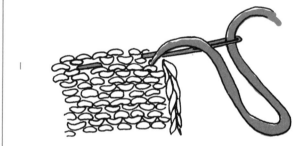

top this
Connecting the Tops of Knit Pieces

'm going to show you two ways to sew the tops of knit pieces together—like the shoulder seam of a sweater, or the toe of a sock. They are both fun. The first is called **fake grafting,** and it's the one you will probably find yourself using the most often. It is an almost invisible way of connecting two bound-off pieces of knitting together.

faking it
Fake Grafting

ake a look at the top edge of a bound-off piece of stockinette knitting in the photo below. You will see rows and rows of knit Vs looking at you, all nestled close together with their arms in the air. Now, turn the piece of fabric (or this page) upside down, and examine that edge. You *still* see rows of Vs. Upside down or right side up, stockinette looks like Vs. What's going on?

Upside down or right side up, stockinette looks like Vs.

Well, think of it this way: How many Vs do you see in a W shape? Two, right? Turn it upside down, and you will see a V shape, but only one, in the middle, with two ski poles hanging by its sides. The same thing happens with your knit Vs when you turn them upside down: You see the Vs that are formed by the sides of your original knit stitches.

Fake grafting takes advantage of this fact. Start by laying the two pieces flat in front of you, face up, with one pointing away from you (we'll call it the *top*), and one facing toward you (we'll call it the *bottom*). Their bound-off top edges should be next to each other. Look at the Vs on the bottom piece, the Vs on the top piece, and the gap in between. Now, with your yarn, you're going to create a row of Vs across this gap, connecting these two pieces together. Here's how:

First, tack a length of yarn to your work by bringing your needle up through the center of the right-most V on the bottom piece, just below the bound-off edge (leave a 6-inch tail). Now come back up through the center of this V again (the yarn can go around the outside edge of the piece).

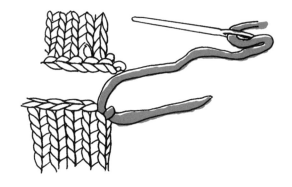

2 Bring your yarn down to the right of the bottom of the right-most V on the top piece, and back up to the left of that V, like you are wrapping a scarf around the neck of that stitch.

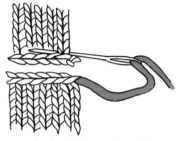

3 Insert the needle back down into the center of the same V in the bottom piece of fabric where your yarn originated, and come up in the center of the next V to the left. Repeat across.

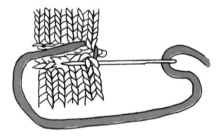

4 Now, unlike for the mattress stitch, where you pull the yarn so tight it disappears, here you pull the yarn only as tight as needed to make your stitches approximately the same size as the knit Vs in the fabric.

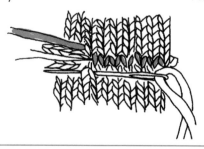

And don't you feel like some magical, alchemy-performing wizard right about now?

if you can stand the heat
The Kitchener Stitch

t o do "real" grafting—also called the **Kitchener stitch**—you need two sets of stitches that are not bound off—sometimes called **live stitches**. Grafting is often used to close off the toe of a sock, but it can also be used to sew a shoulder seam (if that edge is just a straight row of stitches, and hasn't been shaped by decreases). You just have to plan ahead, so when your pattern tells you to bind off your pieces, don't do it. Instead, put them on a stitch holder so you can graft them later. You will want to do this especially for baby stuff, since grafting makes a truly seamless seam, and the fewer bumps on those teeny-tiny garments, the better.

Grafting is simple, but it will require your full concentration. So turn off your music and sit somewhere quiet.

And here's one more grafting caveat: *Grafting can only be done on two sets of stitches that have the exact same number of stitches in each set.*

Before grafting, transfer your live stitches onto two needles, if they are on stitch holders. Hold your knit pieces with their wrong sides facing each other and the points of both needles and the end of the yarn you were working with to the right. (From here on out, the needle in front will be called the *front* needle, the needle in back, the *back* needle.)

Thread the yarn through a needle. If you haven't left a long enough tail on either of your knit pieces to sew this seam, simply make a slip knot on the end of a piece of yarn about 12 inches long, slip the old yarn through it, tighten the knot, and slide it as close to the last stitch as it will go.

1 Slide the yarn needle through the first stitch on the front needle *as if to knit.* Pull the yarn through and drop that stitch off the needle.

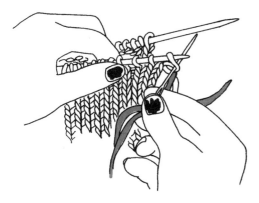

2 Pass the yarn needle through the second stitch on the front needle as if to purl. Don't drop the stitch off the needle.

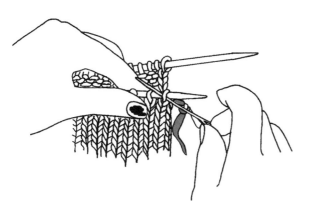

3 Pass the yarn needle through the first stitch on the back needle *as if to purl.* Drop the stitch off the needle.

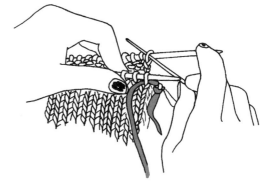

4 Pass the needle through the second stitch on the back needle *as if to knit.* Leave that stitch on the needle.

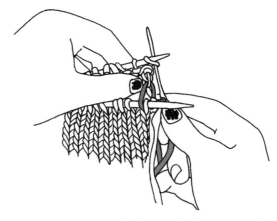

Repeat steps 1–4 until all the stitches are grafted together. It's easy to make mistakes on these, so really try to pay attention for the full fifteen minutes (or less) that it will take you to execute the Kitchener stitch.

Now take a look at your work. Like turning water into wine, grafting two pieces of fabric together with the Kitchener stitch seems nothing less than miraculous. Take a bow, turn on some music, and do a jig.

ménage à trois
The Three-Needle Bind-off

if you really hate to sew seams, try this one. You'll need two sets of live stitches on your needles and the same number of stitches in each set.

1 With the right sides of your work facing each other, hold the two knitting needles in your left hand with their points facing to the right. Then, take a third needle and insert it, knitwise, through the first stitch on the front needle and knitwise through the first stitch on the back needle.

2 Knit the two stitches together. Do the same on the next stitch, then leapfrog the first stitch over this second one. Repeat to the end, turn your work right-side out, and you'll wind up with a relatively flat, neat seam that didn't even require threading a needle. Hot diggity!

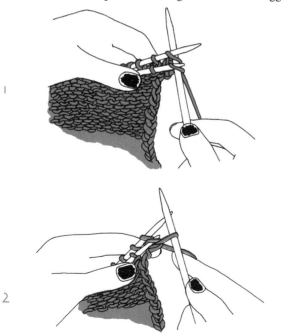

Sewing behind bars
Joining a Top to a Side Edge

When you sew a sleeve to the body of a garment, you are connecting a bound-off edge (the top of the sleeve) to a side edge (the side of the front or the back of a sweater). The stitch you need for this is a special combo of the mattress stitch and the fake grafting you learned above.

Start by pinning the pieces together. Now, thread a yarn needle with a nice long piece of yarn, and get ready to start stitchin'.

Lay the two pieces flat in front of you on a table, or on your lap with the sleeve at the right and the side piece at the left. Tack the yarn in place at the bottom left corner of your seam, just like always.

1 Now, draw the needle up through the center loop (or "head") of the bottommost bound-off stitch on the sleeve piece.

2 Pass it under one or two running bars on the side piece.

3 Then, go back down into the center of the same stitch on the bound-off edge and come up in the center of the next stitch.

4 Push the needle through the same space you came out from on the side piece and pull it back up one (or two) bars later. Repeat until you're done. As you're sewing, take one or two bars from the side, as needed, to make the seam sew up flat.

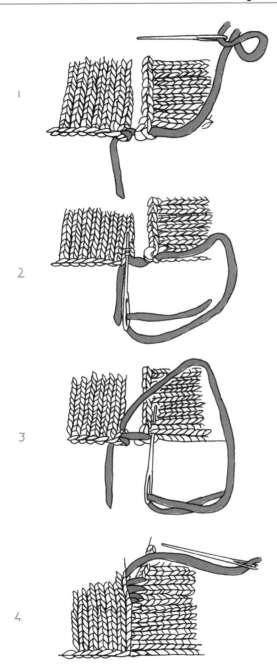

1

2

3

4

NEVER LOOK A GIFT HAT IN THE MOUTH: THE FINE ART OF KNITTING FOR OTHERS

Remember how, before you knew how to knit, you thought it was so easy? Remember how you never appreciated those lime-green-and-orange-striped sweaters your grandmother made you? Well, you'll be reminded of all of that when you start knitting presents for your friends and relatives. Give a girlfriend a hat you made, and she may figure you spent an hour on it (instead of a week). And if it's not exactly her color, her style, or her head shape, she is likely never to wear it. Same goes for scarves, gloves, and especially the time-consuming sweaters that you've knit for others. The recipients won't give you the oohs and aahs you were hoping for, since they can't possibly know how much work you've put into the thing.

SO DO YOURSELF A FAVOR: Stick to small items, like hats, for your friends, if you knit for them at all. And save your really extensive knit gifts for your knitting friends—they're the only ones who will really know what that gift means, and they'll wear that mohair sweater loud and proud, even if it makes them look like a gorilla.

pickup Lines
Learning to Pick Up Stitches

Sometimes you'll need to pick up stitches from a finished edge to create the collar of a sweater or add a fancy edge to the bottom of a piece. Say you want to add a turtleneck to a sweater: You'd pick up stitches around the entire neckline, and then knit till your neck is as turtley as you want it. You might also pick up stitches along the bottom of your sweater to make it a little longer. And some folks pick up stitches from the armholes and knit the sleeves downward from there, connected right to the sweater from the get-go.

The following are different circumstances in which you have to pick up stitches. But don't let the task bother you any; it's as easy as the old in-and-out.

From the Top

Hold your fabric in your left hand and one needle in your right.

With the front of the piece facing you, insert your knitting needle through the center of a stitch (your pattern will usually tell you where to begin).

2 Wrap your yarn around it.

3 Draw this new loop from the back of the fabric to the front. One stitch picked up. Now, it's true that you didn't really "pick up" a stitch; instead, what you did was make a new stitch by pulling a loop of yarn through an old stitch.

TIP: Here's an important thing to remember, which they never tell you in knitting instructions: *When a pattern tells you to "pick up and knit" a stitch, they really just mean "pick up" a stitch.*

Your pattern will tell you how many stitches you need to pick up from a given area, and you'll want to space them evenly. Just measure the area and figure out how many stitches you'll need to pick up per inch. If you have to pick up more stitches than you have stitch heads, just pick up some stitches from the space in between your stitch heads. If you have to pick up fewer, just skip over some of the stitch heads. But whatever you do, try to pick up the stitches *evenly* around the edge.

From the Side

Again, this is easy. With your work facing you, just stick your right needle between the running bars along the sides of your edges, loop your yarn around the needle, and pull it through. And because stitches are wider than they are tall, you'll usually have more spaces between bars than stitches you'll need to pick up. To keep things nice and even, just pick up the number of stitches that your pattern tells you to, skipping a bar here and there as necessary, and you'll be good to go.

From the Bottom

You won't have to do this very often, but sometimes, as with gloves and mittens, you might have to pick up stitches from the bottom, cast-on edges of the fingers or from the cast-on edge of a sweater, either to lengthen it or to add edging.

To do this, first remember what you learned about how you can still see Vs created by the "arms" of the knit stitches when you turn your fabric upside down (page 77). Now, you want to pick up your stitches from the heads of *these* Vs; in other words, pick up the stitches from *in between* the cast-on stitches, and not in the centers of them.

bLocking for bLockHeads

blocking is the almost alchemical process of taking your completed project, which is beautiful but will most likely have a couple of lumps and bumps, and turning it into a professional-looking, finished piece. Blocking, you should know, only works on fabrics made of natural fibers. Many patterns will tell you to block your knit pieces to size before you sew them together. Pay them no mind; I don't know a single person who does it this way. Go ahead and sew your pieces together, then block the whole thing after it's all done.

The following method is the one I like best. You'll need a couple of clean towels and a place that's flat, such as a floor, a table, or even your bathtub, and big enough that you can lay your garment out flat on it.

Fill a sink with lukewarm water. Never use hot water, because hot water can really make wool go nutso. Add a bit of mild shampoo or special wool wash to the water, mix it up a bit, then dunk your piece in there. Gently swirl it around in the water just a bit. Remember, agitation is as deadly to wool as garlic is to a vampire. Squeeze the piece to get the suds through it, then let it soak for about five minutes.

Empty the sink and refill it with clean, cool water and rinse your piece. Squeeze all the suds out, refill the sink, and rinse once more. Your piece is now ready to be blocked.

Get out a big thick towel. Lay the piece on it, flat, in the shape you want it to be. Roll up the towel, squeezing it and squeezing out the water at the same time. Toss that soaked towel in the laundry and get out another towel. Lay the towel down flat somewhere (on your kitchen table, for instance) and lay your piece out on top of it. Pull the piece lightly at its opposite corners to "set" the stitches. And now, as if the piece were a rag doll or a big lump of clay, lay it out on the towel in the perfect shape and dimensions you want it to be (you can refer to the diagram—or schematic—included in most patterns to see what the measurements should be). Straighten out the seams, scrunch up the sleeves so they are the right length for you (instead of for an ape), and pull down the body of the sweater so it's the right length too. Then just leave it be.

You probably won't believe this, but when you come back to it, about twenty-four hours later, your piece will actually *be* the shape that you blocked it to. It will be perfect, and even, and lovely. Stick a fork in it, baby, because it's done!

getting knitty
FANCY THINGS TO DO
with it
WITH NEEDLES AND YARN

the problem with knitting—once you get good at it—is that it can get boring. And while it's great to be able to knit large expanses of fabric while watching TV or sitting in a movie theater with nary a glance at your hands, it's also good to have a couple of tricks up your sleeve to break up the monotony. I, for one, am convinced that this is why knitters of yore invented cables and ways to add colorful patterns to their knitting projects. In this chapter, you'll learn tricks to spiff up your work. I'll also show you the few crochet techniques that every knitter should know. Try them, and before you know it, you'll be a happy hooker.

beLLs & whistles

the easiest way to add a little sumpin' sumpin' to your knitted projects is to hang something from them. Fringe, pom-poms, and tassels can look great dangling from the ends of a scarf, the top of a hat, or even at the bottom of a sweater for that Pocahantas look.

Fringe Benefits

1 Wrap yarn around a sturdy rectangular thing that's a bit longer than the length you want your fringe to be, such as a book, a DVD, a pack of cigarettes, or whatever. To make lots of fringe, wrap the yarn a whole bunch of times, then cut it at one end.

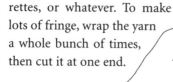

2 You now have a stack of strands for your fringe. Grab a few strands and fold them in half. This is how thick your fringe will be. Add or take away a few strands until it feels like what you want. Don't worry about the ends not lining up exactly; you'll trim them later. Stick a crochet hook *from back to front* through the space in your knitting where you want to add fringe. Hang your folded yarn over the hook and pull it through to the back of the fabric.

3 With a crochet hook or with your fingers, pull the tails of the yarn through the loop. Tighten. Et voilà! Le fringe!

4 Keep hanging fringe until your piece is all fringed up. Then trim the bottoms so they all line up like little toy soldiers.

The No-Hassle Tassel

tassels are a more mature, slightly fancier version of fringe. Cute and jaunty whether hung from the top of a hat or the corner of an afghan, tassels are also easy to make. And of course, few things are more fun than twirling them!

1 Get a piece of heavy cardboard that is a bit longer than the tassel you want to make. In a pinch, a deck of cards or anything else that's rectangular and sturdy will do. Then take your yarn and wrap your little heart out.

2 Stop when your wrapped yarn is about ¼ inch thick all around, then cut the yarn at one end. Take another piece of yarn about 8 inches long, thread it through a needle, and pass it along the edge of your rectangular object, underneath the wrapped yarn. Take out the needle and make a square knot—a very, very tight square knot—leaving a long tail on one end of the yarn. This has to hold all the yarn together, so don't be afraid to pull it really tight and choke the life force out of that thing. Then cut through the loops of yarn that are on the opposite side of the rectangle.

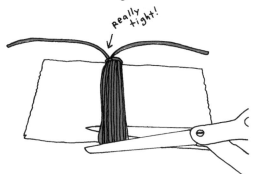

3 Tuck the short tail inside the tassel, take the long yarn tail, and wrap it around the folded top of the tassel about ¼ to ½ inch from the fold. Again, do this nice and tightly. Thread the yarn through a needle and stick it up through the "head" of the tassel, right up the center. This is the bit of yarn you'll use to attach the tassel to your piece. Sew it on.

I CORD, YOU CORD, WE ALL CORD FOR I–CORD

I-cord, invented by Elizabeth Zimmermann (see page 120), is short for "idiot cord"— because it's what you might make if you knit the wrong way. I-cord is great to use as a drawstring, a tie cord for a hat, or even as handles on a purse. To make it, you'll need a pair of double-pointed needles. Start by casting on 3 stitches (or as many as your knitting pattern tells you to). Knit those stitches. Then, instead of turning your work and knitting back the other way, switch the needles in your hands without turning your

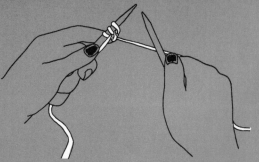

work. Slide the stitches to the other side of the needle in your left hand—with the yarn still hanging from the left, instead of the right, as it usually would—and knit across. Be sure to pull the yarn tight when you make your first stitch so that the fabric rolls in on itself, like a teeny-tiny little tube. Keep knitting and what will you get? I-cord! Doesn't everybody?

Shake Your Pom-Pom

Some folks insist on calling these fuzzy balls "pom-pons," but to me that final *n* makes this item sound like some kind of feminine protection product. I have no idea what the derivation of this word is, but if you want to know how to make a pom-pom, follow the instructions below.

1 Pom-poms require that you first create a little pom-pom maker, which is nothing more than two doughnut-shaped pieces of cardboard or plastic (you can also buy these ready-made at your local yarn store). The hole in the center should be about half the size of the circle itself—that'll give you a nice, full pom-pom. (There are few things more pathetic than a wimpy, wispy, thin-haired pom-pom.) Then take your yarn, either threaded on a needle or with your fingers, and wind it around the two stacked doughnut shapes, until the center hole is filled with yarn.

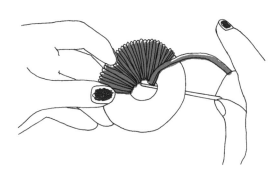

2 Cut through the loops all the way around the outside of the doughnut.

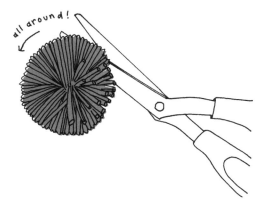

3 Pull an 8-inch length of yarn up between the two halves of the pom-pom maker, wrap it tightly around the core of the pom-pom, and make a sturdy square knot to hold the whole thing together. Pull or cut the cardboard rings out, fluff up your pom-pom, and trim it as necessary to even up the ends.

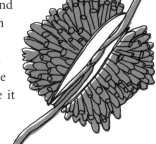

Attach the pom-pom to your knitting with the same yarn you used to tie it together.

ſew pretty
Using Embroidery

below are two cute 'n crafty ways to add color to your knit pieces, as an edging or as a design right on the body of your work. Both of them are done using a yarn needle and a bit of yarn. Best of all, it won't take you very long to learn either of these techniques.

blanket ſtatement
How to Make the Blanket Stitch

blanket stitch is a very simple stitch that was once used to keep woven blankets from unraveling. Often done in a contrasting color yarn, the blanket stitch can be made around the bottom of hats and mittens or even along the entire border of a cardigan—and don't be afraid to use a different yarn texture, either. Mohair, for instance, would make a very nice blanket-stitch edging on a wool sweater.

1 Thread a yarn needle with a long length of yarn. Begin by passing the needle from back to front as close as possible to the bottom edge of your work. Leave a 6-inch tail at the back, which you can work away later.

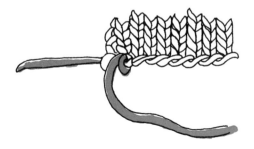

2 Insert the needle into the fabric about ¼ to ½ inch above the edge, and about ¼ to ½ inch to the right of where the first stitch was made. At the same time, hold this loop of yarn down and slip the point of the needle over it (the needle is now coming from behind the fabric). Pull the yarn through till the stitch is taut but not tight.

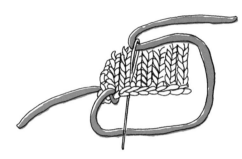

3 Continue in this way all around the edge of your work. Keep the stitches evenly spaced and make sure that the point where your needle enters the fabric is the same distance from the edge each time. Use your knit stitches as a guide to keep the blanket stitching even.

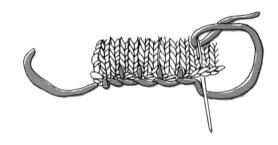

juʃt dupe it
The Duplicate Stitch

Now here's a fun trick: You can add colorful stitches to your knit pieces *after* you've finished knitting them by simply tracing over each knit stitch with a different color yarn. Use duplicate stitches to add small designs and pictures to your knitting, such as a skull head on the front of a knit cap or a ladybug on a child's sweater. Duplicate stitch should not be used for really large areas of color, however, because it will make your fabric too thick. Here's how to do it:

1 Duplicate stitch is best done on stockinette. Simply take a length of yarn in a contrasting color, thread it through a yarn needle, and come up from the back to the front of your work through the bottom point of one of your knit Vs. Pull the yarn up and through to the right, leaving a nice 6-inch tail at the back that you can work away later.

pull through with needle

2 Now pass the needle under the bottom two legs of the stitch above the one you are duplicating, from *right to left*. Pull the yarn through, gently.

3 Insert the needle back down into the first hole you came up through. Come back up at the base of the next stitch you need to duplicate. Continue to do this with all the stitches you want to color in, pulling the yarn through so that the new stitch just sits on top of the original stitch.

2
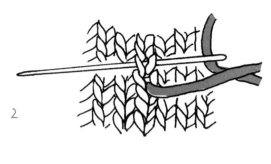

3

twiʃt and ʃhout
Making Cables

Cables are those twisty, snakelike things you've seen on countless sweaters. You may not like the look of them—I didn't when I started knitting—but they are fun to do and can make a large knit piece more interesting to work on. Cables are pretty and decorative, but they're also functional: They thicken up fabric by squeezing it together widthwise, thereby making sweaters and hats warmer than they would be if knit in something like plain stockinette.

The trick to making a cable is to knit your stitches in a different order than they appear on the needle. To do that, you need something called a **cable needle** (see page 22),

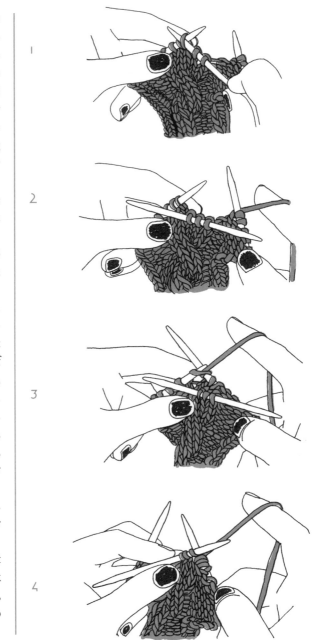

Hooked up to cable

which lets you put some stitches on hold and then come back to them later. But don't let it scare you; knitting a cable sounds more difficult than it is, and the results can be pretty thrilling. Plus, you only have to do the fancy cable-twisty thing every six rows or so—all the other rows are knit the regular old way.

So let's lay down some cable already. Here are instructions for making what's called a 6 × 6 front-crossed cable.

Begin by casting on 18 stitches. On row 1, purl 6 stitches, knit 6 stitches, purl 6 stitches (p6, k6, p6). On row 2, knit the knits and purl the purls (k6, p6, k6).

Row 3 is where the magic happens. Purl 6 stitches. Then, slip the first 3 knit stitches purlwise onto a cable needle (**figure 1**). For a front-crossed cable such as this one, let the cable needle with the stitches dangle to the front of your work (**figure 2**). Knit the next stitch on the needle, pull the yarn tight, and knit the next 2 stitches (**figure 3**). Now knit the first stitch off the cable needle (**figure 4**). (You may have to tug and stretch to get to those stitches, but don't worry—it comes with the territory for cables), pull the yarn tight, and knit the last 2 stitches. Put your cable needle aside, and purl the last 6 stitches.

For rows 4–6, just knit the knits and purl the purls. Then start over again with row 1, and at row 3, do your cable twist again.

Sometimes when you're knitting a cable, it's difficult to tell when it's time to do the twist. You should keep track of the rows, but, in general, if it looks like it's time to twist, it probably isn't yet. When it looks like you've forgotten to twist, it's actually the right time to make the twist.

Cables can also be made to twist in the opposite direction; just hang your cable needle *to the back* of your work while you knit the next few stitches in the row, then knit the stitches from the cable needle.

Other configurations of cables can be 6 stitches that are twisted every 8 rows, or 4 stitches twisted every 4 rows, and so on.

coLor me impreʃʃed
Advanced Color Knitting

You see them every winter: Women of a certain age sporting cheery hand-knit cardigans with snowflakes circling the collar, or bright green sweaters with a giant, smiling reindeer on the back. Well, the next time you see one of these ladies, you should rush right up and and congratulate her, or at least give her a high five, because knitting designs into a sweater like that is damn hard work. It requires patience, skill, and lots of practice to work with so many different colors and keep a sweater from turning into a big, lumpy mess as you do so. I'm now going to introduce you to the two methods you'll need to make similarly fancy knit projects. And if your taste doesn't run to snowflakes and reindeer, you'll want to learn these techniques so that you can knit yourself, say, a Hello Kitty hat or a sweater with a tribal tattoo design around the sleeves.

Intarsia? I Hardly Know Ya!

Intarsia is an ugly name for the pretty method you'll use when you want to knit a heart in the center of your bikini bottom or create a large picture on a sweater or backpack. Sometimes it is called "picture knitting,"

which isn't really any nicer and sounds cornier. But whatever you call it, intarsia can be trickier than it seems.

The effect you want with intarsia is to have your knitting look as if your yarn magically changed color from one stitch to the next. What you're really doing is introducing a new piece of yarn for every patch of color you're knitting, and you constantly have to twist the old yarn and the new yarn together at the back of your work to link the stitches together. Otherwise you'll wind up with disastrous holes between the old and new stitches. (Imagine a chain-link fence where the chains aren't linked!) This technique is pretty straightforward when making simple shapes, like a circle inside a large square, or straight blocks of color. But try making something fancier—like a strawberry with green pointy leaves on a yellow background or a daisy in the center of a field of green—and things quickly get more complicated.

Okay, here's how it's done:

To add a second color of yarn in a row:

Slide your right needle into the first stitch as if to knit (or purl if that's what you're doing), but don't make the new stitch. Instead, lay the *new* color of yarn across the tip of the needle, leaving about a 6-inch tail hanging to the left and the ball end of the yarn to the right.

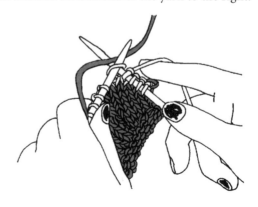

2 Bring the ball end of the yarn *around and underneath* the old color, then wrap it around the needle to make a knit (or purl) stitch. Finish the stitch in the usual way, dropping both the old loop and the tail of the new yarn over the newly formed stitch.

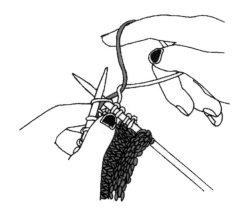

To change from one color to the next in the middle of a row:

Bring the old color up and to the left, then bring the new color up *from under* the old color, and make the new stitch. This hooks the two stitches together, like they're standing arm in arm for all eternity. Aw, ain't that sweet?

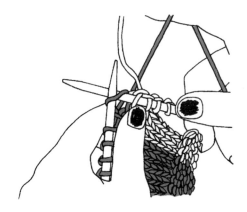

That's it, basically. You should know that the edges of your color blocks are probably going to look crappy—the edges of intarsia always do. Just wait until you're all done knitting, then take a little double-pointed needle and tug on the edges of each of those stitches to make 'em look nicer (see page 109). Also remember that the ragtag look of freshly knit intarsia patterns can be vastly improved and evened out with a bit of blocking.

And when you're done, yes, you really do have to work away each and every one of those yarn ends. Just try, if it's at all possible, to work each color away in an area that's the same color—otherwise your ends may show through on the front of your work.

Not-So-Fair Fair Isle

Let me be honest with you: I don't especially like Fair Isle knitting. Despise it, actually. Yet quite beautiful knit fabric can be made with this technique, and I feel it is my duty to at least show you how it's done.

Fair Isle (also known as jacquard knitting or stranded knitting) is the technique used to knit with two colors of yarn (sometimes more) in the same row to create patterns and pictures. It's this business of knitting with two colors at the same time that makes it so tricky. You can drop one color and pick up the other each time you need it; you can hold two different yarns in one hand; or you can hold one color of yarn in your left hand, one in your right, and knit with both at the same time. That last one is a real doozy—akin to patting yourself on the head and rubbing your tummy—but it's the most popular method going. We'll start with the easiest: the picking-up-and-dropping method.

GOODNESS, GRACIOUS, GREAT BALLS OF COLOR: TIPS FOR SUCCESSFUL INTARSIA

EACH AREA OF COLOR SHOULD HAVE ITS OWN BIT OF YARN: That means, if you are knitting a yellow block in the center of a blue background, you will be working with three lengths of yarn: one to knit the section of blue before you get to the block, one to knit the yellow block, and one to knit the blue section after the block.

SNEAK IN SOME FAIR ISLE: Unless you're a balls-out purist, you will use the Fair Isle technique (see page 93) to knit small areas of color in your intarsia and thus have fewer pieces of yarn dangling from the back of your knitting. So don't sweat it if you decide to carry yarn from one area in your picture—say, an eyeball—across a few stitches to knit the other eyeball. But try not to do it too often. If you have more than, say, 5 stitches between areas of color, it's probably best to cut a new piece of yarn for each one.

LET IT ALL HANG OUT: Use bobbins to wind up yarn for your color areas, but for small areas of color (a nose made of 6 stitches, for example), just cut a length of yarn and let it hang loose at the back of your work.

DON'T FORGET TO BREATHE: More than any other knitting technique, intarsia requires an almost Zen-like composure. The multiple strands hanging off the back of your work will inevitably turn into a mass of tangles, and you'll frequently have to stop knitting to untangle them. But hang in there, try to remain even-tempered, and the results will be worth the trouble—I can promise you that, Grasshopper.

just drop it already
Simple Fair Isle

1 Knit a stitch with the first color. When you need the second color, add it in as you would a new ball of yarn (see page 92), and knit the required number of stitches with it.

When you need the first color again, just let go of the second color, pick up the first color and bring it *underneath* the second color, and start knitting with it again.

2 When you need the second color again, drop the first color, bring the second color *over* the first color, and start knitting with it.

When knitting more than an inch of stitches in only one color, you should twist that color with the color not in use about halfway through the area. Do this by carrying the yarn in use *under* then *over* the yarn not in use before making your next stitch. The next time you have to twist your yarns midstream like this, do the reverse: Carry the yarn you're using *over* then *under* the other yarn. This will keep your balls from becoming a big tangled mess. (Your balls of yarn, I mean.) Doing this twisting stuff serves to catch the not-in-use yarn and keeps it from forming long "floats" (the pieces of yarn that get carried behind your work). Long floats are not only unsightly but they also catch on fingers, hands, and anything else in their path.

It is very important, when carrying yarn at the back of your work, that you leave enough of it between stitches so that it lies flat but still allows the fabric to stretch. Try this: After you've inserted your needle into the first stitch to be knit with a new color, stretch out the stitches on the needle before you make the next stitch. As you go on knitting, stop every once in a while and stretch the fabric a bit. You won't get quite as much stretch as you do with regular knitting, but you need to get some.

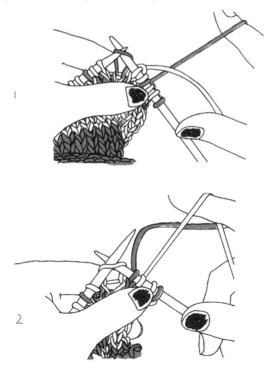

Look, ma! two Hands
Two-Fisted Fair Isle

1 Take the main color of yarn in your right hand and hold it as you would for English knitting (see page 34). Take the other color in your left hand and hold it as you would for Continental knitting (see page 36).

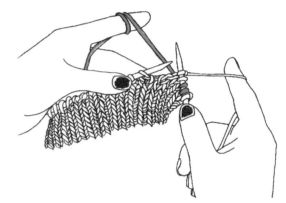

2 As each color is needed, knit it with the hand that is holding that color yarn. Be careful not to pull the yarn too tightly, as mentioned above. You will see that the yarn coming from your right hand will always be above the yarn coming from your left hand.

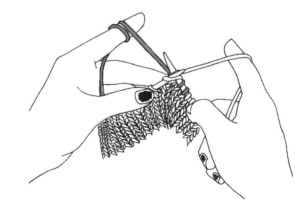

So far, so good—if you can get comfortable knitting with the yarn in both hands, and if you don't pull the yarn too tightly.

Things get *really* interesting when you start needing to weave the yarn in order to avoid getting long floats (if you are using one color for an inch or more of stitches). Let's start with the methods for doing this on the knit side.

To weave in yarn from the left hand on the knit side:

1 Put the needle through the next stitch as if you're going to knit it, only don't just yet. Bring the yarn on your left hand around the front of the right needle tip and lay it across the needle.

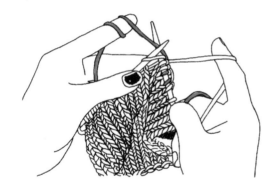

2 Knit the stitch.

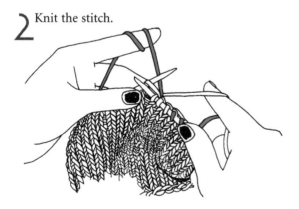

To weave in yarn from the right hand on the knit side:

1 Put the needle into the next stitch as if you're going to knit it, but don't. Wrap the yarn in the right hand around the needle as if you're going to make a knit stitch—then stop.

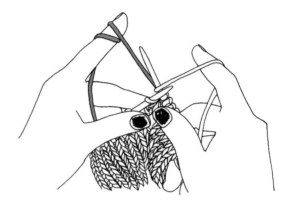

2 With your left hand, wrap the yarn around the needle point the way you would for a knit stitch.

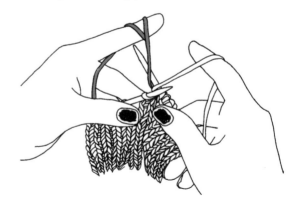

3 Now *unwrap* the yarn in your right hand from the needle (go in the opposite direction from the way you wrapped it). Finish making the stitch. You have "caught" the yarn from the right hand, and you may kiss the bride.

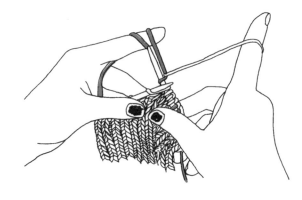

To weave in yarn from the left hand on the purl side:
Traditional Fair Isle knitting is worked in the round—meaning, no purl stitches at all, and thus none of the following headaches. However, if you're not working in the round, you'll need to learn this. You have my sympathy.

1 Insert your right needle into the stitch as if to purl—then stop. Take the yarn in your left hand, and bring it over the top and across the tip of the right needle.

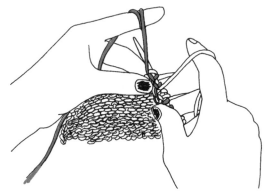

2 Wrap the yarn in the right hand around the needle the usual way for purl, and make the stitch.

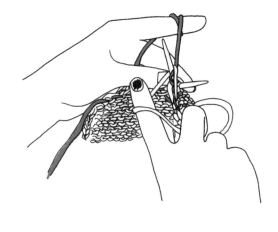

To weave in yarn from the right hand on the purl side:

Okay, this is so mind-warping it gives me a headache. But it can be done with a bit of practice.

1 Put your right needle into the stitch as if to purl—and stop. Take the yarn in your right hand and wind it around the tip of the right needle *in the opposite direction of how you would wrap it to make a purl stitch.* (Ouch!)

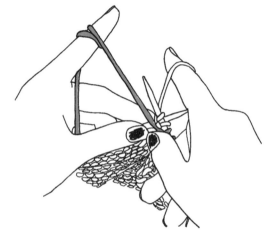

2 Wrap the yarn in the left hand around the needle as if you're going to make a purl stitch.

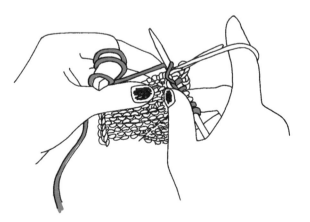

3 Now *unwind* the yarn from the right hand.

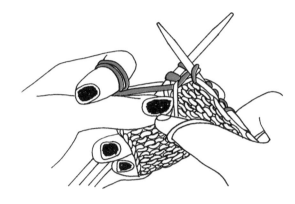

4 Finish the purl stitch. Take two aspirin and call me in the morning.

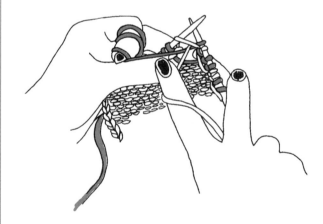

voulez-vous crochet avec moi
Crochet for Knitters

there's just no avoiding it, you're going to have to crochet at some point in your knitting career. So grab some yarn and get hooked up with the few crochet stitches needed in knitting—the chain stitch, single crochet, and crab stitch. You'll be able to use these to stabilize necklines, add decorative stitching around edges, and create tie cords. But here's the good news: Crocheting is a lot easier than knitting, so it shouldn't take you long to learn.

back on the chain gang
The Chain Stitch

the **chain stitch** is the foundation for most crochet work, but you can use it in your knitting to make drawstrings or tie cords to attach to your projects. Here's how it's done:

IN THE LOOP: CROCHET TIPS

✦ In knitting, your wrists stay pretty much stable as you manipulate the yarn and knitting needles, but a crochet hook is twisted, turned, and pulled, all by the motions of your wrist.

✦ Crocheting requires you to constantly pull loops of yarn through your previously formed loops. So, you want to leave enough space in those loops to pass a crochet hook through. When you start out, you might try leaving them purposely loose until you get the hang of how small they can go and still allow your hook to fit through.

✦ When you make a chain stitch or a single crochet, you are always working from right to left—like reading Hebrew. The crab stitch is the one exception: It is made from left to right.

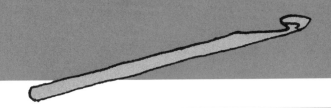

1 Make a slip knot about 6 inches from the end of your yarn and hang it over your crochet hook. Tighten the slip knot at the neck of the crochet hook, but leave it a bit loose, like the way the sales rep at the office Christmas party might wear his tie after his third eggnog. Hold the crochet hook in your right hand and the ball end of the yarn in your left, as you would for Continental knitting. With the thumb and middle finger of your left hand, lightly grasp the knot part of the slip knot.

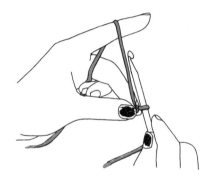

2 With the hook facing up, wrap the yarn over the front of the needle clockwise, from right to left.

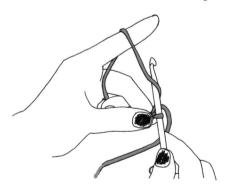

3 Twist the crochet hook so that the hook faces down and toward the knot, and pull the yarn through the loop.

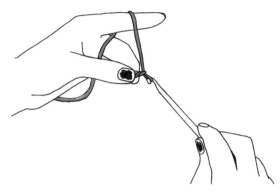

4 Twist the hook so that the hook part is facing up again, wrap the yarn as in step 2, and pull another loop through. In this way, each loop becomes part of a "chain" of stitches. And that's all there is to it.

Single Crochet

Single crochet can be used to add a decorative edge, but it must be made into already existing loops, like the edge of your knitting, or a crochet chain. To learn this technique, first make a foundation chain of about 20 stitches, so you'll have something to crochet into.

1 Slip your crochet hook through the second chain stitch from the hook, wrap the yarn around it clockwise, from right to left, and pull the loop through one loop. You now have two loops on your crochet hook.

2 Wrap the yarn around the crochet hook again, and this time pull it through *both* the loops on the hook.

Single crochet made. Move on to the next chain stitch.

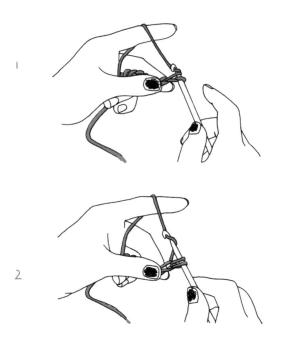

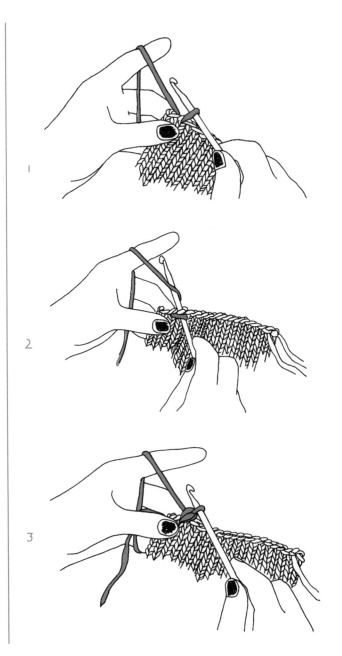

Crab Stitch

basically, the **crab stitch** is single crochet, but going from left to right instead of right to left, as you normally would. It's used around the edges of very open or loosely knit fabric, to stabilize it.

1 Insert a crochet hook into the edge of your knitting. Wrap the yarn around your hook clockwise, and pull a loop through.

2 Slide your crochet hook back into the fabric, in a space to the right of your last crab stitch. Wrap the ball end of the yarn clockwise around your crochet hook.

3 Pull the yarn through, so that you now have two loops on your crochet hook. Wrap your yarn one last time around the crochet hook, clockwise, then pull it through both loops. That's all, folks.

oops, i knit
THE STITCH DOCTOR'S GUIDE
it again
TO FIXING MISTAKES

n my Stitch 'n Bitch group, I am known as the "stitch doctor." Whenever anyone realizes that they suddenly have one stitch too few on their needles, or that they purled when they should have knit, they hand their work over to me. With my trusty crochet hooks at my side, I roll up my sleeves and go about performing my special brand of corrective surgery, setting mismade stitches right again. I find it strangely satisfying to puzzle out tangled stitches, re-create a stitch lost long ago seemingly out of thin air, or magically retwist incorrectly twisted cables.

Sometimes knitting problems are beyond the remedy of simply saving stitches: A sweater may end up too long or too short, for instance. But even these mistakes can be repaired by an experienced stitch doctor, although the patient may require an overnight stay.

You don't have to go through years of training to be a stitch doctor. Here, I'll let you in on some of my secrets and the procedures I practice with greatest success.

five, six, pick up stitch
The Dreaded Dropped Stitch

ven people who've never knit a stitch in their lives are familiar with the concept of "dropping" a stitch. When my mother was a child and was told she had dropped a stitch, she would look around her chair on the floor, expecting to find a small U-shaped piece of yarn—the dropped stitch. But a dropped stitch doesn't actually fall to the ground, and, regardless of its reputation, it isn't really such a big deal. A dropped stitch is simply a loop that comes loose—usually by slipping off the tip of your needle as you work—and unravels downward, like a stocking run, one or more rows.

Dropped stitches befall even the most seasoned knitter, but they are much easier to repair when they slip just a row or two down. So, especially when you're first beginning, keep a close eye on your knitting and count your stitches frequently to make sure that you still have the correct number on your needles.

To pick up a dropped knit stitch that has slipped down only one row, do the following:

1 Insert your right needle from front to back into the fallen loop to stop it from unraveling any further.

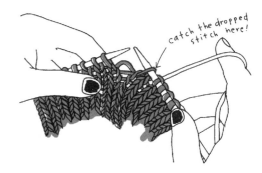

catch the dropped stitch here!

2 Slip the point of the right needle, from front to back, under the loose strand of yarn that remains above the dropped stitch.

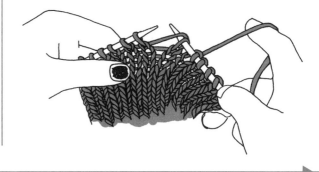

3 With the left needle, lift the dropped stitch over this strand and off the tip of the needle.

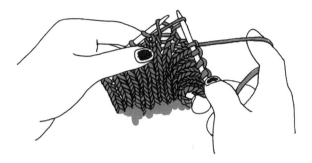

4 Transfer the stitch from the right needle back to the left needle by inserting the point of the left needle through it from front to back.

To pick up a dropped purl stitch that has fallen just one row down, you use similar steps:

1 Insert your right needle from back to front into the fallen loop to stop it from unraveling any further.

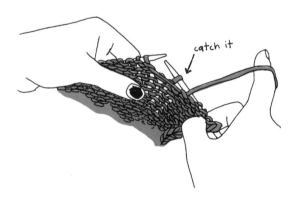

catch it

2 Slip the point of the right needle from back to front under the strand of yarn that remains above the dropped stitch.

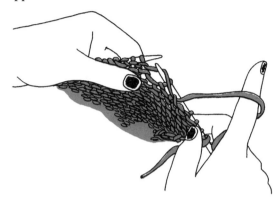

3 Then, with the left needle, lift the dropped stitch over this strand and off the tip of the needle.

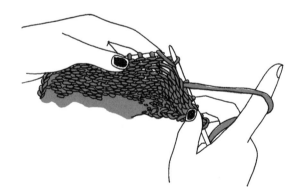

4 Transfer the stitch from the right needle back to the left needle by inserting the point of the left needle through it from front to back.

Hook and Ladder
Picking Up Several Rows of Dropped Stitches

Sometimes a stitch will drop and unravel a number of rows before you notice that it has gone. If this happens, you'll need the stitch doctor's equivalent of a scalpel—a crochet hook—to pick that stitch back up. Crochet hooks come in a large variety of sizes, but you really only need two: a small one for finer yarns, and a large one for coarser yarns.

To pick up a knit stitch that was dropped many rows ago:

Knit up to the last stitch before the dropped stitch. Look at your work. You will have a loop a few rows down, and a "ladder"—with rungs corresponding to each dropped stitch—between your stitches.

1 Insert a crochet hook from front to back through the loop.

2 Grab the first ladder rung and pull it through the opening in the loose stitch. Then grab the next ladder rung and pull it through, and so on until you have carried the stitch all the way back up. The rungs will be very tight, especially if the stitch was dropped a ways back, but just go ahead and force them through. Later you can straighten out those stitches and make it look all better.

3 Transfer the loop from the crochet hook onto the left needle.

If you've dropped a **purl** stitch, just turn the work around so that the knit side is facing you, and pick up the stitches, using the directions above. Make sure to turn the work the right way around before you start purling again.

the grim repair
Picking Up Knits and Purls

If you've dropped a stitch in a fabric that uses both knit and purl—for instance, in garter stitch or seed stitch—picking up the stitch becomes a bit more complicated, and involves removing and reinserting your crochet hook at each ladder rung.

For each **knit** stitch you are picking up, insert the crochet hook into your loop from front to back and pull a ladder rung through to the front. For each **purl** stitch, you must first remove the crochet hook from the loop and reinsert it from back to front (**figure 1**). Then pull the next yarn rung through this loop (**figure 2**). For your next knit stitch, you'll have to remove the hook and reinsert it again. It's annoying, I know, but far less annoying than the alternative—unraveling all your work to the point of the dropped stitch and knitting it all over.

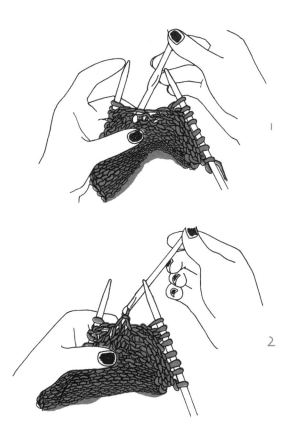

turning water into wine
Changing Knit and Purl Stitches

Now that you can pick up a yarn rung as either a knit or a purl stitch, you're ready for one of the stitch doctor's greatest secrets: re-creating mismade stitches. If you accidentally knit when you should have purled, or vice versa, you can fix it, even if you don't discover the problem until many rows later. Start by purposely dropping the stitch that's in the same column as the bad stitch and letting it unravel to the place where the mistake was made. Now, using your crochet hook, pick that stitch up correctly (making it a knit or a purl, following the instructions on page 105), then pick up the rest of the stitches in the column all the way back to the top of your knit piece. Of course, at a certain point you have to ask yourself whether it would be quicker just to unravel your work and reknit it correctly, but I've used this technique many times to make time-saving corrections to my work.

too much of a good thing
Fixing Extra Stitches

Sometimes when you count your stitches, you discover you have one too many. This can happen for a number of reasons. If you're not careful, it's easy to knit twice into the stitch at the beginning of a row. (See page 38 for how to avoid this.) You might also have accidentally treated stitches made with two strands of yarn—like when you're joining new yarn—as two separate stitches. Or you may have split your yarn so that it looked like two stitches instead of one, and you knit each one. You can easily fix these mistakes in a couple of ways:

Figure out where the extra stitch was created, then drop both the extra stitch and the stitch just before it down to the place where the error was made. Next, pick up the rungs as a single stitch. (See instructions for picking up dropped stitches on page 105.) If you end up with some floppy extra yarn before and after each stitch, don't worry about it. Later in this chapter, I'll show you how to give saggy stitches a face-lift. You can also correct the problems when blocking your garment.

If you're using fine wool, or if the extra stitch was added way back and didn't leave a hole, you might be better off just decreasing a stitch at either end of your work, one or two stitches in from the edge, to correct for the error. (See page 63 for how to decrease stitches.) And if the extra stitch left a hole in your work (which can happen very easily), you can sew it closed with a short piece of yarn after you're done knitting.

if i could turn back time
Unknitting

Sometimes you will need to unknit part of a row so you can get back to correct an error. Unknitting is the easiest way to undo your work if you have to unravel only one or two rows. Here's how: Hold your yarn and needles in the usual way. Then insert the left needle from front to back into the loop *below* the last stitch you made (**figure 1**). Slide the stitch off the right needle and pull out the yarn (**figure 2**). Carry on until you get to the point where you made your mistake. Keep at it, and soon you'll find that unknitting can be done just as quickly as knitting.

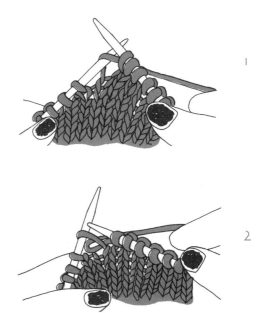

SHe'S come undone
Unraveling Your Work

When you need to undo a large number of rows, it's too time-consuming to unknit them stitch by stitch. Instead, you can just unravel them. The most common way to do this is to simply pull the needle completely out of your stitches, unravel a number of rows until you get to a point before you made your mistake, then reinsert the needle into all of the stitches. I always feel kind of panicky when I'm trying to catch all those stitches again or see some loops dropping farther down than I intend them to. Using a smaller-sized needle to catch the loops can make this task easier, but I still feel safer using the following method when I need to unravel a number of rows:

Using a needle substantially smaller than the one you were using, weave the needle under the right-hand loop of each stitch in the row you will unravel to. Here's the tricky part, though: You have to make sure that all the stitches you pick up are from the same row; carefully following the path of the yarn can help you do this correctly. Also, count the stitches you have on the needle to make sure that you have gotten them all.

2 Pull out the other needle, and unravel the yarn back to the row where your thin needle is. If you did it correctly, you will have a needle full of stitches. Jump up and kiss yourself.

At this point you may find that your needle is pointing in the wrong direction. Just take a regular-sized needle and transfer all the stitches by slipping them purlwise from the tiny needle to the regular one. As you do this, check for stitches that may have twisted the wrong way, and set them straight. Remember that the correct way for stitches to sit on the needle is with the leg on the right side of each stitch in front of the needle, and the leg on the left in the back. Your little friends below are happy to demonstrate this for you one more time.

wrong! Yay!

A knitting face-lift
Tightening Saggy Stitches

You may find, at certain points in your knitting, that you are left with saggy, wacked-out stitches. It happens a lot in intarsia projects, where it is almost impossible to make all your stitches come out perfectly, or when you've picked up a dropped stitch and are making two stitches back into one, or at other points in your knitting. Not to worry; this too can be fixed.

1 A number of rows after the loose stitch (or even after the entire piece is done), take a smaller needle and pull the stitch tighter by pulling up on the right-side arm of the stitch. You may end up with quite a big, slack loop.

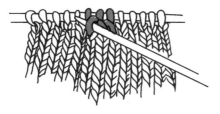

2 Then follow that stitch along to the right by pulling up the left-side arm of the next stitch, then the right-side arm of that stitch, and so on, making each stitch just slightly looser than it was originally (remember—just slightly, and imperceptibly) and distributing the slack across 10 or more stitches. Now your stitch is purty as can be.

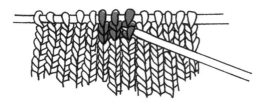

Shortfalls
The Unintentional Crop Top

even if you've checked your gauge carefully, sometimes a sweater just doesn't come out right—maybe it was supposed to reach your hips, but instead your belly is hanging out. If this happens, you sure don't want to unravel the whole sweater and reknit it. Instead, you can undo the cast-on stitches at the bottom of the sweater and put the freed-up stitches on a needle. Then just knit from there. In effect, you are now knitting downward, therefore adding length to your knit piece.

There are some things to keep in mind with this method, however. As I explained on page 77, when you are grabbing stitches from the bottom of your work, you are really getting the Vs that are in between the original knit Vs, and, as a result, you will end up with one stitch less than you started out with. This means that your new knitting will be offset by half a stitch from your original knitting. For many types of stitches, this doesn't matter, but in ribbing and other knit-and-purl designs, it will matter a lot—you'll never get your new ribs to line up with your original ribs. Therefore, if you are extending a sweater that has a ribbed bottom, you should first unravel all the ribbing. Then, when you knit downward, you will need to create new ribbing. If you're extending a sweater with some other kind of knit-and-purl pattern, consider adding a couple of decorative purl or seed stitch rows before continuing on in your pattern. That way, no one can tell that the bottom part doesn't match up exactly with the top part.

Unraveling a cast-on edge is not as easy as unraveling regular knitting. If you have used the slingshot or double cast-on method, you should find the end of your yarn, pick it free from where you worked it away, then follow its path to undo one stitch at a time. As you undo

QUICK-FIXIN' TRICKS

YOUR SMILEY-FACE BACKPACK IS MISSING AN EYE?

If you discover mistakes in your color knitting, you can simply make a duplicate stitch over the wrong color stitch with the right color yarn.

SWEATER GIVING YOU A FLASHDANCE LOOK?

You can tighten up or stabilize a scoop-neck sweater that's too loose or floppy by crocheting a crab-stitch edging around it (see page 101). Try using one crab stitch for every one or two knit stitches around the neckline.

SOCKS TWO DIFFERENT SIZES?

Another problem that can be fixed with the magic of blocking: Just lay both socks on a towel when damp, and scrunch the larger one down to the size of the smaller one. Of course,

if you've made one sock so large it could only fit Bigfoot, you will have to rip it out and start over again.

SWEATER TOO WIDE AND TOO SHORT?

Try stretching the sweater vertically while blocking it. This will make it both longer and narrower.

YOU WANTED A SWEATER, NOT A DRESS?

This one's easy. Just unravel the bottom (see page 109), pick up your stitches, and bind them off at the length you want the sweater to be. If you still want a ribbed bottom, unravel to the point above where the ribbing should start, then knit new ribbing in the downward direction.

stitches, put the freed-up live loops on a needle (preferably a circular one that can hang safely from your work as you go along). Again, use a needle a couple of sizes smaller than the one you used to knit the piece. Once you've picked up your stitches, count them to make sure they're all there (minus one, of course). Then, chop the unraveled yarn off, leaving a 6-inch tail, and just start knitting in the opposite direction with new yarn until the piece is as long as you need it to be.

This method can also be used to change the bottom of a sweater even if it's not too short—for instance, if you decide that your ribbed bottom is too tight or unflattering and you'd prefer a loose, rolled edge at the bottom. Just unravel all the ribbing and reknit the bottom of the sweater in stockinette stitch until it's back to the length you want—this time with a rolly edge.

i say rip it, rip it good
Frogging Your Work

despite all the fixing tricks, sometimes you just have to throw in the proverbial towel. Entire sleeves, fronts, or backs may need to be taken out. It's a very painful moment when you realize you just can't salvage a knitted piece any other way. But remember that it's better to unravel the piece and redo it correctly than to wear it unhappily for years, always noticing where the problem is. Or, worse yet, never wear it at all.

In knitter's parlance, unraveling a large part of knitting is called frogging. Get it? A frog goes "ribbit, ribbit," and you're going to "rip it, rip it." Hey, I couldn't make these things up.

Even cornier is when people speak of putting a project in the "frog pond," which means it's been set aside to be completely unraveled, and the yarn will be recycled for a different project. When that royal blue sweater that looked so good on the model in the magazine makes you look like Cookie Monster, or the sparkly scarf is so itchy around your neck it's become a torture device, it's time to take a trip to the frog pond.

Just like hair that's been sitting in braids for a while, unraveled yarn will have lots of little kinks in it, and it will need to be straightened before you can reuse it. To do that, wind the unraveled yarn into hanks—you can do this around the back of a chair or around your feet held about a foot apart. Secure the hanks with pieces of yarn in three or more places. Then immerse them in warm water with a bit of soap, swish them around, rinse them out, and hang them up to dry. Loop them over the hook of a hanger or over a shower head and put a weight at the bottom of the hank (a can of food works well for this) to help pull out those kinks.

When the yarn is good and dry, you can wind it back into balls until you're ready to use it again. That sparkly yarn might work well as a pillow, or the blue yarn could be knit on larger needles to make a loose, flattering tunic.

a loosely knit group

A GUIDE TO THE WONDERFUL WORLD OF KNITTERS

t's a freezing cold Tuesday night in January, and the gals at my office can't wait to head home, but I'm happy to face the biting winds and make my way to the Java 'n Jazz café. After all, tonight is Stitch 'n Bitch, and I've been looking forward to it all week.

By the time I get there, the ladies have already staked their claim to the rocking chair and the coveted couch at the back of the café. The low coffee table in front of them is covered with mugs of cappuccino and tea, and the women themselves sit thigh-to-thigh on the couches in a tight circle, their heads bent over their latest knitting projects, bags of yarn and needles scattered at their feet. With a bit of rearranging, I find a way to join the circle as well.

I settle in and greet the regulars: There's Marney, a meeting planner who learned to knit as a way to soothe her nerves after having escaped from the seventy-ninth floor of the World Trade Center on that day in September, and who has since established herself as the group's most prolific knitter (the girl whips through socks and sweaters faster than a speeding bullet). There's Jessica, a university professor and one of the most experienced knitters in the group, who not only designs many of her projects, but also dyes and spins the wool for them. There's Betsey, an advertising copywriter who's been knitting bridesmaids' tops ever since she got engaged a few months ago; Jackie, a graphic designer who started knitting in the '80s (and has the embarrassing photos of her in big poofy sweaters and big poofy hair to prove it); Johanna, a book editor who is known for tackling fine, lacy projects; Susannah, a public radio producer and determined new knitter whom we watched knit—and then frog—her very first sweater; and Sonya, a Web programmer who once knit a pair of cat pants (they were a bigger hit with the group than with her cat). Meema, a documentary filmmaker and knitter who is our resident felting queen, is there as well; besides myself, she's the only member who's been with the group since its inception back in September of 1999. Finally, there's Dennis, a premed student and the only regularly attending male member of the group. An ambitious newcomer to knitting, he's already made himself a pair of intricate socks, which he is wearing—and showing off—tonight.

Then there are the many knitters whom I do not yet know by name: the ones who are attending for their first time, who are just learning to knit, or who drop in only once in a while. The gaggle of fresh faces always energizes the regulars as we all get down to the business at hand: working on our own projects while checking out each other's progress and offering advice on dealing with knitting tragedies like too tight collars and crappy-looking buttonholes.

For the most part, more stitching than bitching takes place at these sessions, but talk has ranged from Martha Stewart's status as a feminist icon to whether people who wear low-slung jeans should wear knit "belly warmers" and which of the Muppets we would choose to sleep with (I picked Animal). We bring show-and-tell items—projects that we've completed or our latest knitting book purchases—and we bring our problems. A discussion about a sweater that's too big for a current boyfriend soon becomes a discussion about whether said boyfriend really deserves a hand-knit sweater. By the evening's end, I've usually made good progress on whatever I'm working on, and I've shared some laughs with a bunch of smart, funny ladies (and gentlemen). I always leave looking forward to the next week's meeting.

No matter how loosely it's organized, a Stitch 'n Bitch is fun. For the obsessed knitter, there's nothing as exciting as finding like-minded people who share your passion and with whom you can discuss the craft. (I can just imagine how my friends' eyes would glaze over if I ever started raving about a great new yarn store or some knitting technique I'd just learned.) But even new knitters who aren't yet consumed by the craft can enjoy an evening spent stitching with others—aside from the opportunity to learn things from the old hands, be inspired by them, and get advice. Best of all is the fact that a Stitch 'n Bitch group makes knitting, which can be a very solitary activity, a communal one.

I started the New York City Stitch 'n Bitch for exactly that reason: I had become so obsessed with knitting that I wanted to do little else, and I soon found myself feeling rather isolated. Why not start a group, I thought, where I could spend time in the company of others while engaging in my favorite pastime? A weekly knitting session would also be a great way to involve the many girls I knew who'd expressed an interest in knitting. I could just tell them to show up, and I—or one of the other knitters—could give them a quick lesson.

I chose a local café as the location for our group, set up an e-mail list, and invited friends to join and to spread the word. I also mentioned the group's e-mail address in an issue of *BUST* magazine. Soon we had a group of about twenty women meeting every Wednesday night. I dubbed the group "Stitch 'n Bitch," but the name dates back to at least the 1950s, when housewives held these types of get-togethers in an effort to mix the business of chores with the pleasure of each other's company.

Shortly after she heard about our NYC group, knitter Brenda Janish began a Stitch 'n Bitch in her native Chicago, created a Web site for it, and even developed a cartoon mascot. "Purl" is a combat-booted knitter who proudly brandishes her knitting needles, representin' for the new generation of knitters and gracing canvas knitting totes. Today the Chicago group is one of the largest

Stitch 'n Bitches going, and their e-mail list boasts close to five hundred members. Brenda's bunch, in turn, inspired other knitters to begin Stitch 'n Bitches in such places as Los Angeles; Portland, Oregon; Washington, D.C.; and Toronto, as well as Melbourne, Australia; Aberdeen, Scotland; and even Zurich, Switzerland, all of which can be contacted via Brenda's Web site, www.stitchnbitch.org, which lists information for twenty-eight different groups.

the inter-knit
Virtual Knitting Communities

Maybe you'd really like to start a Stitch 'n Bitch, but it's just not practical: You live in the Arctic Circle, you are the only knitter in a hundred-mile radius, or you're a hermit who doesn't like people enough to get together with them once a week. With a computer and an Internet connection you can still be a part of the knitting community without ever having to leave your house.

five thousand knitters can't be wrong
The KnitList

One of the oldest knitting communities on the Internet, the KnitList is a worldwide knitting e-mail list, and boy, do these knitters have a lot to say. Signing up to be part of the list means getting an inbox full of knitting-related posts on a daily basis—some of which will be helpful, and some of which will be frustrating. Limit

STARTING A STITCH 'N BITCH

Starting a Stitch 'n Bitch is easy—after all, it's just a bunch of folks getting together to knit, nothing more, nothing less. It's pretty much guaranteed that if you plan it (and get the word out in the right places), they will come. Here are some ideas to get your knitting party started:

LOCATION, LOCATION, LOCATION: Choose a meeting spot where it will be easy to find seats for a varying number of people—the most popular café in town is probably not the best choice. A café off the beaten track, or one that isn't known for serving the best coffee in town, is a better idea. Next, you want it to be someplace where it's okay to nurse a cup of tea or coffee all night long. Case the place to make sure that they have empty tables on the night you plan to hold your group. (That way, you can be certain that your group won't be putting a large dent in the waiters' wallets.) You want a place that is relatively well lit. Finally, if you live in a big city, it should be somewhere central, close to public transportation (and to available parking).

I don't recommend holding meetings at anyone's home, because it makes it difficult to establish a regular night and time for your Stitch 'n Bitch. If your host has a conflicting engagement, or isn't feeling well, that's the end of your meeting that week. Plus, newcomers might not feel as comfortable dropping in to a stranger's house as they would to a random café.

GET THE WORD OUT: Let the world know about your group by setting up an e-mail list online that makes it easy to e-mail everyone at the same time (yahoogroups.com offers a good way to do this, as do some other Web servers). Go to www.stitchnbitch.org and get your group listed on the Web site. Then, see if your local knitting shops will let you post notices about the group. Include the time, place, and the e-mail address for signing up and getting info. If you're active on any Web-based bulletin boards and think the members are right for your group, post the information there as well. And of course, if you see someone on the bus or in your local bar who's knitting, ambush her and invite her to join.

STAY REGULAR WITH FIBER: No matter what evening you choose, there will always be a few people who won't be able to make it—so don't drive yourself crazy trying to please everyone. Monday, Tuesday, or Wednesday nights are your best choices. We start our meetings at 7:00 P.M., since that gives people enough time to get there after work, without a lot of empty time in between. Once you've decided on a time and place, try not to change it. Since many members of Stitch 'n Bitches won't come every week, it's good to establish yourself at the same Bat time and the same Bat channel every week—it makes it easier for people to show up whenever they can make it.

DECODING THE KNITLIST ACRONYMS

One highly entertaining aspect of the KnitList is the acronyms used, which can make a KnitList post look like a secret FBI missive.

LYS: Local yarn store.

SEX: Stash enrichment expedition. It means going to a knitting store. Really.

UFO: Unfinished object.

FO: Finished object, natch!

DH or DW: Darling husband or darling wife, as in "Today my DH took me to my favorite LYS for SEX!" Ew.

DS or DD: Darling son or darling daughter, as in "Tonight, after bingo, I got working on that UFO for my DD."

WIP: Work in progress.

KIP: Knitting in public.

MIL OR FIL OR DIL OR SIL: Mother-in-law, father-in-law, daughter-in-law, son-in-law, as in, "On the bus this morning, I caught my MIL KIPing on her latest WIP. Fa shizzle!"

your messages to technical types of questions, however, and you'll be greeted with a wealth of useful information. I'd advise you to receive the posts in "digest" form—meaning you'll be e-mailed one file a day of all that day's posts—because the KnitList can easily overwhelm your inbox.

read this blog
Online Knitting Journals

the KnitList is a great source of knitting info, but for more personal content, I recommend reading any of the ever-expanding crop of Weblogs dedicated to the subject. Weblogs, or "blogs" for short, are online journals created by folks who are willing to share their lives and experiences, diary style, with Internet users worldwide. Reading a person's knitting blog, where she has posted, often on a daily basis, information about her current knitting projects, her current knitting challenges, and, frequently, pictures of her completed projects (or works in progress), can be a really intimate experience. Many Weblogs are interactive, with space for visitors to leave comments. Today there are well over a hundred knitting Weblogs, and more are being created every day—just type "knit blog" into any Internet search engine to find the current batch.

It isn't hard to start a Weblog of your own—you can set one up for free at www.blogger.com, or you can download software to help you create a blog on your own Web server at www.movabletype.org. Having a digital camera (or access to one) is also helpful, since putting up pictures of your projects is one of the coolest things about blogging, and it also makes your site more interesting to readers. And once you've got it set up, adding an entry is about as easy as writing an e-mail.

money for nuthin' and your knits for free

Free Knitting Patterns

the Internet is a great source of free knitting patterns. **About.com's** knitting site (www.knitting.about.com) has a ton of them, many (but not all) of which are accompanied by photos. The **KnitList's** Web site (www.knitlist.com) contains the many patterns that are contributed each year to a knitting "giftlist"—contributions from the members of the KnitList for everything from afghans to washcloths to mittens and sweaters. Then there's the spankin' new online knitting magazine *Knitty* (www.knitty.com), which has awesome free patterns contributed by some of the hippest chicks on the net. And don't forget to do a simple Google search for any knitting pattern you might be hunting. Putting in the words "free legwarmers knitting pattern" brings up quite a few sites that contain such a pattern, and simply typing in "free knitting patterns" brings up over six thousand matches.

There are also a couple of sites that actually make use of the main function that computers were invented for—computing!—on their pages. These sites let you type in certain numbers, press a button, and whammo—they spit out instant, customized patterns. Here are a few to try:

CREATE YOUR OWN GRAPH PAPER

www.thedietdiary.com/knittingfiend/KnittersGraph.html
Since knit stitches are wider than they are tall, if you want to sketch a picture of your boyfriend to knit on your sweater, you'll need to do it on what's called "knitter's graph paper"; otherwise your beau will knit up short and fat. On this page, you can enter your yarn gauge, then generate paper that's the actual size you need.

GRAPH PAPER PDF GENERATOR

www.tata-tatao.to/knit/matrix/e-index.html
This Web page basically does the same as the previous site, but it also allows you to print the paper at a reduced size. But what's even cooler is the fact that it generates the paper as a PDF file, which means you can save it on your computer and print out as many sheets as your heart desires.

CUSTOM DOG SWEATER

www.thedietdiary.com/cgi-bin/chart_dog.pl
Just type in your dog's measurements, and your yarn gauge, and this page will generate instructions for a form-fitting frock for Fifi.

THE SWEATER MACHINE

www.apocalypse.org/pub/u/liz/sweater.html
Amazingly simple, this Web page only asks that you decide on a style for your sweater (bottom-up or top-down drop-sleeve, or top-down raglan) and choose a size, and it pumps out a pattern for you.

THE SWEATER PATTERN GENERATOR

www.thedietdiary.com/knittingfiend/OrderForms/Top Form.html
Much more complex than the Sweater Machine, this page lets you choose from a wide variety of sweater styles and also requires that you enter a good amount of information before it will give up the goods—that is, a custom pattern.

THE SOCK CALCULATOR

www.panix.com/~ilaine/socks.html
This lovely page lets you enter your yarn gauge, the length you want your sock to be, and certain measurements from your foot (such as calf and ankle circumference and foot length), then produces a pattern that's perfect for your peds.

THE SCARF PATTERN CALCULATOR

www.girlfromauntie.com/patterns/clothing/yasp/yasp2.html

The Girl from Auntie makes scarves even easier with this page for generating a pattern for a striped scarf in stockinette stitch. You choose how wide and how long you want your scarf, whether you want stripes lengthwise or widthwise, and enter your stitch gauge. Make a pattern for a long, skinny scarf or a short, fat one—the scarf generator doesn't care, as long as you're happy.

software for softies
Computer Programs for Knitters

While those Web sites can get you started generating patterns, they are very limited as to what you can make. Happily, there are a number of computer programs out there that can help you design a much greater variety of projects, even if you're not a designer.

Programs such as **Stitch Painter, AranPaint**, and **Stitch & Motif Maker** allow you to create and print out complicated stitch patterns for your projects incorporating colorful designs and textures such as cables, braids, and bobbles. Stitch Painter will even take a digital image and transform it into an intarsia knitting chart.

Other programs, such as **DesignaKnit, Sweater Wizard, Garment Styler,** and **Garment Designer,** let you generate patterns for knit sweaters—and even knit skirts—of your own creation. Garment Designer, for instance, will make you feel like you've died and gone to knitter's heaven. Say, for example, you walked by your favorite shop and saw an awesome tunic hanging there, with bell-shaped sleeves, a bit of a fitted waistline, and a wide boat neck. You know you could knit it yourself, and you even know that you have some yarn at home that would look great done up in that style. But where on earth will you find a pattern for a sweater exactly like that? Even if you did find one, there's no guarantee it would be designed to work with the yarn you have.

Enter Garment Designer (www.cochenille.com). With a piece of software like this, you can rather quickly pull together a pattern for that exact sweater—choose the style, the sleeve type, how the sleeves are set in (raglan, drop shoulder, or shaped), the length, the fit (loose or fitted), the size, and even the gauge of the yarn you want to use. Then, just like a fairy godmother, Garment Designer will pump out the pattern for you, with the instructions written out all nice-like with little schematics you can refer to as you knit. The possibilities are endless, making Garment Designer a great and fun toy for grown-up girls. (At $165 it's a bit pricey, though, so you might want to remember it when your next birthday rolls around.)

get off the Net already!
Knitting Organizations in Real Life

Of course, a Stitch 'n Bitch is a great way to get together with the gals and knit your little hearts out. But sometimes you need a little extra guidance from the experts—and more than you can get from all those Web sites. That's when it's time to hook yourself up with a local or national knitting guild. **The Knitting Guild of America** (TKGA) offers conferences and even knitting correspondence courses (how old school!) to help you learn to become a Master Knitter. They send you instructions, you send in swatches and essays, and their panel of knitting experts reviews your work and either awards you the certificate or makes you do it over again. Their Web site (www.tkga.com) also lists all the local branches of the guild—which are, essentially, high-end or more serious versions of Stitch 'n Bitch groups. Some of them, like New York's Big Apple Knitting Guild, offer classes, field trips, and a lending library.

But TKGA isn't the only group that organizes conferences: *Knitter's,* a magazine published by XRX, Inc., holds **Stitches** conferences, big old meet-ups for knitters of every persuasion, a few times a year in a variety of locations: East Coast, West Coast, and Midwest. In the summertime, they even have something called Camp Stitches (www.knittinguniverse.com). I've been to Stitches East the past two years, and I have to say that it's the funnest thing ever. Grab your girlfriends and share a hotel room: This is a weekend that's jam-packed with classes, shopping, and even a banquet and fashion show. Not only do you get to meet and learn from the most famous knitters out there (yes, they exist), but you also get to spend a few days doing nothing but talking and thinking about knitting. Yay!

Finally, in September and October, the Craft Yarn Council of America organizes what they call **Knit-Outs** in various locations across the country. Thousands of knitters show up at these things, and it's a great chance to mix and mingle with your local knitting community. Visit www.craftyarncouncil.com for more information.

ALL the knit that's fit to print
The Best Knitting Books

I love knitting books almost as much as I love knitting. I'm especially enamored of knitting books that go into the history of knitting or some specific technique, although I adore pattern books as well. In fact, my bookshelf at home is bulging from the weight of my giant knitting book collection. Here, then, are just a few of the favorites from my shelves:

KNITTING IN PLAIN ENGLISH, Maggie Righetti (1986, St. Martin's Press)
Righetti is my personal knitting guru: She's funny, she's smart, and she really helped me understand some of the knitty-gritty. She's also got sass: The lame but extremely instructive projects at the back of her book are called things like "the dumb baby sweater" and "the stupid baby bonnet," and her "Buttonholes Are Bastards" chapter is unforgettable. Unfortunately, Maggie has faded from the knitting scene since her books were first published, but this is the one I always recommend to beginning knitters who want to learn more.

THE READER'S DIGEST KNITTER'S HANDBOOK, Montse Stanley (1986, 1993, Reader's Digest)
If you buy only one knitting book in your lifetime (besides the one you're holding in your hands right now), it should be this encyclopedic resource of knitting techniques. This knitter/author knows more tricks of the trade than anyone going (and I've read them all). In fact, I've found solutions to some of the most obscure knitting problems here that aren't addressed anywhere else.

Stanley's writing can be as dry as dust, and her they-came-from-the-'80s patterns are pretty cheesy, but who really cares about all that when this lady can teach you over forty (count 'em!) cast-on methods?

KNITTING WITHOUT TEARS, Elizabeth Zimmermann (1971, Simon & Schuster)

Just as James Brown is the godfather of soul, and Iggy Pop is the godfather of punk, Elizabeth Zimmermann is the godmother of American knitting, and this book is the perfect introduction to her smart 'n snarky "opinion-ated knitting" philosphy. A mistress of "unvention"—she loved to find new and easier ways of doing things—Zimmermann has convinced thousands of American women to drop the yarn from their right hands and throw away their straight needles in favor of Continental-style knitting in the round, which she's con-vinced is easier and more efficient. *Knitting Without Tears* is not for an absolute beginner, but if you've knit your way around the block a couple of times and want to learn some great and innovative knitting tricks, this book is a must.

HOW TO KNIT and **KNITTING WORKBOOK,** Debbie Bliss (1999 and 2001, Trafalgar Square)

Debbie Bliss is the Queen Mum of British knitters. Known for her simple, attractive patterns, especially her sweet baby items, Bliss is one of the most prolific design-ers around. These two books are more inspirational than they are informational, as Bliss sometimes leaves out important details in her knitting method descriptions. But even if you thought you'd never want to knit cables, intarsia designs, or lace, you will once you see what Bliss can do with them.

THE ULTIMATE KNITTER'S GUIDE, Kate Buller (2000, Martingale)

Buller is another knitting Brit, and her book of knitting lessons and techniques is set up in a most unusual way: Each page is cut into two parts, with the bottom fourth containing illustrated knitting techniques, and the top three-fourths consisting of patterns. The idea is that when you are working on a pattern and get to a part where you need to know a technique, there it is on the same page. The most valuable part of her book is the knitting methods themselves, especially the more advanced ones: intarsia knitting, short-row shaping, stranded and woven two-color knitting, and various fin-ishing methods, all accompanied by instructive photos.

Mag Hags
Magazines for Knitters

each of these magazines is published only quar-terly, so if you've really got a knitting pattern jones you'll end up subscribing to all five.

Family Circle Easy Knitting

Don't let the *Family Circle* moniker scare you away—the name is just licensed. Great assortments of basic knitting patterns (as well as a few clunk-ers) are, indeed, included for every family member: women, men, children, babies, and pets. But my favorite thing about *FCEK* is that so many of its patterns are reprinted from European knitting magazines.

Vogue Knitting

As in its namesake, the emphasis here is on patterns by big-name designers: Todd Oldham, Calvin Klein, Marc Jacobs, Donna Karan, and Oscar de la Renta have all contributed patterns. While that sounds like a great idea in theory, in practice—well, let's just say that few  things go out of vogue more quickly than some of the sweaters in *Vogue Knitting*. Nevertheless, there are always a number of great patterns, as well as instructions for various professional techniques.

Interweave Knits

Independently published out of Loveland, Colorado, Interweave Knits is beautifully designed and always includes interesting, often intricate, patterns. Articles for the knitting obsessed describe various yarns, techniques, and tidbits of knitting history. More than the  others, *IK* seems to really capture the larger knitting culture. If you subscribe to only one knitting magazine, I'd suggest this one.

Rebecca

Because *Rebecca* is put out by the German yarn manufacturing company Muench, all its patterns are made using their yarns. But the stuff is so fun—hip, trendy, colorful, sexy, and modeled by attractive Aryans frolicking on the beach—that you won't be able to resist. And you  can always replace the yarn called for with something different. This one's the coolest mag going.

Rowan

Another magazine put out by a yarn company, *Rowan* is so British you'll want to invite it to tea. Featuring beautiful classic sweaters modeled by young people who look so much more cultured than you, these patterns will appeal to the Banana Republic and J Crew crowd. And while the patterns are simple, they're often constructed in lighter-weight yarns, so expect them to take quite a while to complete.

A Field Guide to Knitters

"HURTS SO GOOD" KNITTERS: These folks just like to knit—and the more complicated and challenging the project, the better. Also known as "process" knitters, they look at sweaters in knitting magazines and think, "I'd like to knit that," before they think, "I'd like to wear that." Complicated cable patterns, color work, and odd, angular knitting methods are what get them going. Lots of garments made by process knitters are unloaded as gifts.

"SHE'S GOTTA HAVE IT" KNITTERS: It's all about the finished product for these project knitters. Leafing through a knitting magazine is like reading a mail-order catalog for them: If it's a sweater they want to wear, they'll make it, even if it means night after night of boring, unchanging knitting on tiny needles. The things they make do get worn to death; unfortunately, no matter how long they knit, these knitters often don't learn much beyond knit and purl.

"GET YOUR FREAK ON" KNITTERS: Throwing away their knitting magazines and relieving themselves of the shackles of a pattern, these knitters, also known as artsy-fartsy knitters, like to grab some yarn, grab some needles, and just make something up. Many of them are so busy expressing themselves that they can't be bothered with knitting rules or techniques. The sweaters they make are one-of-a-kind, gorgeous concoctions, though you might not be able to get your head through the collar.

OLD-SCHOOL KNITTERS: Only antiquated patterns and, often, acrylic yarns will do the trick for these types. They abhor anything that smacks of modern, "hipster" knitting; aluminum needles snatched up from the local craft store and leftover balls of yarn from projects that some stranger made ages ago fill their stash. Their preferred colors are orange, green, and brown, and their favorite projects are afghans and baby hats.

DILETTANTE KNITTERS: They just learned to knit last week, but already they've spent more money on luxurious yarn than you did in the past year. Dilettante knitters throw themselves and their money at the craft of knitting for a short while and maybe manage to complete two thirds of a sweater before they get bored with the whole thing. The good news is that they'll probably sell you their leftover yarn for next to nothing.

HOLIER-THAN-THOU KNITTERS: These are the snobs of the knitting world, the ones who turn up their noses at knitting trends and prefer those times when knitting has fallen out of fashion. "We've seen it all before," they sigh as they watch the parade of newbie knitters marching through their local yarn store. "They'll be gone soon enough." They make fun of the folks who ask beginner questions, and they look any completed project up and down, thinking they could have done a better job than you did. Although these folks like to think that they are the true-blue knitters, it is the very way they associate knitting with privilege—instead of recognizing it as a genuine craft of the masses—that betrays them. Whenever a sneer from one of these folks gets you feeling down, just recall the centuries-old history of knitting and remind yourself, "They'll be gone soon enough."

the basics

ribbed-for-her-pleasure scarf
(left, see page 58)

go-go garter stitch scarf
(center, see page 45)

kitschy kerchief
(right, see page 70)

coney island fireworks scarf
(left, see page 158)

windy city scarf
(right, see page 159)

alien illusion scarf
(left, see page 160)

adults-only devil hat and official kittyville hat
(right, see page 165)

Sparkle Hat &
Loopy Velez
Cowl

(left, see pages 163 & 167)

Hot Head

(right, see page 162)

chinese charm
bag
(left, see page 169)

meema's felted
marsupial tote
(right, see page 172)

punk rock backpack

(left, see page 174)

cricket's technicolor techno-cozy

(right, see page 178)

zeeby's bag
(left, see page 170)

fluffy cuff
mittens
(right, see page 180)

powerful wrist protection

(left, see page 185)

pippi kneestockings

(right, see page 182)

big bad baby blanket
(left, see page 187)

umbilical cord hat
(right, see page 188)

the MANLY
sweater
& skully

(left, see pages 210 & 190)

under the Hoodie

(right, see page 192)

to dye for
(left, see page 198)

the go-
everywhere,
go-with-
everything
cardigan
(right, see page 196)

big ſack ſweater

(left, see page 203)

cape mod

(right, see page 201)

145

**pinup queen &
tank girl**

(left, see pages 207 & 218)

cowl and howl set

(right, see page 212)

queen of hearts and wonder woman bikinis

(left, see page 224 & detail below)

little black top

(right, see page 220)

peppermint twist

(*left, see page 216*)

princess snowball cat bed

(*right, see page 228*)

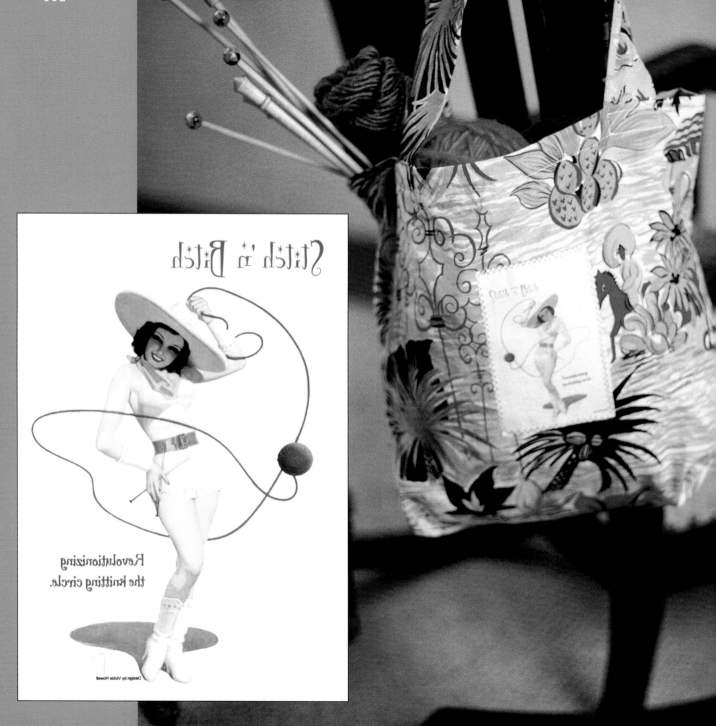

diy tote bag
(left, see page 231)

stitch 'n bitch patch
(far left, see page 233 for instructions on how to make your own iron-on patch)

roll-your-own needle case
(right, see page 234)

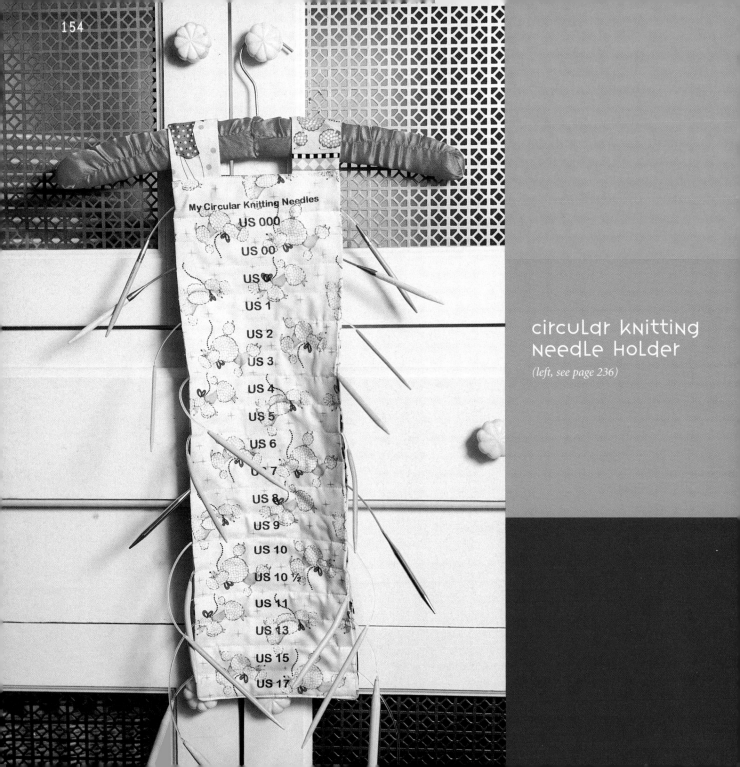

My Circular Knitting Needles

US 000
US 00
US 0
US 1
US 2
US 3
US 4
US 5
US 6
US 7
US 8
US 9
US 10
US 10 ½
US 11
US 13
US 15
US 17

circular knitting needle holder

(left, see page 236)

stitch 'n bitch
part two
patterns

the patterns in the next section were designed by knitters of varying ages, tastes, and levels of experience—from those who have been knitting only a year or less, to professional knitwear designers. (All have been vetted by a technical pattern editor. If you have a question about a pattern, send email to stitchnbitch@workman.com.) I've compiled them from knitters who belong to Stitch 'n Bitches, knitters with Web sites I like, and knitters I've met in person. The skills you'll need to complete these projects range from super-easy to somewhat complicated. But all the techniques you need are included in this book, so don't worry. Sometimes the best way to learn is to take on something complicated and pick up the skills as you go along. On the other hand, if you're the type who's easily discouraged, it might be better to begin with a project that you'll be likely to finish. So grab your needles, get out your yarn, and get ready to stitch a lot, and maybe even bitch a little.

knit one, purl two
How to Read a Knitting Pattern

knitting patterns can be really confusing to beginning knitters. Just like cooking recipes, which may call for 1 t of sugar and 2 T of butter, knitting patterns rely on abbreviations and shorthand to get their message across. However, once you know the lingo, it's all pretty simple.

Most patterns are presented in the same way we present them here. First, the pattern will give you the finished measurements of the garment; these are the finished measurements, not *your* measurements. Thus, if you have a 36" bust (lucky you), you'll be busting out of a sweater with a 34" finished bust measurement; a 36" finished knit measurement size will be nice and snug; a 38" finished measurement will give you room to breathe; and a 42" finished measurement will be downright roomy.

Next comes the list of the materials you'll need to make the project, including the brand and amount of yarn; the size and type of needles; and any additional notions or tools.

After that is the gauge information, which is truly crucial. Here's an example:

$$15 \text{ sts and } 17 \text{ rows to } 4"/10\text{cm over k2,}$$
$$\text{p2 rib using size 11 needles}$$

This means you should whip out your size 11 needles and knit up a swatch that's a bit bigger than the 15 stitches, since edge stitches are difficult to measure—say, 20 stitches—in the stitch pattern requested. In this example, it's k2, p2 ribbing. Knit for about 4", then bind off and lay the swatch down flat. Measure it. Do 15 stitches in fact make up 4"? Or does it come out to 4½" or maybe only 3½"? Your gauge may vary from the pattern's because you are a tighter or a looser knitter than the designer, or because you are using a different yarn than the one recommended. But this can be dealt with. If your swatch comes out bigger than it's supposed to, just reknit another swatch using knitting needles one size smaller—in this case, size 10. If the swatch comes out smaller than it's supposed to, go up a size in your knitting needles (since there are no size 12 U.S. knitting needles, you'd go up to size 13). Keep doing this until you find the size needles you need to knit a swatch to the required gauge. This is super-important, because even a small difference in gauge can make a difference in a sweater. For instance, if your swatch comes out only ¼" under what it should, a piece that's supposed to measure 24", like the front of a sweater, will come out to be only 22", and that means that when you take the front *and* the back together, your sweater will come up a full 4" smaller than it's intended to—which can make the difference between a hot-looking sweater and one that highlights every bubble and bulge, or may not even fit over your boobs at all.

Next come the actual instructions. Knitting patterns often give directions for more than one size. But instead of writing out the pattern over and over again for each size, it's written like this: the first number given will refer to the first, smallest size, and the remaining sizes will be presented, from smallest to largest, in parenthesis, separated by commas. For instance, say you have a pattern for a hat that's made for three sizes: baby bear, mama bear, and papa bear. The pattern might say:

Sized for baby (mama, papa) bears

And the first line of the pattern might read:

CO 24 (30, 38) st.

That simply means that for baby bear's hat you'll cast on 24 stitches, for mama bear's hat you'll make 30 stitches, and for papa bear you'll do 38 stitches.

The next big thing to understand is the abbreviations. On this page you'll find a list of the most common ones. Last, but not least, is the shorthand that knitting patterns use when they want you to repeat something a number of times. It's a little on the funky side, but pretty easy once you understand it. For instance—

K2, *k2, p1; rep from * 6 times, k4

—translates into: Start your row by knitting 2 stitches (k2), then repeat what comes after the asterisks for the number of times given. In this case, you'd knit 2, purl 1, 6 times, and then finish with 4 knit stitches.

Finally, patterns that involve knitting pieces into somewhat complicated shapes will often give you schematics, or diagrams, of all the pieces you'll be making, which can help you visualize what it is that you're doing as well as compare your progress with what you should end up with.

ABBREVIATIONS

Beg	begin(ning)(s)	**Pm**	place marker
BO	bind off	**Pu**	pick up
CC	contrasting color	**Rem**	remain(s)(ing)
Ch	chain	**Rep**	repeat(ed)(ing)(s)
Cn	cable needle	**Rnd(s)**	round(s)
CO	cast on	**RS**	right side
Cont	continu(e)(ed) (es)(ing)	**Sc**	Single crochet
Dec	decrease	**Skp**	slip 1 st, k next st, pass slipped st over k st
Dpn	double-pointed needle		
F&b	front and back	**Sl**	slip
Foll	follow	**Ssk**	slip next st knitwise twice, k sts tog tbl
Inc	increase		
Inc1	bar increase (k in front and back of next st)	**Sssk**	slip next st knitwise 3 times, k all sts tog tbl
		St(s)	stitch(es)
K	knit	**St st**	stockinette st
M1	make 1 increase	**Tbl**	through back loop
MC	main color	**Tog**	together
Meas	measures	**Yo**	yarn over
P	purl	**W&T**	wrap and turn
Patt	pattern	**WS**	wrong side

ELLEN R. MARGULIES

coney island fireworks scarf

A born-and-bred Brooklynite, now living in southern California, I thought I'd make a scarf for those days it does get chilly—only mine would be a little bit off. I went to my LYS (local yarn store) and came across this crazy multicolor yarn that reminded me of the rubber-band balls we used to make as kids. As I unwound the ball, the colored threads flared off in all directions, and I flashed back to my childhood, at the Coney Island fireworks. Every summer we'd sit on the boardwalk, feet dangling above the pitch-black beach, and we'd *ooh* and *ahh* as the sky lit up with an explosion of color. I had found my scarf.

Since the eyelash yarn was too thin to use alone, I combined it with a light cotton yarn to give it structure. Knit together, the yarns produced a scarf that was light and airy, and—*ooh*—really did look like a night at the fireworks!

SKILLS	PAGE
CAST ON	29
KNIT	33
BIND OFF	40

See page 124

SIZE
Approx 6" × 48", unstretched

MATERIALS
A: Trendsetter Yarns *Shadow* (100% polyester; 20g/77 yds), 2 skeins #1 Black Multi

B: Brown Sheep Company *Cotton Fleece* (80% cotton/20% merino wool; 4oz/215 yds), 1 skein #CW005 Cavern

US 15 (10mm) knitting needles, or size needed to obtain gauge

GAUGE
13 sts and 14 rows = 4" in garter st with 1 strand each of A and B held tog

DIRECTIONS
With 1 strand each of A and B held tog, CO 20 sts.

K all rows until both skeins of eyelash yarn are almost used up, leaving enough left over to BO. That's all there is to it.

ABOUT ELLEN
The sound of clicking knitting needles was an ever-present accompaniment to my childhood. I always seemed to wear the most wonderful hand-knit ensembles, courtesy of my mother. But, being a stubborn teenager, I elected to teach myself knitting from a library book. I tend to keep my knitting techniques simple and let the threads' complex personalities shine through. I know I have much to learn, but I've discovered something important: Even the most basic project can be a source of personal expression and deep satisfaction.

JENNIFER MINDEL

windy city scarf

I kept seeing this "keyhole" scarf at stores in Chicago, and thought it would be great for our windy winters because it wouldn't blow away. However, I didn't like the colors or fibers of the ones I saw, so I said to myself,

See page 125

SKILLS	PAGE
CAST ON	29
KNIT	33
PURL	47
CHANGE COLOR	43
BIND OFF	40

"I can do that." I ended up making five last winter as gifts for friends and family (I even made a mini one for a friend's baby girl). What's great about this scarf is that it is quick to make and won't break the bank.

SIZE

Approx 4¹/₂" × 40"

MATERIALS

Classic Elite *Bazic Wool* (100% superwash wool; 50g/65 yds)

A: 2 skeins #2958 Barn Red

B: 2 skeins #2961 Carnation

US 9 (5.5mm) knitting needles, or size needed to obtain gauge

GAUGE

30 sts and 20 rows = 4" in k1, p1 rib

STITCH PATTERN

K1, P1 RIB (OVER EVEN NUMBER OF STS)

All rows: *K1, p1; rep from * across.

DIRECTIONS

With A, CO 30 sts. Work 45 rows in k1, p1 rib.

Divide in half for opening: Rib 15 sts, attach second skein of A, and rib rem 15 sts. Rib 10 rows, knitting both sides at the same time.

Rejoin two sides by working across the next row with one skein only. Cont until 100 rows total have been worked with A.

Change to B and cont in rib for 100 rows. BO. Work away ends.

That's it!

ABOUT JENNIFER

I am an independent graphic and Web designer from Chicago. I learned how to knit when I was seventeen from my great-aunt Bea, and I knit all through college. Whenever I knit for my boyfriends I always seemed to break up with the guy before the project would be finished—and inevitably a sweater with sleeves would quickly become a vest. I stopped for a while because of the bad mojo associated with knitting for boyfriends, but when my nephew was born, I started to knit again, and I joined the Chicago Stitch 'n Bitch. Coincidentally, my mom has been a member of a Stitch 'n Bitch (no affiliation) for thirty years now!

Knitting is a destressor for me, so I don't pick projects with lots of counting or fancy stitches. That's why this nondemanding scarf is perfect for anyone to try.

SHETHA NOLKE

Alien Illusion Scarf

SKILLS	PAGE
CAST ON	29
KNIT	33
PURL	47
CHANGE COLOR	43
READ CHART	55
BIND OFF	40

Illusion knitting was brought to my attention through an online knitting community. Most illusion patterns, however—typically hidden hearts or secret x's and o's—were a bit too cutesy for knitters out there today. Once I figured out how it worked, I realized that any knitter who knows the technique can create his or her own illusion design. As proof of this, I created the alien illusion motif. Now you see him, now you don't!

See page 126

The illusion is the result of two things: knitting texture and positive/negative space images. The texture is created by combining knit (flat) with purl (raised) stitches. In order to create the texture, it's necessary to knit at a fairly tight gauge, but not so tight as to affect the drape of the fabric. Illusion motifs are done with two colors: the positive image color (green in this case) and the negative image, or background, color (black in this case). The image is then created in "slices," and each slice consists of four rows: two knit in the negative color and two in the positive color. Within these rows, the stitches that make up the image (a green alien head on a black background), are made with purl stitches. When the scarf is viewed from an angle, only the raised purl stitches are seen, and the image emerges. Spooky!

SIZE

Approx 7" × 86", including fringe

MATERIALS

Brown Sheep Company *Nature Spun Worsted* (100% wool; 100g/245 yds)

MC: 1 skein #601 Pepper

CC: 1 skein #109 Spring Green

US 7 (4.5mm) knitting needles, or size needed to obtain gauge

Crochet hook for attaching fringe

GAUGE

22 sts and 30 rows = 4" in stockinette st

Note: Because there are only two rows worked in each color, the colors can be carried up the side of the scarf. It's important not to pull these stitches too tightly or that edge of the scarf may be shorter than the opposite edge.

DIRECTIONS

With MC, CO 40 sts. Foll chart beg with row 1 (RS). Rep rows 1–80 five times more for a total of 6 alien motifs. BO loosely in CC.

FINISHING

Cut 33 strands of yarn in each color approx 16" in length. To create fringes, gather 3 strands of yarn, fold in half, and pull loop end through the CO row using a crochet hook. Thread the cut ends through the loop end and pull tightly. Rep across CO edge in alternating colors. Rep with BO edge.

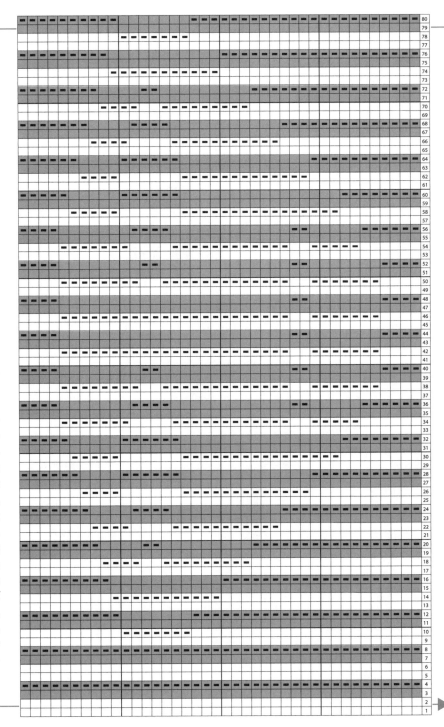

■	MC; knit on RS, purl on WS
⊟	MC; purl on RS, knit on WS
□	CC; knit on RS, purl on WS
⊟	CC; purl on RS, knit on WS

ABOUT SHETHA

I have been knitting steadily for about eleven months. Although I first learned to knit at the age of eight, my short attention span caused my knitting skills to lie dormant for several years. Later, at the age of twenty-one, I decided that knitting was a good way to make use of time while guarding my clothes in the Laundromat (after having had my wash stolen). I read some knitting magazines and realized that I had the skills to create my very own sweater. Since then, I have been sketching my own designs and creating things from others' designs. My love of knitting has grown stronger through the support of local knitting groups in Portland, Oregon, and online. On my knitting blog, www.shetha.com/blog, I share both my knitting successes and failures with knitters around the world.

ALEX ZORN
Hot Head

This hat is a must-have in any knitter's repertoire because what's better than kicking out a warm, snuggly hat in just two hours? The pattern is especially useful if you're an advanced beginner—ready to branch out beyond the rectangle but still a bit intimidated by a circular project. The theme of "fire" came out of my experimentation with crazy red hair. As my hair dye (Manic Panic) gradually washes out, it follows what I affectionately call the "Photoshop flame gradient"—an ever-changing variation of reds, oranges, and yellows. In homage to my crazy hair, I came up with Hot Head—fun, simple stripes in a fiery sequence.

SKILLS	PAGE
CAST ON	29
KNIT	33
PURL	47
CHANGE COLOR	43
DECREASE	63
BIND OFF	40
SEW SEAM	73

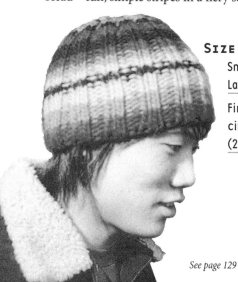

See page 129

SIZE
Small (Medium, Large)

Finished circumference: 20 (21, 22)"

MATERIALS
Brown Sheep Company *Lamb's Pride Bulky* (85% wool/15% mohair; 4 oz/125 yds)

A: 1 skein #M05 Onyx

B: 1 skein #M110 Orange You Glad

C: 1 skein #M155 Lemon Drop

D: 1 skein #M180 Ruby Red

US 10½ (6.5mm) knitting needles, or size needed to obtain gauge

GAUGE
14 sts and 18 rows = 4" in k2, p2 rib, slightly stretched.

STITCH PATTERN
K2, P2 RIB (MULTIPLE OF 4 STS)
All rows: *K2, p2; rep from * to end.

COLOR PATTERN
4 rows D, 4 rows B, 4 rows C, 2 rows A, 2 rows C, 2 rows B, 2 rows D, 4 rows A, 2 rows D, 2 rows A, 2 rows B, 2 rows A, 2 rows C (size Small: work rem rows with C), 4 rows A, 2 rows C (size Medium: work rem rows with C), 2 rows A, 2 rows B (size Large: work rem rows with B).

DIRECTIONS
With A, CO 56 (60, 64) sts.

Work 29 (32, 35) rows in k2, p2 rib foll color pattern.

SHAPE CROWN
Continuing color pattern: Row 1 (RS): *K2tog, p2; rep from * to end—42 (45, 48) sts.

Row 2 (WS): *K2tog, p1; rep from * to end—28 (30, 32) sts.

Row 3: *K1, p1; rep from * to end.

Row 4: *K1, p1; rep from * to end.

Row 5: *K2tog; rep from * to end—14 (15, 16) sts.

Row 6: *K2tog; rep from * to end—7 (8, 8) sts.

FINISHING

Break off the yarn, leaving a 20" tail. Thread the yarn through a yarn needle and thread needle through live sts, drawing them tight and sliding them off the knitting needle. With the RS of the hat facing you, and using mattress stitch, sew back seam invisibly from top to bottom. Weave in ends.

ABOUT ALEX

I live in Pittsburgh with my incredibly handsome dog, my chroma-tastic Honda Rebel 450, and obscenely large stashes of yarn and records. I learned to knit as a child and promptly forgot. Several years ago, on an ill-fated ski trip, I bought some Susan Bates aluminum needles and Red Heart acrylic and started all over again. In addition to being a fanatical knitter, I also (sporadically) publish the lo-fi knitting zine *Needle & Hook: Knitting Our Little Punk Rock Hearts Out.* My current works in progress include a lace shawl in a lovely cashmere/lambswool blend, fingerless gloves for every male friend I have, a queen-sized afghan in a purple colorway, and the "Vegas Bag," which will combine knitting and glass beads and buttons for an exhibit at the Pittsburgh Glass Center. I also make felted handbags and handmade glass buttons, which are sold at Pool, a boutique in New York City, and can be seen on my Web site at www.needleandhook.com.

SONYA LASKA
sparkle Hat

people say this looks like an old-lady hat. I love old ladies, so I consider that the highest compliment. Oddly enough, the hat is also one of the few knitted items that has attracted male attention—men often stop me on the street to say, "Hey, cool hat!" Whether you want to be geriatric fabulous or have the boys follow you home, one thing's for certain—you can never have enough shiny, sparkly clothing.

SKILLS	PAGE
CAST ON	29
KNIT	33
PURL	47
KNIT IN THE ROUND	57
DECREASE	63

SIZE
One size fits most, if not all (approx 24" around bottom end)

See page 128

MATERIALS

Brown Sheep Company *Lamb's Pride Bulky* (85% wool/15% mohair; 4 oz/125 yds), 1 skein #M120 Limeade

US 10 (6mm) double-pointed needles (set of 4)

US 11 (8mm) 24" circular needle or double-pointed needles (set of 4/5), or size needed to obtain gauge

Large sequins (paillettes)—these need to have a large hole in them, not the standard thread-sized hole

GAUGE

13 sts = 4" in St st on larger needles

DIRECTIONS

Before you even CO, thread the paillettes onto your yarn using a yarn needle. It's okay if you put on more than you need. This example uses 90 sequins, but you could definitely use more or less.

Push the paillettes down on the yarn, then with larger knitting needle, CO 60 sts. Join, being careful not to twist the sts, then pm at rnd.

K 4 rnds.

ADD SPARKLE

Rnd 1: *P1 by inserting the needle into the st as to purl, pushing a paillette up as close to the needle as you can; then complete the st, catching the paillette in place. K3. Repeat from * for the entire rnd—15 paillettes.

Rnds 2–3: K.

Rnd 4: K2, *p1, k3; rep from * to last 2 sts, p1, k1—always catching a paillette in each p st. This staggers the paillettes so they're not all in a row.

Rnds 5–6: K.

Repeat rnds 1–6 twice more.

CROWN DECREASES

Change to smaller dpns, k 1 rnd as you are doing this—3 needles holding 20 sts each.

K2tog at the end of each needle every rnd (each rnd will dec by 3 sts) until you are left with 6 sts on each needle. Cut your yarn, leaving a 10" tail. Using a yarn needle, thread through those last sts and pull them tog. At this point you could add one more paillette, for fancy!

Weave this tail, as well as the CO tail, into the sts on the inside of the hat.

Have fun!

ABOUT SONYA

Quilts, beading, clothes, costumes, collages, books, cookies—I love to make things. My whole family is pretty crafty: My mom does rug hooking, my dad is a welder, my brother is a furniture maker, my stepsister is a professional quilter, and Grandma does needlepoint. I always suspected I would love knitting, but it wasn't until I took a class four years ago that it finally clicked.

Now, when I'm excited about a project, I knit every minute I can get—at home, on the phone, on the subway. I particularly enjoy hanging out with a bunch of pals, all of us knitting and exchanging tips and life stories. I also like making things that are a little goofy. Have you ever noticed how serious—in color and function—so many knitting projects are? Knitting is fun, and I think we should all be a little less serious about it. For would-be knitters who are interested and ask me if they can learn, I always say that if you have patience and can read directions, you (yes, you!) can make anything you want.

KITTY SCHMIDT

Adults-only devil Hat and official kittyville Hat

See page 127

t hese hats are the bastard children of the Lil' Devil Baby Hat that I featured on my Web site, www.kittyville.com. Kittyville is an online hodgepodge that I started in 1997 to present my somewhat off-center interests to the rest of the world. I love getting feedback and questions from faraway places, and I got so many requests for an adult version of the Lil' Devil Baby Hat that I adapted it to fit grown-ups. It naturally evolved into the Kitty Hat, which is the official headgear for Kittyville. I like to imagine people wearing it to surf my site, like a kid putting on a Captain Video helmet to watch his favorite show.

You can omit the ears or horns and add your own kind of ornamentation: pom-poms, tassels, ponytails. Or just go minimal—with this basic hat shape, the possibilities are endless!

SKILLS	PAGE
CAST ON	29
KNIT	33
PURL	47
DECREASE	63
KNIT IN THE ROUND	57
CABLE CAST-ON	69
PICK UP STITCHES	82
I-CORD	87

SIZE

One size fits most, approx 23" around

MATERIALS

Mission Falls *1824 Wool* (100% superwash merino wool; 50g/80 yds)

Devil Hat: 3 skeins #011 Poppy

Kitty Hat: 3 skeins #005 Raven

US 7 (4.5mm) 16" circular needle, or size needed to obtain gauge

US 7 (4.5mm) double-pointed needles (set of 4/5)

Stitch markers

GAUGE

17 sts = 4" in St st

STITCH PATTERN

SEED STITCH (ON EVEN NUMBER OF STS IN THE ROUND/FLAT)

Rnd/row 1: *K1, p1; rep from * around.

Rnd/row 2: *P1, k1; rep from * around.

Rep rnds/rows 1–2 for pattern.

DIRECTIONS

BOTH HATS

With circular needle, CO 84 sts. Work 1¾" in seed st. Switch to St st for 3¾" more. Place a stitch marker after every 12th st.

Dec rnd (switch to dpns when necessary): K2tog before each marker around. Rep dec rnd every other rnd 3 times more—56 sts; then every rnd until there are 7 sts left on needle. Break off yarn, leaving a fairly long tail. Thread tail through rem 7 sts, pull firmly, and draw through to inside of hat and fasten.

EARFLAPS AND TIES

**On CO edge, with the outside of the hat facing you, count 12 sts to the left of beg of rnd. Pu 18 sts from this point, making sure to pu through both loops of the st. Turn. With the inside of the hat facing you, k 1 row plain (if you're stuck with the outside of the hat facing you for the first row, p 1 row plain). This leaves a nice beaded line between the earflap and the rest of the hat. Work 2 rows seed st.

Row 4: K1, k2tog, seed st to last 3 sts, k2tog, k1.

Row 5: Seed st.

Rep rows 4–5 until there are 4 sts left. K1, k2tog, k1—3 sts. Work 2 more rows seed st, then knit I-cord for 12" or to desired length. Keep your st on the needles—you're not done yet.

DEVIL HAT ONLY

DEVIL TAIL ENDS

Cable CO 3 sts at one side of the I-cord. K across these 6 sts, turn. Cable CO 3 more sts—9 sts. K 1 row. Cont in garter st, dec 1 st each end every other row until there are 3 sts left. K2tog, k1, turn; k2tog—1 st. Break off yarn. Thread end through last st, pull firmly, weave end up through tail end and I-cord to hide.

Rep from ** for other side, beg pu 30 sts to right of beg of rnd.

DEVIL HORNS

Mark where you want horns with a safety pin. It helps to try on the hat when you do this. Try to place them symmetrically, above earflaps, and slightly to the front. Pu 15 sts in a triangle, using 3 dpns, 5 sts on each needle. Join in the rnd and k 3 rnds St st. Then (k3, k2tog) on each needle. K 2 rnds even. (K2, k2tog) on each needle. K 1 rnd even. (K1, k2tog) on each needle. K2tog on each needle—3 sts. Break off yarn, leaving a fairly long tail. Thread through rem 3 sts firmly to form a point, then pull down through horn to inside of hat and weave in end. Rep for other horn.

KITTY HAT ONLY

End off I-cord. Make pom-poms and attach to ends of I-cord.

Rep from ** (under "Earflaps and Ties") for other side, beg pu 30 sts to right of beg of rnd.

KITTY EARS

Lay hat flat with earflaps at the center. Above the earflap, slightly front of center, meas about ¾"

10"

7¼"

12"

down from the top of the hat. From this point, pu 12 sts down toward the earflap. Work 2 rows in seed st.

Row 3: *K1, k2tog, seed st to last 3 sts, k2tog, k1.

Row 4: Seed st.

Rep rows 3–4 until 4 sts rem. Then k1, k2tog, k1, turn; k1, k2tog, turn; and k2tog. Break off yarn and pull through last st. Weave end through ear to hide. At the base of this ear, pu 12 sts. Rep entire process, so there is a double ear above the earflap. Using a yarn needle, whip st the 2 pieces tog. Rep for other ear.

ABOUT KITTY

When I was eight or nine, my grandmother, Nan, taught me how to crochet. Nan was from the granny-square-vest and bicentennial-themed-daisy-afghan school of crocheting. I didn't learn to knit until I was twenty, while working at a mind-numbingly boring job, taking orders for a catalog company. An older coworker, who would knit through our shift, brought in a spare pair of needles and yarn and patiently walked me through the fundamentals. After a few overly ambitious, expensive, failed projects (a sweater that would fit Bigfoot, a vest for my mom that made her look like Sonny Bono, and so on), I gave it up. Then one day, I came across Elizabeth Zimmermann's *Knitting Without Tears*. I found her technique liberating and inspiring, and I haven't worked with a commercial pattern since. I take my inspiration from vintage girlie magazines, thrift-store treasures, drag queens, Saturday-morning cartoons, and old movies. I will always be blown away by the fact that you can make something warm to wear from a piece of string. I am also a graphic designer and play accordion with the Big Mess Orchestra in Philadelphia.

KITTY SCHMIDT

Loopy velez cowl

this cowl has a loopy, shaggy edge that can be worn around the face or around the neck edge for a more sedate look. It fits snugly, and soft merino wool makes it warm and comfortable.

SKILLS	PAGE
CAST ON	29
KNIT	33
PURL	47
KNIT IN THE ROUND	57
LOOP STITCH (SEE BELOW)	
BIND OFF	40

MATERIALS

Karabella *Aurora 8* (100% merino wool; 50g/98 yds), 4 skeins #0008 Orange

US 7 (4.5mm) 16" circular needle, or size needed to obtain gauge

GAUGE

19 sts = 4" in St st (k all rnds)

STITCH PATTERN

GARTER STITCH (IN THE ROUND)

Rnd 1: K.

Rnd 2: P.

Rep rnds 1–2 for pattern.

See page 128

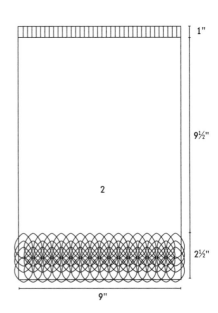

LOOP STITCH (ANY NUMBER OF STS, 5 ROWS)

Note: This loop stitch is not as complicated as it seems. It takes a few stitches to get into the groove, but if you stick with it, you'll be glad you did. It's meant to be shaggy and loopy and kind of crazy-looking, so don't despair if your loopy stitches aren't perfectly uniform. Anyway, you only have to do it 4 times, and then it's smooth sailing.

Rnd 1: K1, *M1, bring yarn to front and back again to make a loop, anchoring it down with thumb; slip M1 onto left needle; k2tog; rep from * around. (Your work will appear to be loose and sloppy and wrong. Don't worry, we're going to fix it with rnd 2.)

Rnd 2: K. As you k, give a tug on one side of the loop below. One side won't budge; the other will tighten firmly. You'll want to tug the side that pulls tight. Do this for the entire rnd.

Rnds 3–5: K. Again, as you knit give an extra little tug to the loops below. Things should be getting back to normal about now.

DIRECTIONS

CO 84 sts. Join, being careful not to twist sts, and pm to indicate beg of rnd.

Work 4 rnds in garter st.

Work loop st patt 4 times.

K every row until piece meas 12" from beg.

Work 1" in k2, p2 rib.

BO loosely in rib.

FINISHING

Go around and give those loops an extra tug. Weave in ends.

ABOUT KITTY
See page 167 for Kitty's bio.

SYLVIA MAHONEY

chinese charm bag

this bag was an accident. I was trying to make my first beanie on circular needles and miscalculated the number of stitches. Needless to say, after 10" of stockinette stitch, I had a beanie that would fit only the Incredible Hulk. My friends and I laughed, but I felt that tossing it aside would have been a waste of my time and yarn. Rather than frog it (rip it out), I noticed it was a nice size for a bag. So I affixed a pair of bamboo handles, sewed in a lime-green lining, then I added a Chinese horoscope charm and gave it to a friend as a birthday gift.

SKILLS	PAGE
CAST ON	29
KNIT	33
KNIT IN THE ROUND	57
BACKSTITCH	76
BIND OFF	40

SIZE

Approx 13^1/$_2$" × 10" without handles

MATERIALS

Noro *Gemstones* (57% rayon/17% acrylic/21% nylon/5% cashmere; 50g/65 yds), 6 skeins #8

US 10 (6mm) 24" circular needle

1 pair circular bamboo handles

^{1}/$_2$ yard lining fabric

Sewing needle and thread

Charm (optional)

GAUGE

12 sts and 18 rows = 4" in St st (k all rnds)

DIRECTIONS

CO 80 sts. K 1 row, then join ends to form a circle. Cont St st in the rnd for approximately 10" or however deep you would like the bag to be, then BO all sts.

Turn the bag inside out. Thread a yarn needle with the yarn and, using back sts, sew the bottom of bag closed. Turn the bag RS out.

Cut a piece of lining fabric approx 20" × 14" (think of making a fabric purse to fit in the knitted bag). Fold it in half with RS tog and hand- or machine-sew the sides. Push the lining down into knitted bag (with WS of lining and bag tog). With matching thread, hand sew the opening of the lining to the opening of the knitted bag, folding the lining over ^{1}/$_4$" for a finished edge as you do so. Remember, the RS of your lining should show inside the knitted bag.

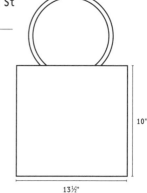

10"

13½"

See page 130

Last, thread your yarn needle and attach the handles by sewing small loops around each handle and the first row of the bag's edge.

Add a charm of your choice to any spot you choose. I put mine right next to where the first stitch of the handle connects to the bag.

Fini!

ABOUT SYLVIA

One day last year, as I was walking down a trendy Los Angeles street, I spotted a small French yarn shop. When I wandered inside, my senses were blown away. Gone were the itchy acrylic yarns of my youth—here was a cornucopia of silk, cotton, wool, chenille, and angora. I bought a pair of bamboo needles and some yarn, had my mom cast on to get me started, and I was off.

Today, I knit in Topanga Canyon, California, where I live with my husband, three dogs, and one bird. When I'm not writing, knitting, or trying to conceive a "crafty child," I work as a producer at Lost Planet Editorial.

TINA PAREDES
zeeby's bag

I posted a picture of the first bag I knitted on my girly-style blog called primp! (www.primp.blog spot.com). A reader admired it and requested one for herself. Her only requirements were that it be dark blue and big enough to hold her 12" × 12" sketchbook. I named the bag after her nickname on the blog, Zeeby, and this is how it's made.

SKILLS	PAGE
CAST ON	29
KNIT	33
PURL	47
BIND OFF	40
SEW SEAM	73

SIZE
Approx 15" wide × 12" tall × 2" deep

MATERIALS
Brown Sheep Company *Lamb's Pride Worsted* (85% wool/15% mohair; 4 oz/190 yds)

MC: 2 skeins #M82 Blue Flannel

CC: 1 skein #M51 Winter Blue

US 8 (5mm) knitting needles, or size needed to obtain gauge

GAUGE
18 sts and 24 rows = 4" in St st

See page 134

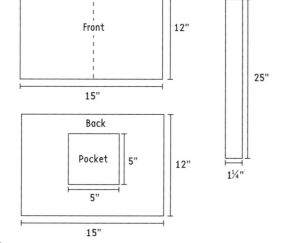

Gusset

Side	Bottom	Side
12"	15"	12"

2"

Front — 12" — 15"

Strap (2) — 25" — 1¼"

Back

Pocket — 5" — 5" — 12" — 15"

Directions

FRONT AND BACK PANELS (MAKE 2)

CO 68 sts in MC.

Work in St st for 11".

Work in garter st for 1".

BO all sts.

GUSSET

CO 10 sts in MC.

Work in garter st for 39".

BO all sts.

STRAPS (MAKE 2)

CO 112 sts in MC.

Work in garter st for 7 rows (approx 1¼").

BO all sts.

INSIDE POCKET

CO 23 sts in CC.

Work in St st for 4".

Work in garter st for 1".

BO all sts.

With MC, sew front and back panels to gusset.

With CC, sew on straps 2 inches in from the left and right edges and add detail stitching to the front (as shown). With MC, sew pocket to inside of back piece 2" from the top edge and centered between left and right edges.

ABOUT TINA

I'm twenty-seven years old and live in southern California (you have to be creative about finding things to knit in this weather!). I first picked up knitting needles and yarn at my local thrift shop, when I was in between Web design jobs and had plenty of time on my hands. I didn't even know what the numbers on the needles meant—I chose mine because they were pink. After getting thoroughly confused by a few online knitting tutorials, I turned to Mom for help. Cast on! My first project was a hat. It was lime green and oh so sassy, but way smaller than I'd planned. Darn cute on my little niece, though. Next I started a sweater in a pretty pink thrift-store yarn. I ran out of yarn and ended up with a bag instead. Ta-da!

It's been four months since that first pair of pink needles, and I've been sticking to the small stuff—hats, scarves, bags—and adding my own finishing touches. I like the instant gratification they offer. One day, I hope to have the patience to tackle a larger project. Like a bikini.

MEEMA SPADOLA

meema's felted marsupial tote

I was first inspired to make a felted bag when my brother returned from Morocco with a pound of yarn. The fibers were too rough for a garment, so I decided to try to make a bag. The result was way too floppy and not durable enough for daily use. Felting the bag—just throwing it in a hot washing load—completely changed the nature of the fabric, creating a sturdy, less homemade look. I started playing around with different kinds of yarn, colors, shapes, and sizes.

This latest pattern is the easiest yet because the bag itself requires no sewing or assembly (except for the cute little pouch). The pouch was inspired by my habit of misplacing my keys and wallet.

You knit the bottom of this bag first, then pick up stitches and knit in the round "up" to the top of the bag—no sewing is needed at the end! Attach the small pouch to the inside of the bag with I-cord.

SKILLS	PAGE
CAST ON	29
KNIT	33
PURL	47
KNIT IN THE ROUND	57
PICK UP STITCHES	82
CHANGE COLOR	43
I-CORD	87
SINGLE CAST-ON	68
BIND OFF	40

See page 131

SIZE

10" tall at sides and 27" around base of bag, after felting

MATERIALS

Brown Sheep Company *Lamb's Pride Worsted* (85% wool/15% mohair; 4 oz/190 yds)

MC: 3 skeins #110 Orange You Glad

CC: 2 skeins #M38 Lotus Pink

US 15 (10mm) 24" circular needle, or size needed to obtain gauge

4 stitch markers

2 large metal snaps

GAUGE

Approx 10 sts = 4" in St st with 2 strands of yarn held tog

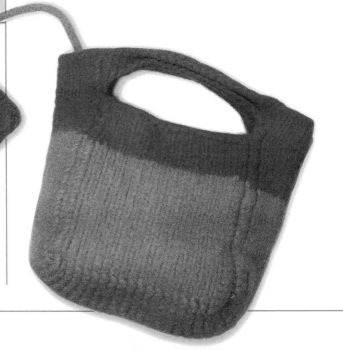

Stitch pattern

RIGHT TWIST (RT)

K 2nd st on needle without slipping sts off needle; k 1st st on needle; then slip both sts off needle.

Directions

Note: Don't be dismayed if your bag looks floppy with loose stitches while knitting. It will shrink anywhere from 15 to 25 percent when felted and will look completely different. The instructions here can be changed to create new versions and new sizes. Use your imagination and experiment.

With 2 strands of MC held tog, CO 16 sts. Work 44 rows in garter st. With 16 sts on needle, place 1st marker; pu 22 sts across long side of bag, place 2nd marker; pu 16 sts along short side, place 3rd marker; pu 22 sts across rem side, place 4th marker and join the rnd. Don't worry if you get 1 more or 1 less st. The idea is to evenly fill the sides of the bag with sts.

*RT, k to within 2 sts of marker, RT, sl marker; rep from * around. Rep this row every row until bag meas 10" from base. Switch to CC and k 4 rnds, then BO 22 sts between markers on each of the 2 long sides of the bag. On next rnd, CO the same number of sts as was BO using single cast-on method and k 6 rnds more. BO all sts.

MARSUPIAL POUCH (WORKED FLAT)

With a **single strand** of CC, CO 30 sts. Work 5 rows in garter st, then switch to MC and work 2" even. On next row, BO 15 sts and work 3" even on rem 15 sts, then BO rem sts. Fold width-wise and sew side and bottom edge. (You should have a small purse with a flap.) Cast on 3 sts in MC and make I-cord 14" long. Attach one end to small purse and the other end to interior of bag near top of MC section.

FELTING

You should do this in a top-loader, not a Laundromat-style machine, because it's best to open the washer frequently to check on the bag. Pop the bag in a half-filled machine with very hot, sudsy water, agitate on the longest cycle, and rinse in very cold water. Pull out your bag from time to time during the hot sudsy part, because if it's felting quickly you want to stop agitation.

If it's not felting, throw in a pair of jeans to add to the agitation process. More agitation will result in a tighter, smaller bag. Roll in a towel to get moisture out, shape as desired, and lay flat to dry completely.

Attach snap to center of tote opening and to flap of small purse. Enjoy!

ABOUT MEEMA

I'm a television and radio documentary maker and a third-generation (at least) knitter living in Brooklyn. I grew up in Maine, where my crafty mother taught me to knit when I was a kid. It took three times, several pairs of socks, and an ugly blue garter-stitch sweater before it really clicked in. Besides experimenting with felted bags of all shapes, sizes, and colors, I love making (and occasionally designing) sweaters for myself, and endless baby booties, hats, and sweaters for friends. My television and radio documentaries have aired on HBO, PBS, and NPR, but this is my first published pattern. A million thanks to my mother—a wonderful guide in knitting and in life.

HEATHER BARNES
Monkey and bunny characters by Adrienne Yan

punk rock backpack

A fter a lot of measuring up and unraveling, I came up with this design for a backpack. Except for the intarsia knitting, it's pretty easy to make—all you're doing is stitching together knitted squares, then throwing in a zipper and some straps. The bag's big enough to fit things that wouldn't usually fit in a purse but small enough and soft enough to take to crowded places. Mine's even accompanied me to a few mosh pits.

SKILLS	PAGE
CAST ON	29
KNIT	33
PURL	47
READ CHART	55
INTARSIA	92
BIND OFF	40
SEW SEAM	73

See page 132

SIZE
Finished measurements: 9$^{1}/_{2}$" wide by 12$^{1}/_{2}$" tall by 3$^{1}/_{2}$" deep

MATERIALS
Brown Sheep Company *Lamb's Pride Worsted* (85% wool/15% mohair; 4 oz/190 yds)

MONKEY

MC: 2 skeins #M120 Limeade

A: 1 skein #M13 Sun Yellow

B: 1 skein #M175 Bronze Patina

C: 1 skein #M05 Onyx

D: 1 skein #M34 Victorian Pink

BUNNY

MC: 2 skeins #M13 Sun Yellow

A: 1 skein #M105 RPM Pink

B: 1 skein #M05 Onyx

C: 1 skein #M52 Spruce

US 6 (4mm) knitting needles, or size needed to obtain gauge

1 yard cotton lining fabric

9" nonseparating zipper

Sewing needle and thread

GAUGE
18 sts and 26 rows = 4" in St st

DIRECTIONS

LOWER FRONT (MONKEY)

With MC, CO 45 sts. Beg with a p row, work 25 rows in St st.

Work 30 rows of monkey chart (including MC rows).

Work 10 more rows in St st.

BO.

LOWER FRONT (BUNNY)

With MC, CO 45 sts. Beg with a p row, work 5 rows in St st.

Work 55 rows of bunny chart (including MC rows).

Work 5 more rows in St st.

BO.

UPPER FRONT

With MC, CO 45 sts. Beg with a p row, work 20 rows in St st.

BO.

BACK

With MC, CO 45 sts. Beg with a p row, work to 13" in St st.

BO.

GUSSET

With MC, CO 18 sts.

Work in St st (or, optionally, in garter st) until piece is 44½" long.

BO.

STRAPS (MAKE 2)

With MC, CO 13 sts.

Work in St st until piece is 16" long.

BO.

LINING

From lining fabric, cut the following pieces (see cutting diagram at right):

Back: 10½" × 13½"

Front top: 10½" × 3¾"

Front bottom: 10½" × 10¾"

Gusset: 4½" × 45"

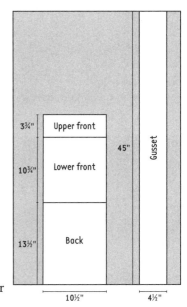

FINISHING

SEW BACKPACK TOGETHER

With RS facing, fold straps in half lengthwise and use mattress stitch to sew center seam.

With RS together, use backstitch to seam narrow ends of gusset piece, ¼" from edge.

Pin straps to top and bottom of back piece, RS together, 1" in from either side edge.

Pin gusset around outside edge of back piece with RS together, with the center seam of gusset at center bottom of back.

Use backstitch to seam ¼" from edge, sandwiching the straps between gusset and back piece at the same time.

Pin lower front to opposite edge of gusset with RS together, and attach gusset to side and bottom edges of lower front, using backstitch to seam ¼" from edge.

Pin upper front to gusset with RS together, and attach gusset to side and top edges of upper front piece, using backstitch to seam ¼" from edge.

Bottom edge of upper front piece and top edge of lower front piece should meet in center. Turn backpack right side out.

SEW LINING TOGETHER

Fold gusset lining in half with RS together, seam narrow ends together ½" from edge.

Pin gusset around outside edge of back piece with RS together, attach gusset to back piece, seam ½" from edge.

Fold bottom edge of upper front piece over ½", WS together, and press.

Fold top edge of lower front over ½", WS together, and press.

With WS of both front pieces facing up, pin zipper, RS up, to folded edge of upper front piece and folded edge of lower front piece (see diagram). Sew zipper in place.

Pin front piece (with zipper sewn in) to opposite edge of gusset, RS together, and attach gusset to front piece, seam ½" from edge.

SEW LINING TO BACKPACK

Insert lining into backpack so that WS are together and zipper is centered at opening. Pin bottom edge of upper front and top edge of lower front to top and bottom of zipper, and hand-sew zipper into center of opening with sewing needle and thread. With short piece of yarn, graft seams on either side of zipper.

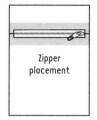

Zipper
placement

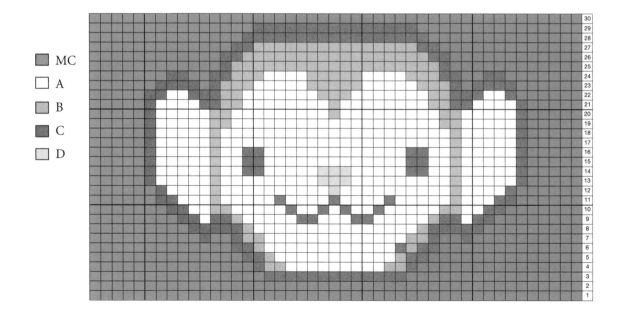

MC
A
B
C
D

ABOUT HEATHER My first knitting project was for a Girl's Brigade badge (New Zealand's Girl Scouts). I quit soon after because I had more holes than stitches. Nine years later, I tried again on a pair of huge wooden needles, and I knit up a chunky-arse scarf in an hour. I can't seem to use a pattern, so I usually knit freshly, which means I can end up with something completely different from what I envisioned. When I knit or sew (another pastime), I listen to loud music; bands like Foo Fighters, Pacifier, and Rage Against the Machine get me knitting at a breakneck pace. At the moment, I'm trying to learn bass guitar so I can make music of my own. My favorite thing is going to rock concerts with friends, but that doesn't happen too often when you live in a small town in New Zealand.

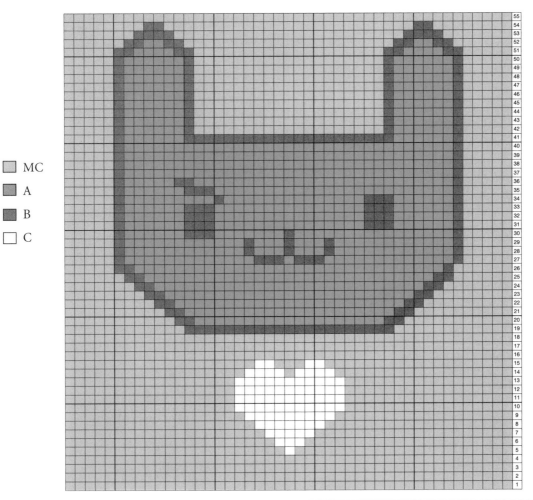

- MC
- A
- B
- C

JESCA SANDER

cricket's technicolor techno-cozy

My friend Cricket had this horribly beat-up cell phone. The battery fell off constantly and the faceplate wouldn't stay on, so I decided that she needed a cozy to protect it. I got to work that night, and after a few revisions, the cozy was just right for that old phone. Then I realized that, with a few adjustments, my piece could hold just about any techno-accessory, including a PalmPilot or an iPod. Now Cricket has three covers and wants even more!

SKILLS	PAGE
CAST ON	29
KNIT	33
PURL	47
BIND OFF	40
CHANGE COLOR	43
SINGLE CAST-ON	68
SEW SEAM	73

SIZES

Cell phone (iPod, PalmPilot)

Finished measurements:
approx 2$\frac{1}{2}$ (3, 3$\frac{1}{2}$)" wide by 5$\frac{1}{4}$" tall

MATERIALS

Tahki•Stacy Charles *Cotton Classic II* (100% cotton; 50g/74 yds)

COLOR SCHEME 1

A: 1 skein #2801 (teal)

B: 1 skein #2401 (orange)

C: 1 skein #2726 (lime)

See page 133, cell phone cozy

COLOR SCHEME 2

A: 1 skein #2459 (pink)

B: 1 skein #2726 (lime)

C: 1 skein #2401 (orange)

US 6 (4mm) knitting needles, or size needed to obtain gauge

1" square Velcro

Sewing needle and thread

One $\frac{1}{2}$" coordinating button (optional)

GAUGE

20 sts and 26 rows = 4" in St st

Then work 4 rows B, 2 rows C, 4 rows B, 2 rows A.

BO all sts. Your piece should meas approx 13".

FINISHING

With RS together, and matching first set of B rows to 8th set of B rows, backstitch seam. Turn RS out, sew button to lower center of flap. Sew one side of Velcro under last set of B rows of flap and other side onto cozy itself.

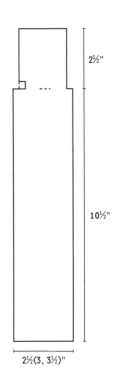

2½"

10½"

2½(3, 3½)"

See page 133, PalmPilot cozy

DIRECTIONS

With A, CO 16 (18, 20) sts.

Working in St st throughout, work 2 rows A, *4 rows B, 2 rows C, 4 rows B,** 8 rows A.

Rep from * 2 times more, then from * to ** once.

Cont with A, work 2 rows. Piece should meas approx 10½".

BO 2 sts, k to end of row.

BO 5 (2, 2) sts, p 0 (6, 0), BO 0 (2, 0) sts, p to end of row.

K 0 (6, 0), CO 0 (2, 0) sts, k to end of row, CO 3 (0, 0) sts using single CO.

Work 3 more rows A.

ABOUT JESCA

As thanks for house-sitting for my aunt and uncle, my aunt gave me a set of bamboo needles and a knitting book. That was last year, now I'm hooked. In real life, I am a leader for "Outdoor School," a program in Oregon where we take sixth-graders on week-long trips into the woods to teach them about the environment. I spend the rest of my time playing piano and flute, surfing, and snowboarding.

KAREN BAUMER

fluffy cuff mittens

I n my yarn stash, I had almost a full skein of Classic Elite *Montera* left over from a tote project, and I bought the GGH *Esprit* just because I liked the color. The two yarns were snuggling near each other, and I liked the way the colors and textures looked together. Since I was using up leftovers, the project had to be small—hence, mittens. Note: You can wear these mittens with the cuff flipped up or down.

SKILLS	PAGE
CAST ON	29
KNIT	33
PURL	47
KNIT IN THE ROUND	57
CHANGE COLOR	43
DECREASE	63
PICK UP STITCHES	82

SIZE

Women's Medium/Large

Finished measurements: approx 9^1/$_2$" around base of fingers; 11^1/$_2$" from bottom of cuff to tip; 9^1/$_2$" from cuff to tip with cuff folded up

MATERIALS

MC: Classic Elite *Montera* (50% wool/50% llama; 100g/127 yds), 1 skein #3887

CC: GGH *Esprit* (100% nylon; 50g/88 yds), 1 skein #15

US 10 (6mm) double-pointed needles (set of 5), or size needed to obtain gauge

Stitch marker

Waste yarn to mark thumb sections

See page 135

GAUGE

MC: 16 sts and 22 rows = 4" in St st

CC: 10 sts and 20 rows = 4" in garter st

DIRECTIONS

LEFT MITTEN

With CC, CO 24 sts; divide sts evenly among four needles and join into a rnd. Pm to indicate beg of rnd/needle 1. Work 2½" in garter st, inc 1 st per needle on last rnd—28 sts. *Remember that garter st in the rnd is alternating one row p, one row k.*

Switch to MC and beg working St st (k every rnd). All measurements from now on should be taken from where the St st section begins. After 2", inc 4 sts evenly spaced all around—32 sts; 8 sts per needle.

When piece meas 4", mark thumb as foll: On needle 2, k 2 sts, then k the next 5 sts with a piece of waste yarn. Slip those 5 waste yarn sts back onto the left needle and k across them with the working yarn.

Cont until piece meas 7½" from beg of St st section. Beg dec at top of mitten as foll: Ssk at beg of needle 1, k2tog at end of needle 2, ssk at beg of needle 3, k2tog at end of needle 4. Work the dec every 3rd rnd twice more, then every rnd until 4 sts rem. Cut the yarn and use a yarn needle to thread it through those last 4 sts and pull them together snugly.

THUMB

Pull out the waste yarn that's marking the thumb. There should now be 5 "live" sts on the bottom and 4 "live" sts on top. Sl these sts onto 3 needles; join your ball of

yarn; and beg working St st in rnds, picking up 1 st between the top and bottom row of sts on each side in the first rnd—11 sts.

When thumb meas 2¾" from base of thumb, *k2tog, rep from * 5 times, then k the last st. Cut the yarn and pull through the rem 5 sts as you did for the top of the mitten. Weave in all yarn ends, making sure to snug up any little holes that might have formed at the base of the thumb.

RIGHT MITTEN

Make exactly the same as the left mitten **except** make the thumb as foll:

On needle 3, k 1 st, then k the next 5 sts with a piece of waste yarn. Cont as for left mitten.

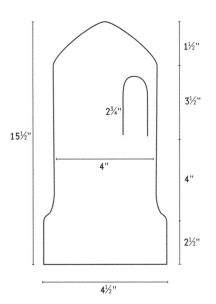

ABOUT KAREN

I asked my mom to teach me to knit when I was fourteen, mainly because I wanted to make things for all the babies that my cousins in Germany were suddenly producing. When I look back, I realize how patient she was, fixing countless screw-ups so I wouldn't get frustrated, and never telling me anything was "too hard" for me to tackle. Thanks, Mom! A good twenty years have passed since then, and knitting has helped keep me sane through college, grad school, and stressful jobs. I do lots of Fair Isle and intarsia because I like zany multicolor and floral designs, but I also do cables and texture work, lace if it's funky enough, and sometimes just plain ol' mindless stockinette stitch so I can read while I knit.

I'm a linguist, and I fund my yarn habit (and life in general) by developing verbal skills tests for educational institutions and testing services.

THERESA V. STENERSEN

pippi kneestockings

These stripy "longstockings" were inspired by Astrid Lindgren's stories about the irrepressible, fiercely independent redhead with pigtails who could handle anything life threw at her. Decreases down the back of the calf and elastic in the ribbing help keep these from sliding down when you're on the go. And when you're wearing them, you just might feel like Pippi—the strongest girl in the world!

SKILLS	PAGE
CAST ON	29
KNIT	33
PURL	47
KNIT IN THE ROUND	57
CHANGE COLOR	43
DECREASE	63
PICK UP STITCHES	82
KITCHENER STITCH	78

Size

To fit average woman's foot

Materials

Brown Sheep Company *Nature Spun Sport* (100% wool; 50g/184 yds)

1 skein each

COLOR SCHEME 1

A: #N46 Red Fox

B: #N85 Peruvian Pink

C: #N48 Scarlet

D: #N54 Orange You Glad

COLOR SCHEME 2

A: #N121 Tornado Teal

B: #N102 Eucalyptus

C: #N03 Grey Heather

D: #N20 Arctic Moss

2 cards K1C2's Rainbow Elastic (100% cotton-covered elastic thread; card/50 yds) to match A

US 2 (3mm) double-pointed needles (set of 4/5)

US 3 (3.25mm) double-pointed needles (set of 4/5), or size needed to obtain gauge

Gauge

26 sts and 34 rows = 4" in St st on larger needles

Color Pattern

A, B, C, D, *B, A, D, C; rep from *.

Directions

RIBBING

With A, CO (very loosely) 64 sts with smaller needles. Divide them onto 3 needles as foll: 19 sts on needle 1, 26 sts on needle 2, 19 sts on needle 3.

Join, being careful not to twist the sts, and pm to indicate beg of rnd.

With elastic and A held tog, work 14 rnds in k2, p2 rib.

Change to larger needles and B (drop the elastic at this point), k first st of rnd with both the old color and new color (rep this at each color change and treat both strands as 1 st on next rnd). Work 14 rnds in St st with B, C, then D.

CALF DECREASES

Change to B and *work 3 rnds in St st.

Rnd 4: needle 1: k1, k2tog, k to end; needle 2: k across; needle 3: k to last 3 sts, ssk, k1.

Work 6 rnds even.

Rnd 11: needle 1: k1, k2tog, k to end; needle 2: k across; needle 3: k to last 3 sts, ssk, k1.

Work 3 rnds even.

Rep from * with A, then D. At this point you'll have 52 sts (13 on needle 1, 26 on needle 2, 13 on needle 3). Cont without dec to the heel.

Change to C and work 14 rnds in St st, rep with B.

See page 137

HEEL FLAP

Note: When slipping sts (sl 1) on RS rows: sl as if to k with yarn in back; on WS rows: sl as if to p with yarn in front.

Change to A.

Row 1: K13 and turn (to work back over sts just worked).

Row 2 (WS): Sl 1, p25 (consolidating 26 heel sts onto 1 needle), turn.

You'll be knitting these 26 sts (the only sts in A at this point) back and forth in St st while the other 26 sts (in B) are being held for the instep either on the rem needle or transferred onto a scrap piece of yarn.

Row 3: Sl 1, k25, turn.

Row 4: Sl 1, p25, turn.

Rep these last 2 rows 13 times more, ending with a WS row.

TURN HEEL

K16, ssk, turn.

*Sl 1, p6, p2tog, turn.

Sl 1, k6, ssk, turn.*

You now have 24 sts on the heel needle—8 center sts and 8 on either side. Rep from * to * until only the center 8 sts rem and you are ready to beg a RS row.

K4, change to D, pm, k4 with needle 1.

*Cont with needle 1 and, holding an empty needle in your right hand, insert the empty needle from front to back in the next elongated st (the sl st of the heel flap) and k tbl; rep from * 13 times more—18 sts on needle 1.

Next, with needle 2, k the 26 sts on hold for the instep.

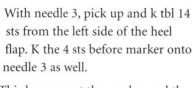

With needle 3, pick up and k tbl 14 sts from the left side of the heel flap. K the 4 sts before marker onto needle 3 as well.

This leaves us at the marker and the beg of the rnd, ready to begin knitting the foot. You should have 62 sts divided onto 3 needles. If you would rather work with 5 needles, divide the instep sts onto 2 needles instead of 1. The next step is to dec back to 52 sts by shaping the gussets.

SHAPE GUSSETS
Rnd 1: K.

Rnd 2 (dec): K to 3 sts from end of needle 1, k2tog, k1; k 26 sts (needle 2); k1, ssk, to end of needle 3.

Rep these 2 rnds 4 times more until there are 13 sts each on needles 1 and 3.

K 3 more rnds in D without dec.

FOOT
Work 14 rnds in St st with C, then 14 rnds with B. Work 2 rnds with A.

Note: To make the foot of the stocking a different length, cont working 14 rnds each color in color patt until the foot (meas from the back of the heel) is 2" less than the total desired length, then begin toe dec.

TOE DECREASES
Arrange sts so first 13 sts are on needle 1, 26 instep sts on needle 2, and last 13 sts on needle 3.

Rnd 1: K to 3 sts from end of needle 1, k2tog, k1; needle 2: k1, ssk, k to 3 sts from end, k2tog, k1; needle 3: k1, ssk, k to end (4 sts dec).

Rnd 2: K.

Rep these last 2 rnds 5 times more—28 sts—then work rnd 1 four times—12 sts.

With needle 3, k 3 sts from needle 1, leaving 6 sts each on the 2 needles and break off yarn, leaving approx 12" tail. Stitch the toe sts tog using Kitchener st.

ABOUT THERESA
I'm a thirty-two-year-old North Carolinian living outside Oslo with my husband and two stepdaughters. I was gripped by a sudden desire to learn to knit three years ago after witnessing a sheepdog demonstration. I began to learn when I relocated to Norway, where I'm knitting up warm woolen garments to survive in the Arctic climate. I dream of having my own fiber-animal farm someday and a Border collie named Fly. In the meantime, I'm making my first forays into the exciting world of hand spinning.

CATHERINE STINSON

powerful wrist protection

everyone says that your very first knitting project should be a scarf. It's true that your first project should be a rectangle in a single color, but that doesn't automatically mean a scarf. Use your imagination a little, and you'll see there are all kinds of things you can make out of rectangles. Wristbands are small rectangles, which makes them a great first project. If they put their minds

SKILLS	PAGE
CAST ON	29
KNIT	33
PURL	47
INTARSIA	92
READ CHART	55
BIND OFF	40
SEW SEAM	73

to it, even the greenest beginners can, in one day, finish a rectangle big enough to go around their wrists, so that cathartic moment of finishing a project comes quickly.

These wristbands are a little fancier and use smaller needles than most beginners can handle, but they're still pretty easy. I came up with this idea out of pure laziness. I had set out to make arm warmers, but after I got a few inches along, I was bored, so they became really short arm warmers. A star pattern and a geek pattern are given, but they can be personalized, if you don't want to advertise your geekiness (or lack of star quality, poor thing).

SIZES

Small (Medium, Large)

Finished measurements: 6 (6^1/$_2$, 6^3/$_4$)" around

MATERIALS

Katia *Mississippi 3* (60% cotton/40% acrylic; 50g/230 yds)

GEEK

MC: #759 Yellow

CC: #760 Olive Green

STAR

MC: #750 Light Blue

CC: #733 Orange

US 5 (3.75mm) knitting needles, or size needed to obtain gauge

GAUGE

20 sts and 32 rows = 4" in St st with 2 strands of yarn held tog

See page 136

☐ MC

■ CC

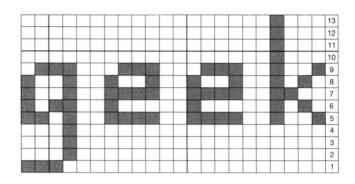

Note: Wristbands are k with 2 strands of yarn held tog throughout. Instead of using the intarsia method which these charts call for, you can cheat and carry the contrasting yarn behind the work when not needed. It'll make this project much easier to do.

DIRECTIONS

With 2 strands of MC held tog, CO 32 (34, 36) sts. For sizes Small and Large, work 3 rows k2, p2 rib. For size Medium, work 3 rows rib as foll:

Row 1: K3, p3, *K2, p2; rep from * to end of row.

Row 2: *K2, p2; rep from * to last 6 sts, k3, p3.

Row 3: Rep row 1.

For the "geek" wristband, knit 2 rows St st. Then k 10 (11, 12) st, k 22 st of chart, k to end of row. Cont with chart until finished, then k 3 more rows St st.

For the "star" wristband, k 2 rows St st. Then k 12 (13, 14) st, k 9 st of chart, k to end of row. Cont with chart until finished, then k 2 more rows St st.

Work 2 rows of rib, using the same instructions as before.

BO in rib.

Sew up the side seams. You're done.

ABOUT CATHERINE

While writing my master's thesis on artificial intelligence, I became bored and unmotivated, so I turned to knitting for help. I knit all night and slept all day until my hands couldn't take it anymore. I organized Stitch 'n Bitch sessions to make my obsessive knitting more social. Soon my pile of hats, bikinis, and wristbands had grown to an alarming size. I started to joke about opening a business to sell wristbands. Then I made a Web site, and the joke became reality.

Now that I've finished my master's degree, I'm avoiding gainful employment in my field. Instead, I'm doing freelance Web design and running www.deadpan.ca, my online knitting and sewing store, from Toronto.

LISA SHOBHANA MASON
big bad baby blanket

See page 138

very mother-to-be appreciates a lovingly hand-knit baby blanket. However, if you are going to knit one special item, why not choose something that is destined to be a cherished heirloom? Don't choose easy care over quality when it comes to selecting a yarn, especially when easy means cheesy (think acrylic). This blanket is made using Koigu *Painter's Palette Premium Merino*, a wonderful hand-painted yarn that comes in hundreds of beautiful variegated colors, suitable for both a wild and wacky mom-to-be or someone whose taste is more traditional. This elegant yet easy-to-knit blanket will garner rave reviews for generations!

SKILLS	PAGE
CAST ON	29
KNIT	33
PURL	47
BIND OFF	40

SIZE
28" × 28" unblocked; 31" x 31" blocked

MATERIALS
Koigu Wool Designs *Painter's Palette Premium Merino* (100% wool; 50g/175 yds), 8 skeins #P118

US 9 (5.5mm) 29"–40" circular needle, or size needed to obtain gauge

Rust-proof pins for blocking

GAUGE
18 sts = 4" in St st with 2 strands of yarn held tog

STITCH PATTERN
SEED STITCH (EVEN NUMBER OF STS)

Row 1: *K1, p1; rep from * to end of row.

Row 2: *P1, k1; rep from * to end of row.

Rep rows 1–2 for patt.

Note: You will be working with 2 strands of yarn held tog throughout.

DIRECTIONS
With 2 strands of yarn held tog, CO 126 sts. Work 20 rows in seed st.

Row 1 (RS): *K1, p1; rep from * 5 times, k53, p53, *k1, p1; rep from * 5 times.

Row 2 (WS): *P1, k1; rep from * 5 times, k53, p53, *p1, k1; rep from * 5 times.

Rep these 2 rows until entire piece meas approx 14" (or until you have finished your 3rd and 4th skeins of yarn). End with a WS row.

Next row (RS): *K1, p1; rep from * 5 times, p53, k53, *k1, p1; rep from * 5 times.

Next row (WS): *P1, k1; rep from * 5 times, p53, k53, *p1, k1; rep from * 5 times.

Rep these 2 rows until entire piece meas approx 25½" (or same number of St st rows as lower half). End with a WS row.

Work 20 rows in seed st.

BO.

FINISHING
Immerse blanket in cool water. Very gently squeeze, then roll the blanket in a towel to absorb excess water. Lay flat on a dry towel. Gently stretch until it meas 31" × 31". Pin with rust-proof pins. Let dry.

ABOUT LISA
I've been obsessed with fashion ever since I visited New York's Fiorucci shop back in the early '80s while on a weekend shopping trip with my mother. Since then, I have gone to ridiculous lengths to obtain unique fashion finds. Some of my favorite pieces are vintage Courrèges and Vivienne Westwood, and both new and old Yohji Yamamoto. During the '90s, every Yvonne, Nikki, and Shari was sporting a label, which made me want to create my own one-of-a-kind designs. Since taking up my needles in 1998, I have knit countless sweaters, socks, scarves, and, yes, baby blankets! A couple of years ago, I turned my obsession into a profession and began teaching knitting classes at Rosie's Yarn Cellar in Philadelphia. I'm a professional astrologer, and my horoscope columns have appeared in several magazines and on Style.com. I live in Philadelphia with my baby, Ashby the Chihuahua.

JENNIFER L. JONES
umbilical cord Hat

everyone I know seems to be having a baby these days, so I designed this easy, quick, and inexpensive hat to give as a gift. It can be made with any worsted-weight yarn, but make sure you use something washable that is soft, since babies need garments that don't itch and that can easily be thrown into the washer. Depending on your gauge, you can probably get two hats from one skein of yarn.

SKILLS	PAGE
CAST ON	29
KNIT	33
KNIT IN THE ROUND	57
DECREASE	63
I-CORD	87

SIZE
Infant to 6 months

Finished circumference: 16"

MATERIALS
Patons *Canadiana* (100% acrylic; 85g/197 yds), 1 skein #81 Gold

US 7 (4.5mm) 16" circular needle, or size needed to obtain gauge

US 7 (4.5mm) double-pointed needles (set of 5)

Stitch markers

GAUGE
16 sts and 22 rows = 4" in St st (k all rnds)

DIRECTIONS

Using circular needle, CO 64 sts. K 1 row. Join ends, being careful not to twist the sts. K until hat meas 5" from the CO row.

Next row: *K8, pm; rep from * to end.

You should have 8 groups of 8 sts between 7 markers.

*With a dpn, k 16 sts off the circular needle and onto the dpn, being careful to slip the st marker between the sts; rep from * 3 times more. When you reach the end of the row, you will have placed 16 sts and 1 marker on each of 4 dpns.

Now, in each successive rnd, you will k tog the last 2 sts before the marker or the end of the needle as foll:

See page 139

Rnd 1: *K6, k2tog; rep from * to end of rnd—56 sts.

Rnd 2: *K5, k2tog; rep from * to end of rnd—48 sts.

Rnd 3: *K4, k2tog; rep from * to end of rnd—40 sts.

Rnd 4: *K3, k2tog; rep from * to end of rnd—32 sts.

Rnd 5: *K2, k2tog; rep from * to end of rnd—24 sts.

Rnd 6: *K1, k2tog; rep from * to end of rnd—16 sts.

Rnd 7: *K2tog; rep from * to end of rnd, remove markers—8 sts.

Rnd 8: *K2tog; rep from * to end of rnd—4 sts.

Slip rem 4 sts onto one dpn. Knit 6" of I-cord. Break yarn, thread it onto a yarn needle, and pull the length through the remaining 4 stitches, drawing the I-cord to a close, then draw the loose end down inside the I-cord to finish. Tie the I-cord into a knot and weave in any loose ends.

ABOUT JENNIFER

I come from a long line of knitters. My grandmother loves to tell about how, at age four, she would walk around the neighborhood knitting. Compared to her, I was a latecomer to knitting, but now I knit almost daily. I knit to relax or while chatting with friends over coffee, so I prefer projects that don't require too much concentration. The attraction of knitting, for me, is designing patterns with differing levels of challenge and then working them up in a variety of yarns.

SAMANTHA BLISS

skully

The first time I made this sweater, I used slubby dark brown and cream yarn that I'd found in a local yarn shop on sale for one dollar a skein. I'd been wanting to make a big, oversized sweater, and the price was right, so I bought eleven or twelve skeins and started brainstorming. I didn't want it to be completely plain (too boring to knit), but generally I don't end up wearing things that have a big emblem on the front. I figured I'd put something cool on the sleeves—and what's cooler than skulls? I made up the pattern as I went along, graphed out the skulls on some graph paper, and just started knitting. "Skully" was my first real sweater project, and it was so damn easy, you all should make one too. What would be even cooler—make your own graph like I did and put whatever you want on the sleeves.

SKILLS	PAGE
CAST ON	29
KNIT	33
PURL	47
INTARSIA	92
READ CHART	55
PICK UP STITCHES	82
3-NEEDLE BIND-OFF	80
BIND OFF	40

Sizes

Small (Medium, Large, Extra-Large)

Finished chest: 40 (42, 47, 50)"

Finished length: 23^1/$_4$ (24^1/$_2$, 26, 27^1/$_2$)"

Materials

Brown Sheep Company *Lamb's Pride Bulky* (85% wool/15% mohair; 4 oz/125 yds)

MC: 6 (6, 7, 7) skeins #M06 Deep Charcoal

See page 140

CC: 1 skein #M10 Creme

US 10^1/$_2$ (6.5mm) knitting needles, or size needed to obtain gauge

Gauge

13 sts and 20 rows = 4" in St st

Directions

FRONT

With MC, CO 65 (69, 77, 81) sts.

Work 7 rows in garter st.

Then work in St st until front measures 17 (18, 19, 20)" from beg.

SHAPE ARMHOLE

BO 1 st at beg of next 6 (8, 10, 12) rows, then work 3" more in St st, ending with a WS row.

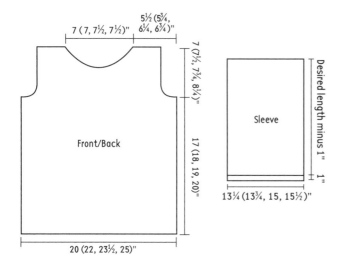

NECK SHAPING

K 26 (27, 29, 30) sts. Join 2nd skein of yarn; BO center 7 (7, 9, 9) sts; k to end of row. Both shoulder sections are worked at the same time with separate skeins.

BO 2 sts at neck edge at beg of every other row until 18 (19, 21, 22) sts rem on each shoulder.

Work 1" more in St st. Leave sts on needles or holder.

BACK

Work same as front, *except* when you have decreased to 18 (19, 21, 21) sts at shoulders, just stop there—don't knit the extra inch. Leave sts on needle or holder.

JOIN SHOULDERS AND MAKE NECKBAND

When front and back are finished, put RS together and join 1 shoulder using 3-needle BO over 18 sts for a strong, compact seam.

With RS facing, and beg at edge of neck, pu and k 54 (54, 58, 58) sts evenly around the neckline. Work 1" in k1, p1 rib. Loosely BO in rib.

MC ☐ CC

Join second shoulder seam using 3-needle BO and sew neckband seam.

SLEEVE

Lay front and back flat.

With RS facing and MC, pu and k 43 (45, 49, 51) sts at armhole.

Work 1" in St st.

Mark center st with a contrasting loop of yarn for center of skull pattern.

Cont in St st, work 6 (7, 9, 10) sts MC, work 31 sts of chart; work 6 (7, 9, 10) sts MC.

When chart has been completed, cont with MC in St st to 1" shy of desired sleeve length (approx 20").

Then work 7 rows garter st.

BO fairly loosely.

Rep sleeve on other side.

FINISHING
With RS facing, sew side and sleeve seams.

ABOUT SAMANTHA

I'm thirty years old and have been knitting for about five years. I'd wanted to learn to knit for a while, and my mom had tried to show me a couple of times, but I just never got it. A few years later when I wanted to learn again, my mom told me about a lady at the local yarn shop who was a "whiz." It took this woman about five minutes to show me all I needed to know—it turns out that my mom and I knit completely differently, and I just needed someone with more general knowledge to push me along. I ended up knitting my first swatch on the plane home, poking the man sitting next to me with my knobby needles, and I've been knitting ever since. I made a lot of scarves at first but quickly branched into more free-form knitting, an ever-shifting cycle of hats, socks, various part-warmers (leg, wrist, knee), handbags, and a custom sweater for a goose(!). Even when I'm not knitting, I work with needles: I'm a tattoo artist working in Purdys, New York.

KRISTIN SPURKLAND
under the Hoodie

this sweater combines several of my favorite design elements: hoods, stripes, and a mix of deep red, pink, and orange. I love making sporty styles in soft, luxurious mohair—the yarn gives the design more versatility. I wear this hoodie as a cover-up in my yoga and dance classes, and then pair it with a low-slung, funky skirt and my favorite red boots for nights out.

I suggest knitting this sweater on a circular needle (even though it is knit flat), because you can join new colors at either end of the circulars—especially important when you work on stripes. Also, it is easier to knit the hood on circulars than on straight needles. You'll see what I mean when you get there!

SKILLS	PAGE
CAST ON	29
KNIT	33
PURL	47
PICK UP STITCHES	82
DECREASE	63
INCREASE	60
CHANGE COLOR	43
KNIT IN THE ROUND	57
3-NEEDLE BIND-OFF	80
SEW SEAM	73
BIND OFF	40

SIZES

Small (Medium, Large, Extra-Large)

Finished bust: 36 (40, 43$\frac{1}{2}$, 47$\frac{1}{2}$)"

Finished length: 20 (21, 22, 23)"

MATERIALS

Rowan *Kid Classic* (70% wool/26% mohair/ 4% nylon; 50g/151 yds)

A: 5 (5, 6, 7) skeins #825 Crushed Velvet

B: 3 (4, 4, 4) skeins #819 Pinched

C: 1 (1, 1, 1) skein #827 Juicy

US 8 (5mm) 24" circular needle, or size needed to obtain gauge

US 7 (4.5mm) knitting needles

Stitch holders

See page 141

GAUGE

19 sts and 26 rows = 4" in St st on larger needles

STITCH PATTERNS

RIB

Rows 1, 3, 5 (WS): P2 *k1, p2; rep from * across.

Rows 2 and 4 (RS): K.

BORDER FOR POCKET AND HOOD (WORKED OVER 5 STS)

WS rows: (K1, p1) 2 times, k1.

RS rows: K.

DIRECTIONS

BACK

With smaller needles and A, CO 86 (95, 104, 113) sts. Work 5 rows of rib patt as indicated, ending with a WS row. Change to larger needles and work in St st until back meas 9½ (10, 10½, 11)" from beg. Change to C and work 3 rows. Change to B and work for 4". Change back to C and work 3 rows. Change to A and work even until back meas 20 (21, 22, 23)" from beg. BO 27 (31, 35, 38) sts; work across center 32 (33, 34, 37) sts and place on holder; then BO rem 27 (31, 35, 38) sts.

FRONT

Work as for back through rib patt, then change to larger needles and work 3 rows St st. Place a safety pin in the 14th (17th, 19th, 21st) st from either end to mark where you will be picking up sts for the pocket later.

Using the row counter to track rows, work another 43 (43, 47, 49) rows in St st. This is very important, as it ensures that the pocket lines up neatly with the body of the sweater! Your last row should be a WS row. Place all these sts on a holder.

POCKET

With the RS of your sweater facing you and a separate skein of A at WS of front, pu the center 58 (61, 66, 71) sts between the safety pins by *inserting the RH needle into the center of the next st from front to back, wrapping the yarn as if to k, and pulling the loop through. Rep from * across the center sts to be pu.

Work 13 (13, 17, 19) rows St st, working first and last 5 sts in border patt, end with a WS row.

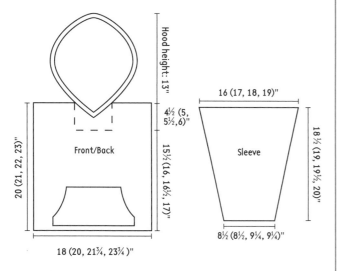

Hood height: 13"

4½ (5, 5½,6)"

15½ (16, 16½, 17)"

16 (17, 18, 19)"

18½ (19, 19½, 20)"

Front/Back

Sleeve

20 (21, 22, 23)"

18 (20, 21¾, 23¾)"

8½ (8½, 9¼, 9¼)"

SHAPE POCKET

Rows 1 and 3 (RS): Work 5 border sts, ssk, work to last 7 sts, k2tog, work 5 border sts.

Rows 2, 4, 6 (WS): P across, working first and last 5 sts in border patt.

Row 5 (RS): K.

Rep rows 1–6 four times more—30 shaping rows worked, 38 (41, 46, 51) sts rem.

JOIN POCKET TO SWEATER

K 24 (27, 29, 31) sweater sts from holder. Now, with the pocket sts in front of the sweater sts, k across the next 38 (41, 46, 51) sts, knitting 1 st from the pocket tog with 1 st from the sweater. Once the pocket sts have been joined, k across rem 24 (27, 29, 31) sts. Congratulate yourself on completing the pocket!

Cont to work front as for back through the stripe section. When rejoining A after completing stripe, join it with the RS of the sweater facing you and at the right-hand side of your knitting, so that the first row worked with A will be a k row (this is where working on a circular needle comes in handy!). Work 3 rows with A.

NECK SHAPING

On next WS row, divide for neck opening.

Right front: P 50 (55, 59, 64) sts, then work border patt over next 5 sts—55 (60, 64, 69) sts. Place rem 31 (35, 40, 44) sts on holder. Next row (RS), work first 5 neck edge sts in border patt, then k to the end of the row. Cont to work in this manner, keeping 5 neck edge sts in border patt, until right front measures 20 (21, 22, 23)", ending with a RS row. BO 27 (31, 35, 38) sts and place rem 28 (29, 29, 31) sts on holder.

Left front: With RS of garment facing you, rejoin yarn and k across 31 (35, 40, 44) sts on holder. Cont across row, pu 24 (25, 24, 25) more sts by knitting into the purl bumps of sts already worked along right front neckline (you are picking up sts on the inside of the garment, but working with the RS of your sweater facing you)—55 (60, 64, 69) sts. Work as for right front, working border patt at neck edge, until left front measures 20 (21, 22, 23)", ending with a WS row. BO 27 (31, 35, 38) sts, and place rem 28 (29, 29, 31) sts on holder.

SLEEVES

With smaller needle and B, CO 41 (41, 44, 44) sts. Work 5 rows rib patt as indicated, ending with a WS row. Change to larger needle and work 1" in St st, end with a WS row.

Cont in St st, inc 1 st each side every 6th row 18 (12, 16, 14) times; then every 4th row 0 (7, 5, 9) times—77 (79, 86, 90) sts. Work even until sleeve meas 18½ (19, 19½, 20)" from beg BO.

HOOD

Sew shoulder seams. Place rem right front, back neck, and left front sts on larger circular needle—88 (91, 96, 99) sts. Work in St st for 13", cont border patt on first and last 5 sts. On final RS row, dec 0 (1, 0, 1) st at center of row—88 (90, 96, 98) sts. Divide sts evenly over 2 needles—44 (45, 48, 49) sts per needle. Working with RS tog, join hood seam using 3-needle BO.

FINISHING

Mark armhole depth by placing pins 8 (8½, 9, 9½)" down from shoulder seam. Sew in sleeves, lining up sleeve edges with pins. Sew sleeve and side seams. Block sweater to shape (especially hood edges, which will want to curl until you straighten them out). Now go out and wear your hoodie with joy!

ABOUT KRISTIN

I became interested in design in the early 1980s when I discovered the work of Vivienne Westwood. During my freshman year at college, my roommate taught me how to knit. Alas, both interests languished while I pursued a more academic path. Then one day, inexplicably, I found myself making for the nearest yarn shop, where I bought the hottest hot-pink mohair, needles, and a reference book to explain it all. I happily went home and knitted my heart out. Later, my two interests merged into an apparel design degree from Bassist College in Portland, Oregon. When I graduated, I knew I wanted to work in knitwear design with a focus on hand knitting, and so I have.

When not knitting, I spend time volunteering at a local animal shelter, practicing yoga, taking hip-hop dance classes, riding my bike, cooking, and reading novels written at least one hundred years ago. My first knitting book will be published in spring 2004.

LAURA JEAN BERNHARDSON

the go-everywhere, go-with-everything cardigan

See page 143

I've made different versions of this pattern for years. I love the chunky mohair trim and enjoy playing with the color combos. Experiment with fun combos to really make it your own. I used handmade flower buttons to match both colors, which you can order from www.freshbakedgoods.com, my Web site, or find your own crazy buttons and use them as an inspiration. Have fun with it!

SKILLS	PAGE
CAST ON	29
KNIT	33
PURL	47
INCREASE	60
DECREASE	63
BIND OFF	40
SEW SEAM	73
CROCHET CHAIN	99
SINGLE CROCHET	100

SIZES

Small (Medium, Large, Extra-Large)

Finished bust: 37 (40, 43, 46)" buttoned

Finished length: 20 (21, 22, 23)"

MATERIALS

MC: Emu *Superwash DK* (100% wool; 50g/130 yds), 8 (8, 9, 10) skeins #170

CC: Katia *Ingenua* (78% mohair/13% polyamide/9% wool; 50g/153 yds), 1 skein #15

US 4 (3.5mm) knitting needles, or size needed to obtain gauge

Seven 1" buttons

G/6 crochet hook

GAUGE

22 sts and 28 rows = 4" in St st with MC

DIRECTIONS

BACK

With MC, CO 102 (110, 118, 126) sts.

Work 84 (88, 92, 94) rows in St st—12 (12½, 13, 13½)".

BO 4 (5, 6, 7) sts at beg of next 2 rows.

Dec 1 st each side every 2nd row 5 (6, 8, 10) times—86 (88, 90, 92) sts.

Cont in St st for 140 (146, 154, 160) rows total—20 (21, 22, 23)".

BO all sts.

FRONT (MAKE TWO, REVERSING SHAPING)

With MC, CO 52 (56, 60, 64) sts.

Work 84 (88, 92, 94) rows in St st—12 (12½, 13, 13½)".

BO 4 (5, 6, 7) sts at side edge.

Dec 1 st at side edge every 2nd row 5 (6, 8, 10) times—43 (45, 46, 47) sts. **At the same time,** when piece meas 104 (112, 118, 126) rows total—15 (16, 17, 18)"—dec 1 st at neck edge every row 6 times; then every 2nd row 14 times—23 (25, 26, 27) sts. Cont in St st until front meas same as back. BO all sts.

SLEEVES

With MC, CO 44 (48, 50, 52) sts.

Working in St st, inc 1 st each side every 5th row 0 (0, 8, 16) times, every 6th row 18 (20, 14, 8) times, then every 7th row 2 (0, 0, 0) times—82 (88, 94, 100) sts.

Cont in St st until piece meas 122 (126, 130, 134) rows total—17½ (18, 18½, 19)".

SHAPE SLEEVE CAP

BO 4 (5, 6, 7) sts at beg of next 2 rows. Dec 1 st each side, every 2nd row 5 (6, 8, 10) times. BO rem 64 (66, 66, 66) sts.

FINISHING

Sew shoulder seams. Sew sleeve caps into armholes. Sew side and sleeve seams.

TRIM

With 3 strands of CC held tog, sc evenly around entire edge of cardigan. Don't match up st for st—the mohair

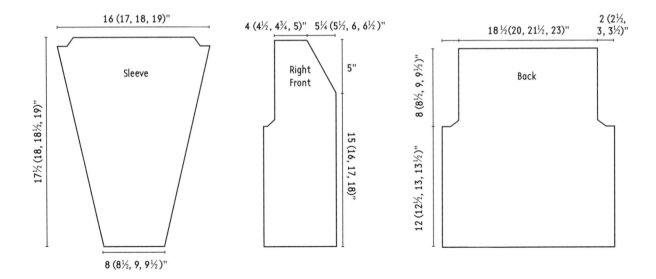

is going to be a way different gauge than the wool. Just do this by eye and feel to make it not too tight and not too loose.

BUTTONHOLE BANDS

Place markers on right front for 7 buttonholes, with first one at beg of neck shaping and last one ½" from bottom.

Now work a 2nd row of sc along the front edges for the buttonhole bands. When you get to a marker, ch 3, sk 1 st, then cont in sc to next marker. Fasten off after finishing the last buttonhole. Work a second row of sc on opposite side as well. Sew on buttons opposite buttonholes.

ABOUT LAURA JEAN

I started knitting in October 1994, and within two weeks I had sold my first sweater. I had so many ideas, I just kept making sweaters. People would stop me on the street and ask me where I got what I was wearing. Desperate for something I could call a career, I decided to start my own business. That's how Fresh Baked Goods was born. The business was small at first, based out of my living room, but today I have my own shop in Toronto, and a Web site (www.freshbakedgoods.com), where I sell all of my knit projects.

I'll admit that I'm a bit results-oriented, which is why I love machine knitting—I can actually get things done before I'm bored with them, and for the business side of things, it's a necessity. That said, I also love the relaxed pace of hand knitting. It's amazing to watch my two hands, needles, and time turn a simple bit of yarn into a wearable item.

MARTHA LAZAR
to dye for

I designed this sweater at the end of a long, cold winter. I'd been suffering from cabin fever and was already thinking about spring, which is why I knit the mohair in a very open, airy gauge. The shaping was inspired by some beautiful Tibetan silk tunics that I was longing to wear as soon as it warmed up.

The yarn for the sweater was dyed with Kool-Aid. Why? Well, it's easy, fun, nontoxic, and you get the most amazing range of colors. Our Kool-Aid classes at Urban Knitter are always fun, and people come up with the greatest color combinations. I chose sedate colors for this project to show that you can get pretty sophisticated with Kool-Aid, but you can go wild, too. There's a whole range of colors, from flaming red to toilet-bowl-cleanser blue. Play around with a few test hanks, or dive in with your whole stash.

SKILLS	PAGE
CAST ON	29
KNIT	33
PURL	47
DECREASE	63
BIND OFF	40
SEW SEAM	73
SINGLE CROCHET	100

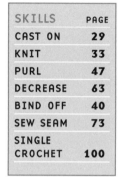

SIZES

Small (Medium, Large, Extra-Large)

Finished bust: 38 (40, 43, 46)"

See page 142

MATERIALS

Halcyon yarn *Victorian Brushed Mohair* (70% mohair/24% wool/6% nylon; 50g/145 yds)

4 (5, 5, 6) skeins #103

2 boxes Kool-Aid, Magic Secret and Changin' Cherry

US 13 (9mm) knitting needles, or size needed to obtain gauge

H/8 crochet hook

GAUGE

10 sts and 14 rows = 4" in St st

DYEING DIRECTIONS

Kool-Aid will work only with animal fibers, so wool, mohair, angora, and silk work well, but cotton, linen, and rayon won't hold the color.

The suggested starting point for mixing the colors is 1 packet of unsweetened Kool Aid mixed with 1 cup (8 oz.) of lukewarm water. (You'll probably end up using about 3 packets of each color.)

You can add 1 oz. white vinegar to help with colorfastness, although some people feel this isn't necessary, as the Kool-Aid contains citric acid. I suggest using clear measuring cups, so you'll be able to see the color clearly.

You can mix different Kool-Aid colors like watercolors; add more water to make lighter colors, or more Kool-Aid for more saturated colors. The grape color is very intense and acts like a black. When you add a very diluted solution of grape to a primary red, you'll get a raspberry color. Play around with the colors; perhaps even knit a swatch to see how the dyed yarn looks knit.

If you are going to use more than 1 skein for a project, take notes about your color mixtures and dilutions so you can duplicate them.

1. Wind your yarn into hanks (see page 111) if it doesn't already come that way. Don't try to dye a ball of yarn, because the middle won't get the color. Try to make the hanks consistent if you are dyeing multiple skeins for a project.

2. Loosely tie the hanks in at least 4 places so they don't unwind and get tangled.

3. Soak the hanks in room-temperature water for at least 20 minutes. Don't stir your yarn or make temperature changes, as this can result in felted fibers, which you won't be able to use.

4. When you are ready to dye your yarn, carefully lift one hank at a time out of the water. Let as much water drain as possible. You can *gently* squeeze the bottom of the hank to get excess water out.

If you are dyeing your yarn more than one color:

1. Lay your hank(s) out on a plastic-covered surface, because Kool-Aid dyes more than just yarn.

2. Pour the Kool-Aid liquid onto your hank a little at a time. You can leave space between the colors, or let them bleed into each other.

3. Place the hank in a medium-sized microwaveable casserole dish. Cover with plastic wrap that has a few holes punched in it.

4. Microwave on high for 2–4 minutes, or until the water in the dish is clear.

5. Put the yarn in your sink or bathtub and let cool. Fill with lukewarm water to rinse the yarn, but don't let the force of the water hit the yarn directly.

6. Hang the yarn in the shower to dry overnight.

If you are dyeing your yarn one solid color:

1. Place the hank of yarn in a medium-sized microwave-able casserole dish. Pour in the Kool-Aid, making sure to coat the yarn evenly. You can use your gloved hands to gently push the yarn down into the liquid to make sure it is evenly dyed.

2. Follow instructions 4–6 above.

KNITTING DIRECTIONS

BACK

CO 48 (50, 54, 58) sts loosely. Work 4 rows in garter st. Work in St st until piece meas 17" from beg. BO 3 sts at the beg of the next 2 rows—42 (44, 48, 54) sts. Cont in St st until piece meas 25 (25½, 26, 26½)". Loosely BO all sts.

FRONT

Work as for back, including all shaping. **At the same time,** when piece meas 22 (22½, 23, 23½)" from beg,

beg neck shaping: Work 17 (18, 19, 22) sts, attach another skein of yarn, BO center 8 (8, 10, 10) sts loosely, complete row. Working both sides at once, dec 1 st at each neck edge, every other row 4 times—13 (14, 15, 18) sts each side. Work even until piece meas 25 (25½, 26, 26½)". BO all sts.

SLEEVES (WORKED FROM THE TOP DOWN)

CO 41 (43, 45, 47) sts. Work even in St st for 4 rows. Dec 1 st on each side next RS row; every 6th row 4 times; then every 4th row 2 times—27 (29, 31, 33) sts. Work even until piece meas 16".

BELL SLEEVE SHAPING

Inc 6 sts evenly across next RS row. Rep this inc every 8th row 2 times more—45 (47, 49, 51) sts. Work even until sleeve measures 23 (23½, 24, 24½)". Work 4 rows in garter st. BO loosely.

FINISHING

Sew shoulder seams. Sew sleeves into armhole shaping. Sew sleeve seams from bell to underarm and continue down side seams. Leave 5" unsewn at bottom of tunic. Work 1 row sc around neck opening.

ABOUT MARTHA

I started knitting four years ago as a way to calm down from a very stressful job in advertising. I taught myself knitting out of a book and went on to become what I call a "freaky knitter." Other people might use the term *obsessive*. A year ago my partner Rebecca Hartranft and I opened Urban Knitter, which is a fiber arts studio in Brooklyn, New York, offering knitting, dyeing, spinning, and crocheting classes (www.urbanknitter.com). I learned how to spin about a year ago and am now trying to see how I can smuggle sheep into my backyard.

5¼ (5½, 6, 7¼)"
6¼ (6¼, 7, 7)"

Front/Back

19 (20, 21½, 23)"

2½"

5½"

17"

18 (18¾, 19½, 20¼)"

Sleeve

23 (23½, 24, 24½)"

10¾ (11½, 12¼, 13)"

16¼ (17, 18, 18¾)"

MELISSA LIM

cape mod

don't worry, this isn't that plaid number they wore in the seventies—it's an updated, hip take on the poncho, knit top-down with a chunky yarn and accented with furry trim and pom-poms. The turtleneck adds extra style and warmth. You can pair it with your favorite jeans, dress, or skirt for a quirky, chic look. I love the simplicity of this garment, which knits up quickly on large needles, and the fact that it can be easily adapted to suit different styles and tastes. You can experiment with various necklines, widths, and other details, like adding fringe or mini pom-poms to the hem.

SKILLS	PAGE
CAST ON	29
KNIT	33
PURL	47
KNIT IN THE ROUND	57
CHANGE COLOR	43
INCREASE	60
YARN OVER	62
POM-POMS	88
CROCHET CHAIN	99

See page 145

SIZES

Small (Medium, Large)

Finished length: 20" all sizes

Finished lower edge: 120 (128, 136)" around

MATERIALS

MC: Rowan *Big Wool* (100% merino wool; 100g/87 yds), 5 (6, 6) skeins #008 Black

Gedifra *Tecno Hair* (100% microfiber; 50g/100 yds)

A: 1 (1, 1) skein #44

B: 1 (1, 1) skein #18

US 15 (10mm) 16" circular needles

US 17 (12mm) 24" circular or double-pointed needles (set of 4-5)

US 17 (12mm) 29" circular needles, or size needed to obtain gauge

I/9 (5.5mm) crochet hook

GAUGE

8 sts and 12 rows = 4" in St st on larger needles

Note: When using *Tecno Hair,* which is knit with 2 strands held tog, work from both ends of the skein, wind up another ball using half the skein, or purchase 2 skeins each of A and B.

DIRECTIONS

With MC and smaller needles, CO 40 (44, 48) sts. Pm and join into a rnd, being careful not to twist the sts. Add a double strand of A. Work 3 rnds in k2, p2 rib with MC and A tog. Cont in rib with MC only until work meas 8"–10", depending on how long or how short you want your turtleneck to be.

Work the eyelet rnd next as foll: *K2tog, yo; rep from * until you get back to the beg marker. (This is where you will thread the pom-pom chain later.)

Switch to larger needles and cont in St st as foll: K20 (22, 24) and pm. You may want to use a different colored marker to distinguish it from the beg of the rnd. Work 3 more rnds even.

On the next rnd, inc as foll: *K to next marker, M1, sl marker, M1 (this makes 2 sts in the same spot); rep from * once more. Rep these incs every other row until there are 132 (136, 140) sts. You will have made 23 total incs.

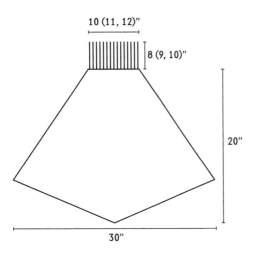

10 (11, 12)"

8 (9, 10)"

20"

30"

At the same time, add the contrasting stripe when the body of the poncho meas approx 10" (measuring from bottom of neck to bottom of V); drop A and add a

double strand of B. Cont for 3 rnds with MC and B tog. You may wish to alter the number of rnds on all the furry trim to suit your stripe thickness preference.

At the same time, when there are 132 (136, 140) sts, ending after an inc row, switch again to smaller needles. Add a double strand of yarn A, and cont incs, work 3 rnds k2, p2 rib with MC and A tog. BO all sts loosely with MC only. Weave in all ends and block if necessary.

FINISHING

Using a 3" pom-pom template, make 2 pom-poms with A. Set them aside. With the same yarn, crochet a chain about 40"–45" long, or whatever length is preferable. Thread this chain through the eyelet rnd at the base of the turtleneck. Attach a pom-pom to each end of the chain.

ABOUT MELISSA

I live in Portland, Oregon, where it doesn't rain nearly as much as people think. My mom taught me to knit when I was a girl, and I started knitting seriously again about five years ago. I began experimenting with knit design and loved how it unleashed my creativity. I document my crafty endeavors on my knitting blog, Action Hero (http://www.action-hero.net/blog/knitblog.html), and I work as an instructional technology teacher. My recent obsessions include NBA basketball, Seattle radio station KEXP, and bulky wool in bright colors.

JENNA WILSON

big sack sweater

Here's an oversized sweater that's just the thing for cozying up and sacking out. It's generously sized for layering over turtlenecks and hangs straight with an easy rolled hem. The extra-long sleeves roll down to keep your hands warm (just in case you lacked the foresight to bring along your mitts), and a collar rolls up as high as you wish—you could end the collar early and have a simple, loose rolled neck, or keep on knitting for a turtleneck. And, to top it off, a great big bulky cable runs right up the center front.

SKILLS	PAGE
CAST ON	29
KNIT	33
PURL	47
CABLE	90
INCREASE	60
DECREASE	63
BIND OFF	40
PICK UP STITCHES	82
SEW SEAM	73

SIZES

Small (Medium, Large, Extra-Large)

Finished chest measurement: 42 (45^1/$_2$, 49, 52^1/$_2$)"

Finished length: 20^1/$_2$ (22, 22, 23)"

MATERIALS

Rowan *Rowanspun Chunky* (100% wool; 100g/ 141 yds), 7 (7, 8, 9) skeins #982 Green Waters

US 8 (5mm) knitting needles

US 10 (6mm) knitting needles, or size needed to obtain gauge

GAUGE

14 sts and 20 rows = 4" in St st larger needles

STITCH PATTERN

CABLE PANEL (20 STS AND 10 ROWS)

Row 1 (RS): P2, k2, p2. Make cable: Sl next 4 sts to cn, hold at back of work; k next 4 sts; k 4 sts from cn. P2, k2, p2.

Rows 2, 4, 6, 8, and 10 (WS): K2, p2, k2, p8, k2, p2, k2.

Rows 3, 5, 7, and 9 (RS): P2, k2, p2, k8, p2, k2, p2.

Rep rows 1–10 for patt.

K on RS, P on WS.

P on RS, K on WS.

8-st cable: Sl next 4 sts to cn, hold at back of work; k next 4 sts; k 4 sts from cn, p2, k2, p2.

See page 144

Note: You'll see in the directions that you will have to increase and decrease stitches at the beginning and end of the cable. That's because cable stitches tend to eat up a lot of width. We need to work these increases and decreases to avoid any unsightly flaring when we make the transition from cables to stockinette at the hem and neckline.

DIRECTIONS

BACK

With smaller needles, CO 74 (80, 86, 92) sts. Work 6 rows in St st. Change to larger needles and work even in St st until back meas 12 (13, 13, 14)" from beg.

BO 4 (4, 4, 6) sts at beg of next 2 rows—66 (72, 78, 80) sts rem. RS should be facing for next row.

For sizes Small (Medium) only: Work 6 (4) rows even, then cont as foll:

For *all* sizes:

Row 1 (RS): K2, k2tog, k to last 4 sts, ssk, k2.

Row 2: P.

Rep these 2 rows 13 (15, 17, 18) times more—38 (40, 42, 42) sts.

NECK SHAPING

On next row (RS): K2, k2tog, k10. Slip these sts onto a holder. Now BO 10 (12, 14, 14) sts from the left-hand needle. Cont to k to the last 4 sts; ssk, k2. You should now have 13 sts on a holder; 10 (12, 14, 14) sts BO for the center of the neck; and another 13 sts on the right-hand needle (that's the left shoulder).

**Now finish the left shoulder and neck shaping with the following 9 rows:

Row 1 (WS): P.

Row 2 (RS): BO 4 sts at neck edge; k to last 4 sts; ssk, k2.

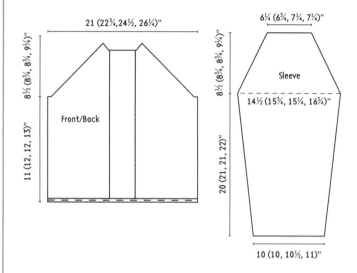

Front/Back — 21 (22¾,24½, 26¼)"
8½ (8¾, 8¾, 9¼)"
11 (12, 12, 13)"

Sleeve — 6¼ (6¾, 7¼, 7¼)"
8½ (8¾, 8¾, 9¼)"
14½ (15¾, 15¼, 16¾)"
20 (21, 21, 22)"
10 (10, 10½, 11)"

Row 3: P.

Row 4: BO 2 sts at neck edge; k to last 4 sts; ssk, k2.

Row 5: P.

Row 6: K1, ssk, k2.

Row 7: P.

Row 8: Ssk, k2.

Row 9: P1, p2tog, then slip the first st over the second st and off the needles. Break off yarn and pass the tail of yarn through the last rem loop and pull tight (you BO and dec 1 st at the same time).

Now return the first 13 sts to a needle, and hold the work so that the WS is facing for the next row—we'll begin knitting from the neck. Finish the right shoulder and neck shaping with the foll 9 rows:

Row 1 (WS): Join the yarn and BO the first 4 sts at neck edge; p to the end of the row.

Row 2 (RS): K2, k2tog, k to end.

Row 3: BO 2 sts at neck edge, p to end.

Row 4: K2, k2tog, k2.

Row 5: P.

Row 6: K2, k2tog, k1.

Row 7: P.

Row 8: K2, k2tog.

Row 9: P2tog, p1, then slip the first st over the second st and off the needle. Break off yarn and pass the tail of yarn through the last rem loop and pull tight.

FRONT

With smaller needles, CO 74 (80, 86, 92) sts. Work 6 rows in St st. Change to larger needles. RS should be facing for next row. Inc row: K 29 (32, 35, 38), p2, k2, p2, k1, M1, k1, M1, k1, M1, k1, M1, p2, k2, p2, k 29 (32, 35, 38)—78 (84, 90, 96) sts.

Next row (WS): P 29 (32, 35, 38), k2, p2, k2, p8, k2, p2, k2, p 29 (32, 35, 38).

Now we have laid the foundation row. The center 20 sts in the row should match up with the cable panel.

From now on, work the center 20 sts using the cable panel patt, beg with row 1 of the patt, and work the first and last 29 (32, 35, 38) sts in St st. Work another 52 (58, 58, 64) rows as established. You should have worked 5 (5, 5, 6) complete rep plus 2 (8, 8, 4) rows of the patt, and the front should be the same length as the back.

Cont in patt, proceed as foll:

BO 4 (4, 4, 6) sts at beg of next 2 rows.

For sizes Small (Medium) only: Work 6 (4) rows even in patt, cont as foll:

For *all* sizes:

Row 1 (RS): K2, k2tog, patt to last 4 sts, ssk, k2.

Row 2: Work even in patt.

Rep these 2 rows 13 (15, 17, 18) times more until there are 42 (44, 46, 46) sts rem. RS should be facing for next row.

NECK SHAPING

On next row, K2, k2tog, k9, p1. Slip these sts onto a holder. Now, BO the center sts as foll:

For sizes Small (Medium) only: BO 1, ssk, BO this ssk st by passing the st already on the RH needle over it, BO 0(1) st, *k2tog, BO this k2tog st as with ssk, BO 2 sts; rep from * once more, k2tog, BO as before, BO 1 (2) st(s)—14 (16) sts BO.

For sizes Large (Extra-Large) only: K2tog, k1, pass the k2tog st over the k1 st; *BO 3 sts; k2tog, BO this k2tog st by passing the st already on the RH needle over it; rep from * twice more, then BO 1 more st—18 sts BO.

Proceed to p1, k to last 4 sts, ssk, k2. You should now have 13 sts on a holder; the center 14 (16, 18, 18) sts BO; and another 13 sts on the right-hand needle (that's the left shoulder).

Now finish shaping neck and shoulders foll instructions for back, beg at **.

SLEEVES

With smaller needles, CO 35 (35, 37, 39) sts. Work 6 rows even in St st, then change to larger needles on next row.

Cont in St st, *inc 1 st each side on next row, then work 7 rows even; rep from * until there are 51 (53, 53, 59) sts across; then work even to 20 (21, 21, 22)".

RAGLAN SHAPING

BO 4 (4, 4, 6) sts at beg of next 2 rows.

Row 1 (RS): K2, k2tog, k to last 4 sts, ssk, k2.

Row 2: P.

Rep these 2 rows until 9 sts remain. BO all sts.

FINISHING

Sew the front to both sleeves along the diagonal raglan edges. Sew the back to the left sleeve along the diagonal raglan edges. Leave the last armhole seam open while you knit the neckband.

NECKBAND

With RS facing and smaller needles, beg at the right back opening, pu 10 sts down the first "slope" of the back neck; 10 (12, 14, 14) sts across the center back; 10 sts up the second slope of the back neck; 7 sts across the sleeve; 10 sts down the first slope of the front neck; 10 (12, 14, 14) sts across the center front; 10 sts up the second slope of the front neck; then 7 sts across the last sleeve—74 (78, 82, 82) sts.

Now you have a choice. If you want to work a short, simple rolled neck, knit 8 rows of St st with the smaller needles. The knit side should be on the RS so that the edge will roll outward. BO.

If you want to work a turtleneck to be folded down, change to larger needles and knit as many rows of St st as you can bear, again with the knit side on the RS. If you want to be able to fold the collar over twice, you should knit at least 6". Then change to smaller needles, k 4 rows even, and BO.

Now sew the final armhole seam between the back and the sleeve, and sew the neckband seam tog. When you sew the neckband seam, make sure it appears neat from the wrong (purl) side, since that's the side that will be facing out.

Sew the side and sleeve seams.

ABOUT JENNA

I taught myself to knit on one of many idle afternoons during my undergraduate days in 1994, and I soon became an addict. Because I was unaware that a beginner should start small and that cotton can be very heavy, my first finished project was a bulky sweater of my own design, knit from several strands of worsted-weight cotton yarn. The sweater still exists, but nobody has the strength to wear it.

In 2001, I launched my Web site, www.girlfromauntie.com, to commemorate my passion for knitting. When I'm not knitting, I spend my time as an attorney in Toronto, Ontario.

ANNIE MODESITT

pinup queen

I'm really tall, but I love short things—my kids, my car, my husband. Here you'll learn how to make short rows—a knitting technique that is feared and misunderstood but just wants to be loved! This sweater is all about curves—making them, hugging them, and loving them! Nothing is as sexy as confidence, and nothing builds confidence like a flattering, well-shaped garment with a plunging neckline. So sit your butt down, knit this baby up, and exult in your mother-given shape!

SKILLS	PAGE
CAST ON	29
KNIT	33
PURL	47
DECREASE	63
BIND OFF	40
SEW SEAM	73

SIZES

Small (Medium, Large, Extra-Large)

Finished bust: 34 (36, 39, 42)"

Finished length: 21¹/₂ (22¹/₄, 23, 23¹/₂)"

MATERIALS

Classic Elite *Lush* (50% angora/50% wool; 50g/123 yds)

7 (8, 9, 10) skeins #4407

US 7 (4.5mm) knitting needles, or size needed to obtain gauge

US 8 (5mm) knitting needles, or size needed to obtain gauge

GAUGE

20 sts and 26 rows = 4" in k2, p2 rib on smaller needles

STITCH PATTERN

K2, P2 RIB (MULTIPLE OF 4 STS + 2)

Row 1 (RS): *K2, p2; rep from * to last 2 sts, k2.

Row 2: *P2, k2; rep from * to last 2 sts, p2.

W&T (WRAP AND TURN)

Slip next st to RH needle, wrap yarn around stitch (bring yarn to back if purling, bring yarn to front if knitting) and return to LH needle. Turn work and begin working back in the opposite direction.

DIRECTIONS

BACK

With smaller needles, CO 86 (90, 98, 106) sts. Work in k2, p2 rib for 13½ (14, 14½, 15)".

ARMHOLE SHAPING

BO 6 sts at beg of next 2 rows. BO 1 st at each armhole edge every other row 6 (6, 8, 9) times—62 (66, 70, 76) sts. Work even until armhole meas 6½ (6¾, 7, 7½)", ending with a WS row.

See page 146

BACK NECK SHAPING

Work 16 (18, 20, 23) sts in rib, k30, work last 16 (18, 20, 23) sts in rib.

Next row (WS): Work 16 (18, 20, 23) sts in rib, k30, *stop,* do not finish row. Turn work to RS and k30, do not finish row. Turn work to WS and p30; work 2 more rows in St st; then BO loosely.

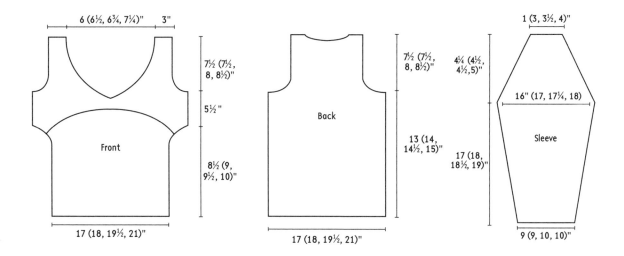

Front

6 (6½, 6¾, 7¼)"   3"

7½ (7½, 8, 8½)"

5½"

8½ (9, 9½, 10)"

17 (18, 19½, 21)"

Back

7½ (7½, 8, 8½)"

13 (14, 14½, 15)"

17 (18, 19½, 21)"

Sleeve

1 (3, 3½, 4)"

4¼ (4½, 4½,5)"

16" (17, 17¼, 18)

17 (18, 18½, 19)"

9 (9, 10, 10)"

SHAPE SHOULDERS

With WS facing, attach yarn to neck edge of left shoulder sts and complete row. Attach 2nd ball of yarn to neck edge of right shoulder. Working both shoulders at one time, BO 2 sts from each neck edge twice, then BO 1 st every row twice. BO rem 10 (12, 14, 17) sts.

FRONT

Work as for back until piece meas 8½ (9, 9½, 10)" from beg.

Start short-row shaping to create empire waist as foll:

First set: (RS) work in rib to last 3 sts, W&T; (WS) work in rib to last 3 sts, W&T.

2nd set: (RS) work in rib to last 7 sts, W&T; (WS) work in rib to last 7 sts, W&T.

Cont short rows, always working to 4 sts from last W&T every row until 8 sts rem between last 2 W&T sts, end with a WS row.

Next row (RS): Work to end of row, k *all* sts, taking care to knit wrap tog with st.

Next row (WS): K the entire row, again working wrap tog with st as above. Work 4 more rows garter st.

BUST SHAPING

Change to larger needles. K3, ssk, k 16 (18, 20, 23), inc 1 in each of next 6 (6, 7, 8) sts, k 32 (32, 34, 34) sts, inc 1 in each of next 6 (6, 7, 8) sts, k to last 5 sts, k2tog, k3—96 (100, 110, 120) sts; p 1 row.

Dec row (RS): K3, ssk, k to last 5 sts, k2tog, k3. Rep dec row every other row twice more—90 (94, 104, 114) sts; p 1 row.

DIVIDE FOR V-NECK

With RS facing, left cup: K 3, ssk, k 38 (40, 45, 50), sl 1 st knitwise, k1. Join 2nd skein of yarn and work right cup: K1, sl 1 knitwise, k to end. Cont working both sides at the same time with separate skeins of yarn.

**Dec row 1 (WS): right cup: p3, p2tog, p to end; left cup: p all sts.

**Dec row 2 (RS): left cup: k3, ssk, k to last 2 sts, slip 1 knitwise, k1; right cup: k1, slip 1 knitwise, k to end. Rep last 2 rows 7 times more, then row 1 once—36 (38, 43, 48) sts each side.

ARMHOLE SHAPING

Row 1 (RS): left cup: BO 6 sts, k3, sssk, k to last 2 sts, slip 1 knitwise; k1; right cup: k1, slip 1 knitwise, k to end.

Row 2 (WS): right cup: BO 6 sts, p3, p3tog, p to end; left cup: p to end.

Row 3: left cup: k3, sssk, k to last 2 sts, slip 1 knitwise, k1; right cup: k1, slip 1 knitwise, k to end.

Row 4: right cup: p3, p3tog, p to end; left cup: p to end.

Rep last 2 rows 3 (3, 5, 7) times more; then rep **dec row 1–2 above (dec 1 st each row) 10 (10, 9, 7) times—10 (12, 14, 17) sts rem each side.

Work even until armhole measures 8 (8¼, 8½, 9)". BO all sts.

SLEEVE

CO 46 (46, 50, 50) sts. Working in k2, p2 rib, inc 1 st each edge every 4th row 10 times, then every 6th row 7 (9, 8, 10) times—80 (84, 86, 90 sts). Work even until piece measures 17 (18, 18½, 19)" from beg, end with a WS row.

CAP SHAPING

BO 6 sts at beg of next 2 rows—68 (72, 74, 78) sts. Cont BO as foll:

BO 3 sts at beg of next 4 rows—56 (60, 62, 66) sts.

BO 1 st at beg next 18 (20, 20, 22) rows—38 (40, 42, 44) sts.

BO 6 sts at beg next 4 rows—14 (16, 18, 20) sts rem.

BO all sts.

FINISHING

Carefully steam-block pieces by holding a steam iron several inches above work. Do not oversteam or press iron directly onto the knitted ribbing or it will lose its elasticity.

Sew shoulders together. Turn under 1 st at either side of front neck opening, turning on the slipped stitch, and stitch in place on underside. Turn back neck facing under, turning on the rev St st row, and stitch in place. Pin sleeve in place, matching center top of sleeve to shoulder seam, and each sleeve cap edge to the start of armhole shaping. Stitch sleeve in place. Sew underarm and side seams.

ABOUT ANNIE

How can I put into words the love affair among my fingers, yarn, and a couple of sticks? A friend taught me the knit stitch and I promptly forgot it. A few days later, I reinvented the stitch for myself, and—without realizing it—began knitting in a totally unconventional style. As fast and easy as my knitting technique is, it looks weird to most knitters who sometimes try to show me the "right way" to knit. I tell my knitting students now, "I don't care how you knit, I only care that you understand why your stitches look the way they do."

Today I knit for a living: I design for most of the major knitting magazines and have an instructional Web site where I offer tips and kits to make knit furniture and other unusual items (http://www.modeknit.com). My advice to new knitters is: Knit with confidence. Don't run with the pack!

KATE WISSON

the manly sweater

A s a self-taught knitter, I never realized that certain things weren't "supposed" to be tackled by beginners. So when I wanted to make a sweater for my husband, I just sketched out a design, took all of the applicable measurements, and figured out the numbers from there. I wanted it to suit him, as well as other body types and tastes, so I went for something both classic and comfortable. The sweater was a big hit. It's not only the first piece I designed, but the first adult sweater I ever knit.

SKILLS	PAGE
CAST ON	29
KNIT	33
PURL	47
CHANGE COLOR	43
DECREASE	63
BIND OFF	40
SEW SEAM	73

Sizes

Small (Medium, Large, Extra-Large)

Finished chest: 41 (45, 50, 56)"

Finished length: 25 (26^1/$_2$, 28^1/$_2$, 29^1/$_2$)"

Materials

Brown Sheep Company, *Lamb's Pride Worsted* (85% wool/15% mohair; 4 oz/190 yds)

MC: 4 (5, 6, 7) skeins #M04 Charcoal Heather

A: 2 (3, 3, 4) skeins #M83 Raspberry

B: 1 skein #M05 Onyx

US 8 (5mm) knitting needles, or size needed to obtain gauge

US 7 (4.5mm) 16" circular needle

Stitch holders

Gauge

19 sts and 26 rows = 4" in k5, p1 rib on larger needles

Color Pattern

Work 1" in B, end with a WS row.

Work 6" in A, end with a WS row.

Work 1" in B, end with a WS row.

Directions

BACK

With MC and larger needles, CO 97 (109, 121, 133) sts.

Set-up row: K3, p1, *k5, p1; rep from * to last 3 sts, k3. Work in k5, p1 rib as set for 16^1/$_2$ (17, 18, 18^1/$_2$)". **At the same time,** work 8^1/$_2$ (9, 10, 10^1/$_2$)" in MC, end with a WS row, then work color pattern.

With MC, work 1 row even.

ARMHOLES

BO 3 (4, 6, 7) sts at beg of next 2 rows. Dec 1 st each side of next row; then every other row 2 (3, 5, 6) times total—87 (95, 99, 107) sts.**

Work even until work measures 7^1/$_2$ (8^1/$_2$, 9^1/$_2$, 10)" from beg of armholes, end with a WS row.

SHAPE NECK AND SHOULDERS

Right side: *BO 7 (8, 8, 9) sts, work 25 (28, 28, 31) sts, turn. Place rem sts on a holder. Dec 1 st from the neck edge every row 4 times; **at the same time,** BO 7 (8, 8, 9) sts from shoulder edge 3 times. Break off yarn.

Left side: With WS facing, join yarn to shoulder edge. Work as for left side from *—23 (23, 27, 27) sts rem on holder for back neck.

FRONT

Work as for back and armholes to **. Work even until work measures 3 (3½, 4, 4½)" from beg of armholes.

SHAPE NECK AND SHOULDERS

Left side: *Work 42 (46, 48, 52) sts, ssk, turn. Place rem sts on a holder. Dec 1 st at neck edge every other row 8 (8, 11, 11) times then every third row 3 (3, 2, 2) times.

At the same time, when the armhole measures 7½ (8, 8½, 9)", work shoulder shaping: BO 7 (8, 8, 9) sts from shoulder edge 4 times. Break off yarn.

Right side: With WS facing, join yarn to shoulder edge and work as for left side from *.

SLEEVES

With MC and larger needles, CO 45 (49, 49, 51) sts.

Set-up row (RS): K0 (0, 0, 1), *p1, k5; rep from * to last 1 (1, 1, 2) sts, p1, k0 (0, 0, 1). Work even in k5, p1 rib, inc 1 st each edge of next and every 4th row 0 (0, 2, 3) times; then every 6th row 15 (18, 19, 20) times—77 (85, 91, 97) sts. **At the same time,** work 10 (11, 11½, 12)" in MC, end with a WS row; then work color pattern.

With MC, work 1 row even.

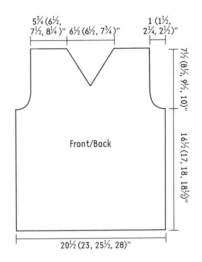

See page 140

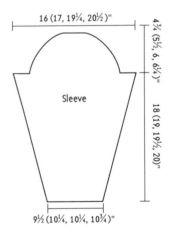

Front/Back

5¾ (6½, 7½, 8¼)"   6½ (6½, 7¾)"   1 (1½, 2¼, 2½)"

7½ (8½, 9½, 10)"

16½ (17, 18, 18½)"

20½ (23, 25½, 28)"

16 (17, 19¼, 20½)"

4¾ (5½, 6, 6¼)"

Sleeve

18 (19, 19½, 20)"

9½ (10¼, 10¼, 10¾)"

CAP SHAPING

Cont in rib, BO 3 (4, 6, 7) sts at beg of next 2 rows. Dec 1 st at each edge of next and every other row 7 (10, 11, 12) times; then every row 14 times. BO 3 sts at beg of next 4 rows. BO rem 15 (17, 17, 19) sts.

NECKBAND

With RS facing, B and smaller needle; pu and k 35 sts up right front, 4 sts down back neck, 23 (23, 27, 27) sts from back holder, 4 sts up back neck, 35 sts down left front—101 (101, 105, 105) sts.

Beg with p1 on WS, work k1, p1 rib for 6 rows. BO loosely in pattern.

Sew down one edge of neckband to the inside of the neck shaping, then overlap the other neckband edge and sew it to the outside of the neck shaping.

FINISHING

Sew shoulder seams, then set in sleeves, matching center p st with shoulder seam. Use mattress st to sew body and sleeve seams. Weave in ends.

ABOUT KATE

I began knitting in 2000 when, on a whim, I purchased a Susan Bates learn-to-knit book on eBay. While I waited for it to arrive, I purchased a few skeins of cheapo acrylic yarn and some needles. Rather than knit a swatch as most beginners do, I followed a pattern for a ribbed hat and taught myself each technique required as I went along. Following my "if it feels right and looks right, it is right" knitting philosophy, I've gone from absolute beginner to professional knitter and freelance designer—a true testament to finding one's passion and letting it blossom. I live in Toronto, Ontario, where I work from home and take care of my children.

DIANA RUPP
cowl and Howl set

I designed this fitted cowl-neck sweater about five years ago, because I wanted to get away from those big, boxy styles that weren't doing anybody any favors (if you know what I mean). A cowl neck was a must (I grew up in the '70s and find myself happily stuck in that decade). I was also determined to make the pattern easy enough so that even a beginner could knit it without having a nervous breakdown. The matching dog sweater, "Howl," came later, but it makes sense: A girl's best friend deserves to be fashionable too.

SKILLS	PAGE
CAST ON	29
KNIT	33
KNIT IN THE ROUND	57
INCREASE	60
DECREASE	63
BIND OFF	40
PICK UP STITCHES	82

See page 147

SIZES

Small (Medium, Large, Extra-Large)

Finished bust: 30^1/$_2$ (32^1/$_2$, 34^1/$_2$, 37^1/$_2$)" Finished length: 23^1/$_2$ (24, 24^1/$_2$, 25)"

MATERIALS

Brown Sheep Company *Lamb's Pride Worsted* (85% wool/15% mohair; 4 oz/190 yds), 5 (6, 6, 7) skeins #M180 Ruby Red

US 11 (8mm) needles, or size needed to obtain gauge

US 11 (8mm) double-pointed needles (set of 5)

US 15 (10mm) double-pointed needles (set of 5)

GAUGE

12 sts and 20 rows = 4" in garter st on smaller needles. (Sweater is worked in a loose gauge, so it is very stretchy.)

Note: Even though you're working in garter st, you'll want to choose a right side/wrong side so all your increases and decreases are worked on the same side.

DIRECTIONS

BACK

CO 46 (49, 52, 57) sts. Work 5" in garter st.

Dec row (RS): K2, k2tog, k to last 4 sts, ssk, k2; rep dec row every 6th row twice more—40 (43, 46, 51) sts. Work even until piece meas 11^1/$_2$" from beg.

Inc row (RS): K2, inc1 in next st, k to last 3 sts, inc1 in next st, k2; rep inc row every 6th row twice more—46 (49, 52, 57) sts. Work even until piece meas 15" from beg.

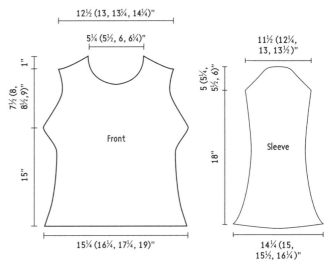

ARMHOLE SHAPING

Dec row (RS): K2, k2tog, k to last 4 sts, ssk, k2; rep dec row every other row 3 (4, 5, 6) times more—38 (39, 40, 43) sts. Work even until armhole meas 7^1⁄2 (8, 8^1⁄2, 9)".

NECK AND SHOULDER SHAPING

BO 3 sts at beg of next 4 rows, then 5 (5, 5, 6) sts at beg of next 2 rows. BO rem 16 (17, 18, 19) sts loosely.

FRONT

Work as for back until armhole meas 6 (6^1⁄2, 7, 7^1⁄2)", end with a WS row.

NECK SHAPING

Next row (RS): Work 14 (14, 14, 15) sts, join another skein of yarn and BO center 10 (11, 12, 13) sts loosely, work to end. Working both sides at once, k one row.

Dec row (RS): K to last 4 sts of first side, ssk, k2; on other side, k2, k2tog, k to end; rep dec row every other row twice more. **At the same time,** when front meas same as back, shape shoulders by BO 3 sts from each shoulder edge twice; then 4 (5, 5, 5) sts once.

BELL-SHAPED SLEEVES

CO 43 (45, 47, 49) sts. Work 2" in garter st.

Dec row (RS): K2, k2tog, k to last 4 sts, ssk, k2; rep dec row every 8th row 3 times more—35 (37, 39, 41) sts. Work even until sleeve meas 18 (18¼, 18½, 18¾)" from beg.

CAP SHAPING

BO 2 sts at beg of next 4 rows. Dec row (RS): K2, k2 tog, k to last 4 sts, ssk, k2; rep dec every other row 4 (5, 6, 7) times more. K 1 row. BO off 3 sts at beg of next 2 rows, BO rem 11 sts.

FINISHING

Sew shoulder seams. Set sleeves into armholes. Sew side and sleeve seams.

COWL

With smaller dpns, pu 52 (54, 56, 58) sts evenly around neck edge. Join and pm indicating beg of rnd. Work St st in the rnd (k all rnds) for 5½". Change to larger dpns and cont until cowl meas 10½" or desired length. BO loosely.

DIANA RUPP

HowL

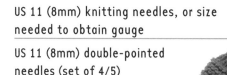

designing your own dog sweater is much easier than following a printed pattern that doesn't take Fido's love handles into consideration. All you have to do is take a few measurements, knit up a couple of rectangles, slap on a turtleneck and cuffs, and voilà!

SKILLS	PAGE
CAST ON	29
KNIT	33
PURL	47
KNIT IN THE ROUND	57
PICK UP STITCHES	82
BIND OFF	40
SEW SEAM	73

MATERIALS

Brown Sheep Company *Lamb's Pride Worsted* (85% wool/15% mohair; 4 oz/190 yds #M180 Ruby Red). One skein was plenty for a chubby Chihuahua; you'll need to guesstimate the yardage needed for a larger dog.

US 11 (8mm) knitting needles, or size needed to obtain gauge

US 11 (8mm) double-pointed needles (set of 4/5)

GAUGE

12 sts and 20 rows = 4" in garter st

DIRECTIONS

Break out a measuring tape and jot down your dog's measurements:

See page 147

A: Length from the top of the front leg over the back to the top of the other front leg.

B: Length from the base of the neck (where the collar would sit) to the base of the tail.

C: Distance around the thickest part of the body.

D: Length from the neck to where you want the sweater to end underneath (remember bodily functions).

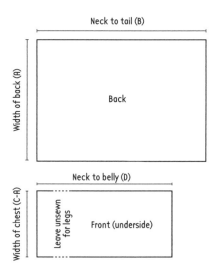

BODY

Begin with the "back" rectangle. CO the number of sts you'd need to match measurement A, deducting 2" for stretch (for a dog with a 16"-wide back, for instance, you'd cast on enough stitches to make a 14"-wide piece—at this gauge, that would mean 42 stitches). Work in garter st to the desired length B. BO loosely.

This next piece is the underside of the sweater (or the distance from the neck to the beginning of the belly), so it'll be several inches shorter than the back. CO the number of sts to make up the amount "missing" from measurement C (C minus A). For example: If you made a 16"-wide back (before 2" deduction), and the dog is 21" around at the widest part of his body, the bottom rectangle will need to be the difference of 5". Work to desired length D. BO loosely.

After you've made the two rectangles, sew them together for 2" from the neck edge, leaving 3" unsewn for leg openings; then sew the rest of the pieces together (see diagram).

CUFFS

With dpns, pu sts evenly (about 3 sts for every 1" of fabric) around the leg openings and work in garter stitch (1 row knit, 1 row purl) for 2".

COWL

With dpns, pu sts evenly (about 3 st for every 1" of fabric) around neck edge and work in St st (k all rnds). The cowl will roll, with the purl side showing. When work measures 5", BO loosely.

ABOUT DIANA

My great-grandmother and my mom were the ultimate craft role models, and I'm still trying to live up to them. A knitter since the age of eight, I have yet to lose my (some would say obsessive) enthusiasm for all things handmade. In addition to designing an eponymous line of knitwear and patterns for kids and grown-ups, I spend my time teaching at MAKE, a knitting and design studio in Manhattan (www.makeworkshop.com).

BECKY DELGADO

peppermint twist

U ntil recently, I had knit things only for my brother's children or for my son. One day, while visiting my local yarn shop, I admired a striped sweater I saw hanging in the display window, and the yarn shop owner—who had by then become my knitting buddy—told me that I could easily knit it for myself. I picked out yarn and she pulled out her calculator, showing me how to estimate yarn amounts for the project. With a bit of help from her and my knitting books, I came up with an easy pattern and knit the sweater. For the first time ever, I had a custom-made sweater! What I love about it is that it has all the colors I've always wanted in a sweater, but couldn't find until I came up with it myself. And it's the only sweater I've ever owned that fits me the way I want— thanks to raglan armholes, waist shaping, and the drape of the cotton yarn.

SKILLS	PAGE
CAST ON	29
KNIT	33
PURL	47
CHANGE COLOR	43
KNIT IN THE ROUND	57
INCREASE	60
BIND OFF	40
SEW SEAM	73

SIZES

Small (Medium, Large, Extra-Large)

Finished bust: 34 (36, 39, 42)"

Finished length: $18^{1}/_{2}$ ($19^{1}/_{2}$, $20^{1}/_{4}$, 21)"

MATERIALS

Rowan *Cotton Glace* (100% cotton; 50g/125 yds)

MC: 7 skeins #724 Bubbles

A: 2 skeins #799 Glee

B: 1 skein #805 Passion

C: Phildar *Sunset* (65% acetate/35% polyester; 25g/219 yds), 1 skein Indien

US 2 (3mm) 16" circular needle

US 2 (3mm) knitting needles, or size needed to obtain gauge

GAUGE

24 sts and 34 rows = 4" in St st with *Cotton Glace*

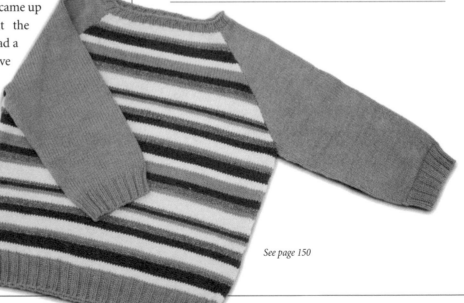

See page 150

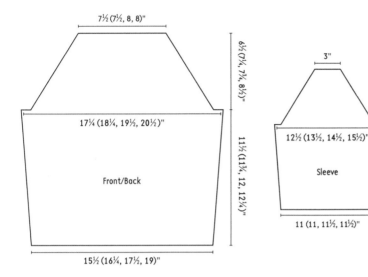

7½ (7½, 8, 8)"

6½ (7¼, 7¾, 8½)"

17¼ (18¼, 19½, 20½)"

11½ (11¾, 12, 12¼)"

Front/Back

15½ (16¼, 17½, 19)"

3"

6½ (7¼, 7¾, 8½)"

12½ (13½, 14½, 15½)"

10 (10½, 11, 11½)"

Sleeve

11 (11, 11½, 11½)"

COLOR PATTERN (IN ST ST)

4 rows A, 6 rows B, 2 rows C, 2 rows MC, 6 rows A, 4 rows B, 4 rows C, 4 rows A, 2 rows MC, 2 rows B, 2 rows C, 8 rows A, 2 rows MC, 4 rows C, 4 rows B, 6 rows MC.

Rep these 62 rows throughout patt.

Note: C is worked with 2 strands held tog.

DIRECTIONS

FRONT AND BACK

With MC, CO 94 (98, 106, 114) sts and work even in k2, p2 rib until piece meas 1½" from beg, end with a RS row. P one row. Cont in St st foll color patt for 18 rows, ending with a WS row.

SHAPE WAIST

Inc row (RS): K2, M1, k to last 2 sts, M1, k2. Rep inc row every 14th row 3 times, then every 12th row 1 (2, 2, 1) time(s)—104 (110, 118, 124) sts. Work even until

piece meas 11½ (11¾, 12, 12¼)" from beg, ending with a WS row.

SHAPE RAGLAN ARMHOLES

BO 3 (3, 4, 4) sts at the beg of next 2 rows—98 (104, 110, 116) sts rem. Cont to work even in color patt; **at the same time,** *BO 1 st at beg of next 2 rows, then work 2 rows even; rep from * once more; then BO 1 st at beg of every row until 46 (46, 48, 48) sts rem. Place rem sts on a stitch holder.

SLEEVES

With MC, CO 66 (66, 70, 70) sts and work even in k2, p2 rib until piece meas 1½" from beg, ending with a RS row. P 1 row. Inc row (RS): K2, M1, k to last 2 sts, M1, k2. Rep inc row every 12th (8th, 8th, 6th) row 4 (7, 8, 11) times more—76 (82, 88, 94) sts. Work even in St st until piece meas 10 (10½, 11, 11½)" from beg.

SHAPE SLEEVE CAPS

BO 3 (3, 4, 4) sts at the beg of next 2 rows—70 (76, 80, 86) sts. *BO 1 st at beg of next 2 rows, then work 2 rows even; rep from * once more, then BO 1 st at beg of every row until 18 sts rem. Place rem sts on a stitch holder.

FINISHING

With MC threaded on a yarn needle, sew raglan sleeve caps to front and back armholes. Sew side and sleeve seams.

NECKBAND

Place all sts at neck edge on the circular needle—128 (128, 132, 132) sts. Join yarn at back left seam.

Rnd 1: **K2tog, p2, *k2, p2; rep from * to 2 sts from next seam, skp; rep from ** around—120 (120, 124, 124) sts.

Rnd 2: K1, p2, *k2, p2; rep from * to last st, p1.

Rep rnd 2 four times more or until neckband measures approx 1". BO all sts firmly in ribbing (but not too tightly) to keep ribbing from flaring out at the neck.

ABOUT BECKY

Most of my life, I've been focused on building my career as a corporate lawyer. I never dreamed that someday I'd be passionate about knitting. I remember chuckling at a partner in my firm when he admitted that he knitted to relieve stress. But in the summer of 2000, I was expecting my first child and confined to complete bed rest. Bored, I told my husband that I wished I knew how to knit so I could make baby clothes. The next day he brought home knitting needles, wool, a beginner's manual, and a layette pattern book. My husband sat down and showed me how to cast on (he remembered seeing his grandmother do it years before). With his help and my beginner's manual, I knit a baby scarf in garter stitch. That's all it took. During the rest of the summer and in the months following my son's birth, I put together several baby sweaters and ensembles. Then I put up a knitting site at www.skinnyrabbit.com, where I blab incessantly about all things knitting. Thanks to my site, I've come into contact with knitters of all ages from all over the world.

KAREN BAUMER

tank girl

I conceived this design as a way to use a bag of *Goa* yarn that was given to me by a friend who owned a yarn shop. I really like tank tops with wide, squared-off necklines—they're a good way to show off muscles and broad shoulders, if you like that sort of thing.

SKILLS	PAGE
CAST ON	29
KNIT	33
PURL	47
DECREASE	63
3-NEEDLE BIND-OFF	80
SEW SEAM	73

SIZES

Small (Medium, Large, Extra-Large)

Finished bust: 33 (36, 39, 42)"

Finished length: 19 (20, 21, 22)"

MATERIALS

GGH *Goa* (50% cotton/50% acrylic, 50g/66 yds), 8 (8, 9, 10) skeins #24

US 9 (5.5mm) needles, or size needed to obtain gauge

Stitch holders

GAUGE

17 sts and 21 rows = 4" in p2, k1, rib

STITCH PATTERN

P2, K1 RIB

Row 1 (RS): *P2, k1; rep from * across, end p2.

Row 2: *K2, p1; rep from * across, end k2.

Rep rows 1–2 for patt.

REVERSE STOCKINETTE

Row 1 (RS): P.

Row 2 (WS): K.

Rep rows 1–2 for patt.

DIRECTIONS

Note: Normally it is preferable to start a new ball of yarn at the edge, especially with a chunky yarn such as Goa. This is what you should do on this garment when you are still below the armhole decreases. However, since the armhole openings are self-edged, once you are working at or above the armhole decreases, it is preferable to add new balls near, but not directly at, the edge of the fabric. This can be done less noticeably if it is done in the 2 stitches forming the "ditch" between ribs (the p2 sections on the right side or the k2 sections on the wrong side). I recommend working with the old and new strands held together for those two stitches, leaving a tail hanging

See page 146

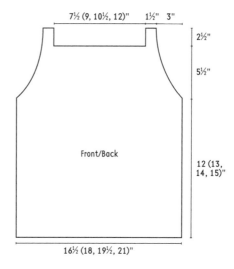

7½ (9, 10½, 12)"   1½"   3"

2½"

5½"

Front/Back

12 (13, 14, 15)"

16½ (18, 19½, 21)"

BACK

CO 71 (77, 83, 89) sts and work even in p2, k1 rib for 12 (13, 14, 15)", ending with a WS row. BO 6 sts at beg of the next 2 rows—59 (65, 71, 77) sts. From this point on, maintain the edge st on each side in rev St st.

SHAPE ARMHOLES

Maintaining rib patt as well as possible at dec points, dec 1 st each side every RS row 7 times as foll: P1, k2tog, rib to last 3 sts, k2tog tbl, p1—45 (51, 57, 63) sts. Piece should now beg p1, k1, p2 and end p2, k1, p1 on RS.

Cont to work even in rib until piece meas 17¾ (18¾, 19¾, 20¾)" from bottom edge, end with a WS row.

SHAPE NECK

Rib 6 sts, BO center 33 (39, 45, 51) sts, rib to end of row. There should now be 6 live sts on each side of the BO section. Work each side separately from this point as foll: Cont in rib over 6 sts (on RS, p1, k1, p2, k1, p1) until strap meas approx 1¼" (on RS). Place sts on a holder and cut yarn, leaving an 18" tail (you can use it later to BO the straps tog). Attach yarn at neck edge of the rem 6 sts and work to match the other side.

FRONT

Work as for back until piece meas 16½ (17½, 18½, 19½)" from bottom edge, end with a WS row. Shape neck as for back and make straps 2½" long, or length needed to match back piece.

FINISHING

Join shoulder seams with 3-needle bind-off. Sew side seams and weave in all ends.

ABOUT KAREN

See Karen's bio on page 181.

JENNA WILSON
Little black top

One of the staples in my wardrobe is the little black top—a plain, black, sleeveless, fitted top that can be worn just about anywhere, with just about anything. This particular little black top has a funnel neck and some subtle texture in a narrow front panel of garter stitch. The simplicity of the pattern keeps finishing steps to a minimum, because the hems and armholes are worked in garter stitch as well. There's a keyhole opening at the back neck, fastened with a button. The design includes an optional knitted tie belt finished with beads. If you find knitting the belt onerous (it is more than six feet long), you can skip it altogether, or cheat and make a tie belt using store-bought cording.

SKILLS	PAGE
CAST ON	29
KNIT	33
PURL	47
INCREASE	60
DECREASE	63
SHORT-ROW SHAPING (SEE BELOW)	
I-CORD	87
CROCHET CHAIN	99
BIND OFF	40
SEW SEAM	73

See page 149

SIZES

Small (Medium, Large, Extra-Large)

Finished bust: 33 (36, 39, 42)"

Finished length: 19½ (20, 20½, 21½)"

Note: The instructions include the option to add short-row shaping to the front to accommodate a larger bust.

Materials

FOR TOP:

Classic Elite *Provence* (100% cotton; 125g/256 yds), 3 (3, 3, 3) skeins #2652

US 5 (3.75mm) knitting needles, or size needed to obtain gauge

One $3/8$" button

FOR BELT:

G/6 crochet hook

Beads with hole large enough to thread yarn through (I used cube-shaped alphabet beads from artbeads.com to spell out "Glam Gal")

US 5 (3.75mm) double-pointed needles (2 needed for I-cord version)

Gauge

22 sts and 30 rows = 4" in St st

Stitch Pattern

WRAP & TURN (W&T)

On RS: K to the point indicated, then slip the next st from the left-hand needle onto the right-hand needle purlwise. Bring yarn to front and turn the work so that the WS faces you. Slip the first st from what is now the left-hand needle to the right-hand needle, then bring the working yarn between the two needles so that it extends to the front of the work. (The one st you've been slipping back and forth is now wrapped with a loop of yarn around its base, and the yarn is now on the side facing you.)

On WS: P to the point indicated in the instructions, then slip the next st from the left-hand needle to the right-hand needle purlwise. Bring yarn to back, and turn so that the RS faces you. Slip the first st from what is now the left-hand needle to the right-hand needle, then bring yarn to back.

TO HIDE WRAPS

On RS: Insert the right-hand needle from the front and under the front of the wrap (not the stitch). Lift the wrap, insert the right-hand needle through the stitch, and k both tog as one.

On WS: Insert the right-hand needle from the front and under the back of the wrap (not the stitch). Lift the wrap onto the left-hand needle, placing it next to the stitch that had been wrapped. Now insert the right-hand needle through both the wrap and the stitch, and p as one.

STRETCHY BIND-OFF

At the neckline, use a stretchy BO to add some elasticity and make sure the garment will fit around your neck.

* Work 2 sts as usual (k or p, depending on whether you're on the RS or WS); then pass the first st you worked on the right-hand needle over the second st you worked on the right-hand needle, and drop this first st off the needles completely (just like a normal BO step), but then return the remaining st from the right-hand needle to the left-hand needle, and repeat from *.

Directions

BACK

CO 92 (100, 108, 116) sts.

Work 2 rows in garter st.

Work 11 rows in St st.

Dec row (RS): Dec 1 st at each end of row. Rep dec row every 8th row 4 times more—82 (90, 98, 106) sts.

Work 5 rows even.

Inc row: Inc 1 st at each end of row. Rep inc row every 6th row 4 times more—92 (100, 108, 116) sts.**

Work 10 (10, 14, 18) rows even, end with a WS row.

ARMHOLE SHAPING

BO 5 (5, 6, 7) sts at beg of next 2 rows—82 (90, 96, 102) sts. From this point until the shoulder shaping, you will be working the first and last 3 sts in garter st.

Dec row (RS): Work 3 garter sts, dec 1 st, work to last 5 sts, dec 1 st, work 3 garter sts. Rep dec row every row 3 (4, 4, 6) times more, every other row 3 (4, 5, 6) times, then every 3rd row 0 (1, 2, 2) time(s)—68 (70, 72, 72) sts.

BACK NECK OPENING

Work even until armhole meas 4 (4½, 4½, 5)", end with a WS row.

K 34 (35, 36, 36) sts, sl rem sts to a holder. Work 19 rows even across the first 34 (35, 36, 36) sts, working the first and last 3 sts in garter st, end with a WS row.

SHAPE SHOULDER

BO 2 sts at the beg of the next row, then every other row 5 times more—22 (23, 24, 24) sts.

Dec 1 st at outside edge of every 3rd row 2 times—20 (21, 22, 22) sts. Work 2 rows garter st, then BO rem sts with a stretchy BO.

To work the other half of the back neck opening, place sts from holder onto needle and join yarn at the back neck opening edge. Work 19 or 27 (as for back neck

opening) rows even, working the first and last 3 sts in garter st, end with a RS row.

Shape the shoulder and the neck in a similar manner to the first half.

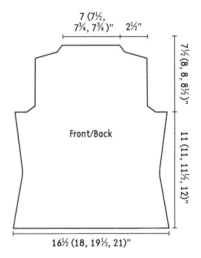

FRONT

Note: When working instructions same as back, your front stitch count should be 1 less than those noted for the back.

CO 91 (99, 107, 115) sts.

Work 2 rows in garter st.

Work 40 (44, 48, 51) St st, pm, work 11 garter st, pm, work 40 (44, 48, 51) St st. Follow instructions for the back to **, keeping the center 11 sts in garter st; end with a WS row.

Optional short-row bust shaping: A short row is a row of knitting that does not extend all the way across the knitted piece. This technique is often used to provide a little extra room for a large bust—without it, the garment might "ride up" at the front hem. By following the instructions below, you'll be shaping the bust and adding about 1½" to the length of the front.

*K until there are 5 sts rem on the left-hand needle, W&T. P back to the beg, but stop when there are 5 sts rem on the left-hand needle again, W&T. This is the first pair of short rows.

Rep from * 5 times more, working each subsequent pair of short rows when there are 7, 9, 11, 13, then 15 sts rem on the left-hand needle.

After the final W&T, work to the end of the row. Pu and k 5 wrapped sts and hide those wraps. Once you reach the end of the row, turn and work back, pu and p the rem 5 wrapped sts and hide those wraps.

Work 10 (10, 14, 18) rows even (if you worked the optional short rows, be sure to pu the wraps and k them with the wrapped sts on that first row across), end with a WS row.

ARMHOLE SHAPING

Work same as back.

Work even on 67 (69, 71, 71) sts until armhole meas same as back, end with a WS row.

SHAPE SHOULDERS

BO 2 sts at the beg of the next 12 rows—43 (45, 47, 47) sts.

Dec 1 st at each edge of every 3rd row 2 times—39 (41, 43, 43) sts. Work 2 rows garter st, then BO rem sts with a stretchy BO.

BELT

The belt was designed to be worn doubled, with 8" dangling ends. Wrap a tape measure around your torso where you intend to wear the belt—your waist or a few inches lower down. The total length of the belt will be twice the length of the tape measure around your torso, plus 16", or about 70"–80". Of course, that's a lot of knitting. If you don't want to wear the belt doubled, then the total length of the belt will be the length of tape measure wrapped around your torso plus 16".

Work 3-st I-cord to desired length.

Thread the bead(s) onto each end of the belt. Once the belt is through, tie a knot in the ends to keep the bead(s) from sliding off.

FINISHING

Block pieces and sew them together at the side and shoulder seams. Sew the button to the upper edge of one side of the back neck opening, then make a small yarn loop with a crochet chain on the upper edge of the other side of the back neck opening.

Make two 1" belt loops using chain st. Sew one belt loop to each side seam in the desired place (which you noted when you measured the length of the belt).

ABOUT JENNA

See Jenna's bio on page 206.

CATHERINE STINSON

Queen of Hearts and Wonder Woman bikinis

See page 148

A lady in my Stitch 'n Bitch got everyone into a tizzy a couple of years ago when she arrived with a pattern for a knit bikini she'd found on the Internet. Well, she knit the bottoms, and they were such a crazy wide shape that they became the "butt" of many a Stitch 'n Bitch joke. We'd sit around brainstorming uses for them, since they obviously couldn't be used as bikini bottoms— slingshot was the favorite suggestion. I tried the pattern myself, and the bottoms ended up so small that I couldn't get them on, even after several tries at making them bigger. We burned that pattern in frustration. Through trial, error, and lots of standing naked in front of the mirror, I came up with something that works. The first prototype was made just in time for a Valentine's Day party, so obviously it had to be red with pink hearts. The Wonder Woman thunderbolts were more of a springtime invention.

This is a cute, slightly slutty string bikini. Make it in a cotton/lycra blend and head to the beach, or make it in something soft and fuzzy for use behind closed doors.

SKILLS	PAGE
CAST ON	29
KNIT	33
PURL	47
INCREASE	60
DECREASE	63
INTARSIA	92
READ CHART	55
CROCHET CHAIN	99
SINGLE CROCHET	100
BIND OFF	40

SIZES

Small (Medium, Large, Extra-Large)

To fit bust: A (B, C, D) cup; hips: 36 (38, 40, 42)"

MATERIALS

Classic Elite *Star* (99% cotton/1% lycra; 50g/ 126 yds)

QUEEN OF HEARTS

MC: 2 skeins #5158 Scarlet

CC: 1 skein #5119 Blush

WONDER WOMAN

MC: 2 skeins #5149 Indigo Bunting

CC: 1 skein # 5168 Firefly

US 6 (4mm) knitting needles, or size needed to obtain gauge

1 yard ¼" elastic for waistband OR bikini-style panties

G/6 crochet hook

Gauge

24 sts and 40 rows = 4" in St st

Directions

Note: The finished bikini pieces are quite small, but they are intended to be worn stretched, to fit. If you're bigger than a D cup, you could try adding a few stitches to make it bigger, though a knit string bikini might not be the thing for you anyway.

Cups

With MC, CO on 31 (35, 37, 41) sts. This will make the base of a triangle about 6 (6½, 7¼, 8)" across the bottom when it's done. Work 22 (24, 26, 28) rows in St st.

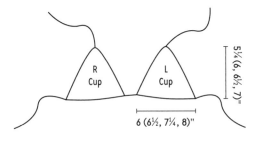

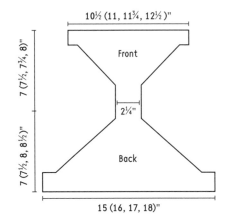

Beg: RS dec row: K13 (15, 16, 18), k2tog tbl, k1, k2tog, k 13 (15, 16, 18).

WS dec row: P 12 (14, 15, 17), p2tog, p1, p2tog tbl, p 12 (14, 15, 17).

Cont as established, dec 2 sts every row and working 1 less st before and after each dec until you have 3 sts left. K3tog or p3tog (depending on which side you're working on)—1 st.

At the same time, beg small heart chart on row 13 (15, 17, 19) as foll: k 11 (13, 14, 16) sts, work 9 chart sts, k 11 (13, 14, 16) sts; OR the small thunderbolt chart on row 11 (13, 15, 17) as foll: k 12 (14, 15, 17) sts, work 7 chart sts, k 12 (14, 15, 17) sts, end with row 22 (24, 26, 28).

Neck Strap

Place the 1 st from the top of the triangle onto your crochet hook. Ch for about 14" to 18", or as long as needed to reach up around your neck and tie. It will be kind of curly at the ends, so it's okay if it's a bit too long. Cut and pull the end through the last st. Parade around in front of the mirror half-naked and imagine how great it will look when it's done.

Finishing

Once you have 2 cups, you need to make the strap that holds them together and ties around the back.

With crochet hook, ch about 48", or whatever length you need to go around your rib cage and tie at the back. Cut and pull end through.

Find the middle of the strap. You're going to want to attach the inside bottom corners of the cups (where your cleavage is) pretty close to the middle of the strap. For skinny ladies with close-together boobs, you won't want to leave any space between the triangles. For bigger ladies, you might want to leave ½" or so in the middle.

Beg at the middle of the strap (or close to it) with RS facing, attach yarn and sc the strap to the bottom of one of the cups, attaching one k st to each ch as foll:

Start with 1 st on the hook. *Insert hook through 1 st of the ch and 1 st of the cup. Make a loop and pull it through both ch and cup (you will have a new st and the original st on the hook). Loop again and pull it through both sts. Rep from * to end of cup. Weave in the ends.

Make sure everything is facing the right way before you attach the 2nd cup. Count back 31 (35, 37, 41) ch sts from the middle (plus whatever you're leaving as cleavage space), and sc the cup to the strap from the outside bottom corner (near your armpit) to the inside.

BOTTOMS

Note: There's a "choose your own adventure" quality to these instructions, because every booty is unique and deserves special attention.

FRONT

With MC, CO 63 (67, 71, 75) sts. Work 17 (18, 19, 20) rows in St st.

BO 5 (6, 7, 8) sts at the beg of next 2 rows—53 (55, 57, 59) sts. Cont in St st, dec 1 st at each end of every row 19 (20, 21, 22) times (k2tog or p2tog)—15 sts.

At the same time, beg large heart chart on row 11 as foll: K 23 (25, 27, 29), work 17 charts sts, k 23 (25, 27, 29) sts; OR the large thunderbolt chart on row 9 as foll: k 24 (26, 28, 30) sts, work 14 chart sts, k 25 (27, 29, 31) sts, working motifs in CC. Remember that you're working upside down. The charts cont into the dec part, so stay alert.

CROTCH PANEL

Work 28 (30, 32, 34) rows in St st, keeping first and last 2 sts in garter st.

BACK

Note: If you have a very round, plump derriere, you can do a few more inc row A and a few less row B. If you have a very flat bum, you can do the opposite. But don't go overboard. Your bum is probably more normal than you think.

Inc row A: Inc 1 st at beg and end of every row. Rep 24 (26, 28, 30) times.

Inc row B: Inc 1 st at beg only of every row. Rep 24 (26, 28, 30) times.

FITTING

Note: This is a crucial stage to make sure it's going to fit around your thighs. You will almost certainly regret it if you don't take the trouble. As you're getting close to the end of the inc rows, figure out which sides are going to turn into the leg holes, and measure one of them around the top of your leg, where the elastic of your underwear goes. (It would work best to strip down to undies before doing this.) Is it going to make it all the way around? Is it going to be too baggy? Adjust the number of inc rows to fit. Making it fit your thighs should also take care of making it fit your butt.

Once you've fixed it to fit around your thighs, cont in St st for 17 (18, 19, 20) more rows and BO *very* loosely.

FINISHING

Sew up the side seams. The elastic isn't in yet, but try it on to make sure you can *get* it on. Don't worry if it's baggy at the hips. But if you can't pull it up, or if won't pull up high enough to cover your crack, you've got a problem and will have to backtrack to the fitting stage to make it bigger.

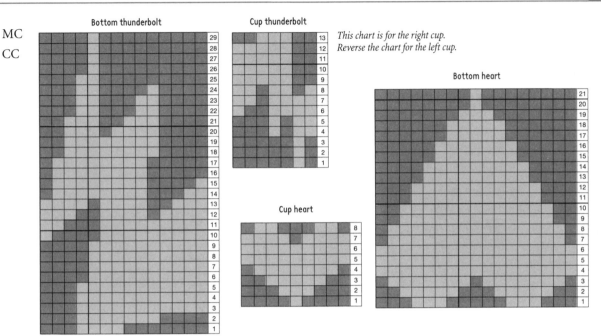

MC

CC

Bottom thunderbolt

Cup thunderbolt

This chart is for the right cup.
Reverse the chart for the left cup.

Bottom heart

Cup heart

Put the elastic in: Attach yarn at the waist seam. With a safety pin, attach the end of the elastic to the inside of the waistband, a little to the right of where you attached the yarn. Now you're going to crochet around the waist, encasing the elastic as you go. With the WS facing you, hold the elastic pretty close to the top of the waistband.

With your crochet hook, pu a p loop a bit below the elastic, then pu a st above the elastic in the top row (elastic is behind hook). You've now got 2 sts on the hook. Pull a loop through both. Chain 1 st. Now keep going around the waist, crocheting into every st and corresponding p loop, rep the following steps:

1. Pu a p loop below the elastic.

2. Pu a st above the elastic (elastic is behind hook).

3. Pull a loop through these 2 sts (2 sts on hook).

4. Pull a loop through both sts.

When you've made it all the way around, take out the safety pin and grab both ends of the elastic. Try it on, and pull the elastic as tight as you want it. Sew or tie the elastic together at the right length. Tuck the ends into the crocheted casing.

Instead of attaching elastic, you can sew a pair of panties to the inside as a liner. This has the added advantage of extra opacity.

And it's done! Parade around in front of the mirror, admiring your fine work.

ABOUT CATHERINE
See Catherine's bio on page 186.

BRENDA JANISH

princess snowball cat bed

● 'm a sucker for eyelash yarns,
and they know it, too—a couple
of skeins mysteriously manage
to jump into my bag every time
I visit my local yarn store. After knitting too many extra-long, skinny,
furry scarves, I decided it was time to
make something more useful with my favorite yarn.
Voilà: a fashionable furry bed for my furry companions.

This project is perfect for beginners—a long garter-
stitch rectangle sewn to the edge of a garter-stitch circle.
That's really all there is to it. Both the pattern and the
intended recipients will forgive any imperfections, so
relax and have fun with it. Your cats will love that you're
finally knitting something for *them*!

SKILLS	PAGE
CAST ON	29
KNIT	33
INCREASE	60
DECREASE	63
BIND OFF	40
SEW SEAM	73

See page 151

SIZES

Standard (Large, for cats over 12 lbs.)

Finished measurements: 14 (17)" diameter, 4" tall

MATERIALS

Lion Brand Yarn *Wool-Ease* (80% acrylic/20% wool;
85g/197 yds)

MC: 1 skein #100 White

CC: 2 skeins #137 Fuchsia

Lion Brand Yarn *Fun Fur* (100% polyester; 50g/
60 yds)

A: 2 (3) skeins #100 White

B: 4 (5) skeins #195 Hot Pink

US 10½ (6.5mm) knitting needles, or size needed
to obtain gauge

Sprayable catnip (optional)

GAUGE

13–14 sts = 4" in garter st with 1 strand each
Wool-Ease and *Fun Fur* held tog.

DIRECTIONS

BASE

With one strand each of MC and A held tog, CO 20
(22) sts.

Working in garter st, inc 1 st each side of the next 7 (9)
rows—34 (40) sts.

Beg with a RS row, inc 1 st each side of next row and
foll 6 (8) RS rows—48 (58) sts.

Work even until piece measures 10½ (12)" from beg,
end with a WS row.

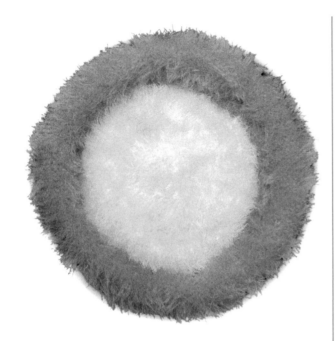

Work in garter st until the length of the side piece meas the same as the number you just wrote down (the circumference of the base) plus ½" for seam allowance.

BO all sts.

FINISHING

With a single strand of CC, sew the short ends of the side piece tog.

Divide the length of the side piece into 4 equal parts and mark each fourth with a pin, placing the first pin at the seam.

Now divide the edge of the base into 4 equal parts and mark each fourth with a pin (imagine it's a clock face and put pins at 12:00, 3:00, 6:00, and 9:00).

With the seam of the side piece facing out, match up the 4 pins in the side piece to the 4 pins in the base and pin together; then match up the rest of the side piece to the edge of the base and pin all the way around, aligning the 2 edges as closely as possible.

With a single strand of either MC or CC, sew the 2 pieces tog.

Weave all ends into the seams.

Now you should have what looks like a giant furry hat!

With all seams facing out, place your cat bed on a flat surface and fold the side piece in half lengthwise to the outside. The side should stand up pretty well on its own and form a cozy all-around wall for your cat bed, but you'll want to make it a little sturdier so it stands up to heavy-duty cat nuzzling.

To do that, use a single strand of leftover B and a yarn needle to sew a single st through both layers of the folded-over side piece, about halfway up from the bottom. Tie the ends of your st into a knot and trim.

Time-saving tip: If you run out of the *Fun Fur* while you're knitting, just tie the end of the new skein to the end of the previous skein with a good strong square knot, and trim the loose ends to match the length of the fur. The knot won't show (honest), and that's one fewer end you'll have to weave in when you're done knitting!

Dec 1 st each side of next row and foll 6 (8) RS rows—34 (40) sts.

Dec 1 st each side of next 7 (9) rows—20(22)sts.

BO all sts.

SIDES

Measure around the edge of the base (the circumference). Write that number down—it should be approx 44 (54)".

With 1 strand each of CC and B held tog, CO 30 sts.

Rep all the way around the wall of the cat bed, placing the sts approx 3" apart.

Now comes the really fun part: Since your cats are probably as well-behaved as mine (ahem) and stay as far away from your knitting as possible (ahem), they may be wary of their new bed at first. To let them know you made it especially for them, spray a little catnip on the bed, let it dry for a few minutes, and put the bed in their favorite napping spot. If your cats are anything like mine, they'll be zonked out in their new bed and having naughty kitty dreams in a matter of minutes.

CLEANING

You don't need to wash cat beds often, because cats actually prefer to have their scent on their stuff. If the bed gets dirty, wipe the spot with a sponge and mild soap and water. If it needs deeper cleaning than that (we cat owners know accidents do happen), wash by hand in cold water and lay flat—folded in half—to dry.

ABOUT BRENDA

I'd been a knitter for more than twenty years, but after spending way too many of those years knitting by myself, I decided to come out of the yarn closet in October of 2000 and form Stitch 'n Bitch Chicago (inspired by Debbie's group in New York City). Almost three years, four hundred members, and a cable access show later, the group is still going strong. The other members are by far my biggest source of inspiration and motivation. Props to my SnB homies for their input on this pattern, and love to my orange tabby Lucy for being the world's best cat bed tester.

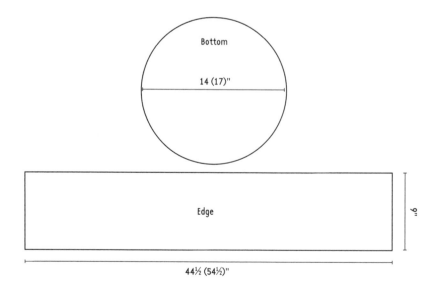

Bottom

14 (17)"

Edge

9"

44½ (54½)"

HILDA ERB AND VICKIE HOWELL
diy tote bag and patch

So you want a knitting bag but feel like you're about three decades too young to be carrying the kind they sell at your local yarn shop? You want something hip, cute, and unique that doesn't use up too much of your precious yarn money? Well, my knitting friend, why not use your craftiness to make a homemade tote with your very own patch? It's easy, it's cheap, and I promise you'll be the envy of everyone at your Stitch 'n Bitch.

See page 152

MATERIALS

FOR THE BAG

About ³/₄ yd fabric; we used Tapatio Floral 100% cotton from Reprodepot Fabrics

Sewing needle or sewing machine

Sewing thread to match fabric

Iron

Pins

FOR THE PATCH

Computer, scanner, and color printer

Iron

Computer-ready iron-on transfer paper

Piece of muslin or other light-colored fabric a bit larger than you want your patch to be

DIRECTIONS

FOR HILDA'S TOTE BAG

Cut 1 piece of fabric 16" × 31" for the bag, and 2 strips of matching or coordinating fabric, each 4½" by 25", for the handles.

You may use the pattern layout below for cutting out these pieces:

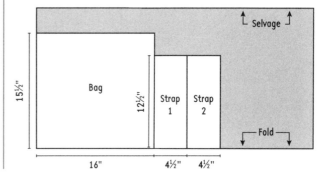

RS tog, fold the larger piece of fabric in half so that the fold forms the bottom and the bag meas 16" × 15½". Stitch up the sides using a ⅝" seam (**figure 1**).

While bag is still inside out, turn the top edge over ¼" and press. Then fold over another 1" for the hem, press down, and stitch ⅝" in from the fold (**figure 2**).

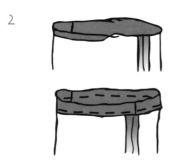

For the handles, fold the 2 smaller pieces of fabric lengthwise with RS tog. Sew a seam ⅝" in from the edge. Stitch across one end, then turn RS out to form handle. Hem the other end (**figure 3**).

To square up the bottom of the bag, turn the bag inside out, fold the side seam against the bottom seam, and stitch a 4"-long line at the bottom of the triangle (2" at center of side seam) (**figure 4**).

Attach the handles 2½" in from each side seam. Stitch a rectangle from the bottom of the trim to the top of the bag to attach the handles (**figure 5**).

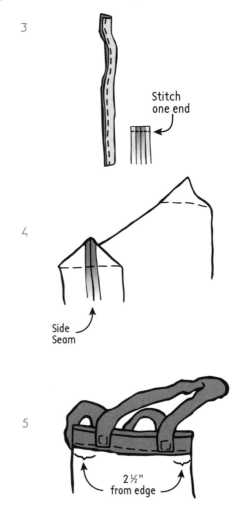

FOR VICKIE'S DIY PATCH

Using your computer, download an image that you'd like to use as your patch, or scan the artwork on page 152. If the picture has text on it, it will need to be reversed before you print it. Flip the picture horizontally using your image-editing software.

Next, print your image onto a sheet of iron-on transfer paper (you can find this at any office supply store). To do this, just open up a file in any word-processing program, and insert the image into it (in Microsoft Word, this means using "Insert Picture From File" on your tool bar). If you center the picture onto the document, you'll be sure that none of the image will be cut off during the printing process, since the transfer paper is the same size as standard letter paper.

Cut the image out, leaving about ¼" all around.

Cut out a square of light-colored cotton or muslin larger than your picture. Following the directions on the transfer paper package, iron the image onto the fabric scrap. There are two reasons to do this instead of ironing the patch directly onto the bag: (1) If the bag's fabric is not plain and light-colored, the transfer will not show up (I found this out the hard way); and (2) if something goes wrong during the ironing process, you've only ruined an inexpensive scrap of fabric and not your kick-ass knitting tote.

Once you've ironed on the transfer, cut the excess fabric off around the picture.

Finally, pin the finished patch onto the desired place on your bag. Sew it on either by machine (I recommend using the zigzag stitch for effect) or by hand, using the blanket stitch (see page 89). Voilà! You have made a knitting bag worthy of your crafty grrl self.

ABOUT HILDA *(right)*

I'm a bohemian child of the '70s. I grew up in Hollywood, where I still live today, with my boyfriend and our three kids. When I was eleven years old, I learned to knit and sew, and I spent my teenage years sewing wrap dresses, lacing inset tees, and knitting scarves from vintage linens and unraveled afghans. My passion for perusing thrift shops, sewing, and knitting has carried over into adulthood. Practicing the three has allowed me to create fun, funky, and whimsical designs.

ABOUT VICKIE *(left)*

I'm a twenty-nine-year-old mother of two and founder of an online business for hip mamas called Mamarama. I've been sewing and crocheting for years, but I didn't start knitting until early 2001, when a friend insisted that I take a class with her at a popular Los Angeles boutique. Enamored of the fabulous yarn textures and soothed by the act of knitting, I was immediately hooked. In order to meet up with other hip, funky, feminist knitters, I started an L.A.-based Stitch 'n Bitch group. Hilda and I met there and collaborated on this bag.

I moved to Austin at the end of 2002, but the L.A. Stitch 'n Bitch continues to flourish. And the Austin Stitch 'n Bitch is off to a great start.

ECHO DEVORE

roll-your-own needle case

'm into accessories, so when I began accumulating knitting needles, I wanted something to carry them in. Anything ugly, like a plastic tube or a cheap box, was out of the question. I thought about canvas paintbrush cases, but the price was too high and they weren't great-looking. Finally, I decided to visit my favorite fabric store and pick out the prettiest, funkiest, and coolest upholstery fabric I could find. My case was easy to make, and I have gotten tons of compliments on it. Now I just need more needles!

MATERIALS

³/₄ yd each of 4 different fabrics (It's a good idea to pick thick fabrics like upholstery if possible. If you can't get upholstery or don't like any, double up the fabric you do choose.) For the case shown here, I used a variety of prints from Reprodepot Fabrics.

Sewing needle or sewing machine

Sewing thread to match fabric

Iron

Pins

Fabric pencil or tailor's chalk

60" piece of ribbon for tying bag closed

DIRECTIONS

Cut your fabric as follows:

A: For the outside of the bag, cut one piece of fabric 26" wide and 17" long.

B: For the inside surface of the bag, cut one piece of fabric 26" wide and 17" long.

C: For the inside needle holder, cut one piece of fabric 26" wide and 24" long.

D: For the flap, cut one piece of fabric 26" wide and 24" long.

Take piece C and fold it in half, WS tog, so that the folded side is 26" long and the edges are 12" long. Press.

Lay piece B down, RS up, and lay piece C on top of it, with the open edge at the bottom. Line up the bottom edges of B and C. The folded edge of piece C should be about 5" from the top of piece B.

Iron them both like that, with one on top of the other, and decide where you want your needle pockets to be. Use a tape measure or a yardstick to measure lines on the top piece of fabric (C), and draw them on with tailor's chalk. These will be the lines you will follow

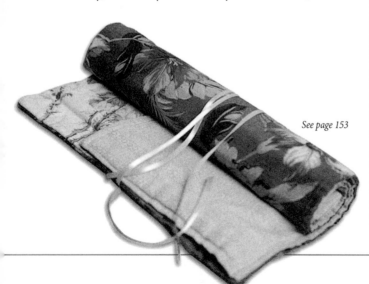

See page 153

when you stitch the pockets. Make as many pockets as you want, keeping in mind the sizes of your needles. I made some lines close together so my size 0 and 1 needles could fit comfortably without sliding around. I also made some bigger pockets for my 13s and 19s. Pin or baste pieces B and C together to keep them from slipping apart.

This is the dullest part: Sew in your pockets. Just follow the lines you drew. Okay, dull part over.

Lay piece A on top of the other piece you just sewed, RS together. (You are going to sew this all together like a pillow, so all pieces should be inside out.) Pin them together and sew a ½" seam around the edges, leaving about a 6" opening so you will be able to turn the case RS out. Turn the case RS out and iron it flat. Stitch ¼" away from the edge all around, folding in and closing up the open area as you do so.

Get out piece D. This will be your flap to protect your needles from falling out of the top of your case. Fold it in half, with RS together, so that it measures 26" × 12"; press. Sew ½" seam around the edges, leaving 6" opening for turning. Turn the flap RS out and press. Stitch ¼" all around, folding in and closing up the open area as you do so.

Line up the top edges. Put the flap on top of the innermost piece of fabric with the pockets facing up. Pin the pieces together on the top and stitch across, ¼" from the top.

Hand-stitch the ribbon to the outside of your case, centered between the top and bottom edges and about 2" in from each side. Pick up only the top layer of fabric with your needle when securing the ribbon.

ABOUT ECHO

I live in Louisville, Kentucky, and have been artsy most of my life—I've been into oil painting, sewing, and decorating. When I decided I wanted to learn to knit, I knew only that it looked hard and that it was one of my mother's favorite pastimes. But since she lived two thousand miles away, I found a local yarn shop where the ladies got me started with garter stitch and some muslin-colored wool. A few weeks later, my grandfather was put in the hospital after having a stroke. During the days and nights my family and I spent in the waiting room, I knitted and frogged the same pink acrylic scarf over and over. The knitting helped me through the stressful time, and I actually got a lot better! I love to knit, and in the last year I have made many hats, scarves, and doll stuff for my two girls. I taught my husband to knit and hope to pass the art on to my children.

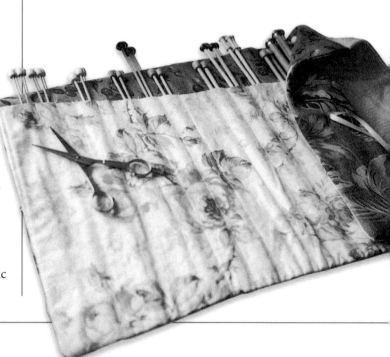

JENANNE HASSLER

circular knitting needle holder

When I started knitting again, I did it by pieces. I would buy a bag of yarn and the needles necessary for each individual project. Very reasonable, I thought. A couple dozen projects later, I realized my system was flawed. (I mean, how many sets of 10½ needles does one knitter need?) Now I wanted ways to hold and organize my sticks and circular needles. Since I'm also a quilter, I dug through my fabric stash, and soon a circular knitting needle holder was born. You too can birth one—even if you're a novice seamstress. Trust me. This is easy.

MATERIALS

¹/₂ yd each of 2 coordinating fabrics. I used Fifties Poodles and Fifties Glamour Gals Stripe (100% cotton, 45" wide) from Reprodepot Fabrics. (Your fabrics should have a simple pattern so that iron-on labels will be legible.)

Small clothes hanger

Sewing thread

Computer printer

Iron

Computer-ready iron-on transfer paper

10" piece of 2"-wide iron-on Velcro (or 2 pieces 5" long each)

Disappearing marking pen

DIRECTIONS

From each piece of fabric, cut 2 rectangles that are 22" × 7½", and two that are 2½" × 9½".

Note: All seam allowances are ⅝" unless otherwise noted.

Begin by creating your iron-on labels. Using a painting program on your computer, type your labels in a bold, large (about ½" tall) font (I used Arial Bold, size 36). Make each label 1" tall. This holder was made to hold needles from size US 000 to US 17, but you can customize your labels to suit your own needs. Now, before you print your labels, take your entire image and flip it so that the words are the mirror image of what they should be on your fabric. (Go ahead, ask me how I know. Sigh.) You may want to test-print a word and iron it on to your intended fabric near the edge (where it would fall within the ⅝" seam allowance) to see if the print is legible. Then cut the labels out and set them aside.

Take one of the two larger rectangles from the "plain" fabric and fold it in half lengthwise. Press lightly to mark this center fold. Open it back up and begin placing your labels, lining up the US on the left of the fold and the number on the right of the fold. Place the first label so that the bottom edge of the type is 1" from the bottom of your

See page 154

fabric. Each successive label is placed 1" from the bottom edge of the label below. Continue until all labels have been placed. Using your pressing cloth, iron the labeled piece lightly to remove the center fold.

Place this piece of fabric and the matching rectangle tog with RS facing. Stitch around the two sides and bottom. Trim off a bit of fabric so that when it's turned it will lie flat. Turn RS out and, using a pressing cloth, press. Set aside. Repeat the previous step with your other material.

Now it's time to put the front and the back together.

With your disappearing marking pen, mark your stitching lines on the labeled piece. You'll be stitching first at only $\frac{1}{8}$" inch from the bottom. The other stitching lines should fall exactly between the edges of each label—about 1" apart. Place the two pieces together, with bottom and side edges matching, and stitch all lines.

Now mark a line 2" above the top line of text. Cut evenly across this line. Set the holder aside.

Now we're gonna make the straps that hold this baby on your hanger. Using the smaller pieces of fabric, stitch one of each print together along three sides with RS tog, and with only a $\frac{1}{4}$" seam allowance. Clip corners; turn RS out. Press.

Grab the needle holder again. Turn the raw edge at the top under by approx $\frac{1}{2}$". Press. Insert the raw edge of the two straps so they are even with the sides of the needle holder, one on each side. Pin to hold this together while you stitch across the top opening.

Iron a 5" × 2" piece of Velcro to the back of the needle holder. To see where to place the Velcro on the straps, simply fold the straps over the top of a hanger. I used

a 2" wide, 4" long piece of Velcro and applied it to the back of each strap beginning $\frac{1}{2}$" from the bottom edge.

And now—the moment of truth! Fold the straps over your hanger, stick the Velcro together, and you have a great, personalized needle holder.

If you find, after adding more needles, that you need more support, cut 5" × $\frac{1}{2}$" pieces of heavy poster board and slip them into each needle slot.

ABOUT JENANNE

I am a thirty-four-year-old designer, living out my dreams in the mountains of North Carolina. Together with my husband and children, I operate a successful Internet business. My days are filled with order fulfillment, home-educating my two children, and pursuing my love of all things crafty. I first succumbed to the creative bug as a child, crafting art from scraps of wood and fibers, and later, when my high school English teacher (thank you, Mrs. Maples) taught me to weave baskets and encouraged me to sell them. From there, I've played with quilting, needlework, dyeing, and even stained glass. These days, I mostly knit.

resources

A Stitch 'n Bitch Guide to Yarn Stores

I asked some Stitch 'n Bitchers to recommend their favorite yarn stores. The consensus was that the best yarn stores offer more than good selection (though that's always important)—they also create a sense of community and make you feel like knitting matters.

If you can't find a yarn store in your area, www.knitting.about.com and www.woolworks.org have listings for hundreds of yarn stores in the U.S. and beyond. If you find any terrific stores, please send me their names, addresses, and a brief description of them, so I can include them in any future editions.

Write to:
STITCH 'N BITCH: THE
KNITTER'S HANDBOOK
c/o Workman Publishing
708 Broadway
New York, NY 10003-9555

ATLANTA, GEORGIA
Neases Needlework
345 West Ponce de Leon
Avenue
Decatur, GA 30030
404-377-6875
www.neasesneedlework.com

The woman who owns and runs Neases will sit down and help anyone with his or her knitting needs, and she carries a great selection of yarn including Manos del Uruguay (my favorite), which is made by a collective of women abroad. Neases also holds silent auctions to raise money for charity.
Mahsa Yazdy

AUSTIN, TEXAS
Hill Country Weavers
1701 South Congress
Austin, TX 78767
512-707-7396
Don't let the country-folk-sounding name scare you off. This is actually a fairly hip little cottage with a decent variety of yarns. I'm from L.A., where there tends to be a little bit of knitting snobbery in some of the shops. You won't find that here! *Vickie Howell*

BOONVILLE, INDIANA
The Village Knitter
8A West Jennings
Newburgh, IN 47630
812-842-2360
Docia, the owner, is very knowledgeable, is always willing to help, will order anything she can get from suppliers, and will even carry lines that you suggest.
Chris Behme

BOSTON, MASSACHUSETTS
A Good Yarn
4 Station Street
Brookline, MA 02446
617-731-4900
A colorful shop with reasonably priced yarns and a welcoming feel. The owner, Beverly, really takes the time to help you with projects and has a big table where people are always working on things.
Amy Corveleyn

Mind's Eye Yarns
22 White Street
Cambridge, MA 02140
617-354-7253
The owner, Lucy, carries mostly natural-fiber yarns. She even stocks some of her own hand-spun yarns, and she spins in the store. The atmosphere is cozy, and even though the shop is small, it never feels overcrowded. Lucy's a good teacher and a fabulous enabler!
Dyana Fine

Windsor Button
35 Temple Place
Boston, MA 02111-1305
617-482-4969
Charming in a quirky, anti-yuppie way, Windsor Button has an interesting vibe, and it's located right off the Common in a forgotten block near wig shops and an antique bookseller. It's an old button and sewing shop that has

expanded its yarn selection by leaps and bounds. *Aimee Dawson*

Woolcott and Company
61 JFK Street
Cambridge, MA 02138
617-547-2837
www.woolcottandco.com
Next door to the Redline Bar (where a Stitch 'n Bitch is held weekly), Woolcott and Company focuses on natural fibers but also carries some novelty yarns. The people who work there are obsessive about knitting, and the wool overflows from the shelves. Knitters like to stop by and show off what they've made. *Jessica Marcus*

BURLINGTON, VERMONT, AREA
Kaleidoscope Yarns
15 Pearl Street
Essex Junction, VT 05452
802-288-9200
www.kaleidoscopeyarns.com
Just outside Burlington, this store is an embarrassment of riches. Beautiful custom yarns and a huge selection of knitting supplies make this a favorite in the area.
Rebecca Schiff

CHICAGO, ILLINOIS
Arcadia Knitting
1211 West Balmoral Avenue
Chicago, IL 60640-1308
773-293-1211
www.arcadiaknitting.com

In the lovely Andersonville neighborhood on Chicago's North Side, Arcadia is owned by two delightfully quirky sisters. They have lovely yarn. Also, they spend time with you if you need help or advice trying to figure things out. My favorite part of the store is their clearance bin, where all yarns are only $4. *Jennifer Mindel*

Knitting Workshop
2218 North Lincoln Avenue
Chicago, IL 60640
773-929-5776
Knitting Workshop carries lots of designer yarns as well as good old standards. This shop has more books than other city shops and displays projects that inspire you to knit. Shop owner Mary offers classes as well as a weekly knit night. *Michele Cullom*

COLORADO SPRINGS, COLORADO
Green Valley Knitters & Weavers Supply
2115 West Colorado Avenue
Colorado Springs, CO 80904-3305
719-448-9963
800-457-8559
This store is absolutely fabulous! It's not big, but very cozy. The class schedule is excellent, and the owners are kind and down-to-earth. They even have a shop dog and shop-dog-in-training.
Melanie Wallace

EDMONTON, CANADA
Knit & Purl
10412 124th Street
Edmonton, AB T5N 1R5
780-482-2150
Knit & Purl carries a wide variety of domestic and international yarns in all price ranges and has great novelty yarns. The staff will help you customize your garment so that it is a "one-of-a-kind" piece. Or if a pattern doesn't fit, they will adjust it for your body type.
Penny Erickson

LAWRENCE, KANSAS
Yarn Barn
930 Massachusetts
Lawrence, KS 66044
785-842-4333
Yarn Barn has a great selection, and the staff are quick to adopt new things. They also stock weaving yarns, fleece, looms, and spinning wheels. I am glad it's such a ways away from me, or I'd be spending more money there than I already do.
Roberta Bragg

LONG BEACH, CALIFORNIA
Alamitos Bay Yarn Company
174 Marina Drive
Long Beach, CA 90803
562-799-8484
www.yarncompany.com
This store has a very helpful staff, a beautiful selection, and even a birthday club. *Tina Paredes*

LOS ANGELES, CALIFORNIA
Knit Cafe
8441 Melrose Avenue
Los Angeles, CA 90069
323-658-5648
Susan Mischner's brightly colored store is much more than a place to purchase yarn and needles. Knit Cafe is also a cozy hangout, a favorite for those in the entertainment industry who want to knit in the company of others and talk shop. *Julia Rubin*

Suss Designs
7354 Beverly Boulevard
Los Angeles, CA 90036
312-954-9637
Their selection is yummy and still competitively priced, and all the yarns are swatched (which really gives you a taste of what these yarns will do). The finished articles around the store are incredibly inspiring. Suss also has her own line of easy and hip patterns.
Hilda Erb

MIDDLETOWN, RHODE ISLAND
Knitting Traditions and More
1077 Aquidneck Avenue
Middletown, RI 02842
401-847-2373
Recently redesigned, with a big sign boasting "the largest scarf bar in New England," this yarn and bead shop is owned by a handful of women who really love to knit. They encourage you to come in and touch everything.
Rubi McGrory

MINNEAPOLIS, MINNESOTA
Needlework Unlimited
3006 West 50th Street
Minneapolis, MN 55410
612-925-2454
888-925-2454
www.needleworkunlimited.com
The staff in this cozy shop is quintessential Minnesota Nice. They are widely respected for their fiber and stitching expertise as well as for their willingness to aid and teach knitters of all levels. Their wonderful selection of knitting inventory also includes supplies for crocheting and tatting (a Scandinavian tradition). They have a frequent buyer program that makes me feel a bit less guilty about indulging my knitting obsession. *Susan Devoe*

MONTREAL, CANADA
Magasin de Fibre L. B. Inc.: La Bobineuse de Laine
2270 Mont-Royal East
Montreal, QC H2H 1K6
514-521-9000
Here they sell yarn by the pound and they'll spool together a selection of different fibers from their vast assortment for you. The staff is really warm and the prices are super-cheap.
Alanna Lynch

NEW YORK, NEW YORK
Downtown Yarns
45 Avenue A
New York, NY 10009
212-995-5991
This shop is like a little piece of western Massachusetts snuggled up in the East Village. They don't have a compost heap out back, but they do have a terrific selection of yarns in different price ranges and an adorable dog who will wag his tail for free. *Susanna Goldfinger*

Knitting Hands
398 Atlantic Avenue
Brooklyn, NY 11217
718-858-5648

This place *rocks!* It's one of the many reasons to go to Brooklyn. They have both high- and low-end yarns—*and* good karma.

Kathleen Woodberry

Knitting Salon
8 Windsor Place
Brooklyn, NY 11218
718-499-0135
718-499-2782
This store offers a touch of the spiritual: The owner, Prophet, hosts silent meditation and needle-work sessions as well as unraveling parties. After all, as the true knitter knows, it's the process, not the product.

RS

P&S Fabrics Corps
355 Broadway
New York, NY 10013
212-226-1534
866-740-0316
www.psfabrics.com
Not just a knitting store, but a cheap-yarn bonanza. Lots of Lion Brand (some of the best prices around), Red Heart, and other brands. They also stock Patons booklets, books, needles, and supplies.

Olugbemisola Amusashonubi-Perkovich

Purl
137 Sullivan Street
New York, NY 10012
212-420-8796
The walls are painted a soothing mint green and the floor-to-ceiling shelves hold a rainbow assortment of mostly luxury yarns. Purl's SoHo location makes it the prime desti-

nation for crafty fashionistas, and the women who work there are hip and friendly. *Susanna Goldfinger*

School Products Co., Inc.
1201 Broadway
New York, NY 10001
www.schoolproducts.com
212-679-3516
If you're from out of town, this should be the first yarn store you visit in NYC. In addition to some of the usual suspects, you'll find cheap cones of mohair, angora, cashmere, and other specialty yarns left over from designer knitwear factories. Only in New York, kids, only in New York.

DS

Seaport Yarn
135 William Street, near Fulton
New York, NY 10038
212-608-3100
www.seaportyarn.com
It might not look like much from the outside, but once inside the store, you won't be disappointed. There are several rooms of yarn, everything from Artful Yarns to Adrienne Vittadini, and the prices are the lowest in the city.

Elaine Hamilton

The Yarn Company
2274 Broadway, 2nd floor
New York, NY 10024
212-787-7878
888-YARNCO1
www.theyarnco.com
The Yarn Company carries a wide selection of imported and hand-dyed yarns and a large variety of

patterns. The staff are very helpful and welcome you to come in, take a seat, and knit, knit, knit.

Kathleen Woodberry

Unique Knitkraft
257 West 39th Street
New York, NY 10018
212-840-6950
www.BUTTONS.TV
Unique Knitkraft carries lots of European and Asian yarns and some Patons at great prices. You'll be able to pick up a nice surprise every time you visit.

Olugbemisola Amusashonubi-Perkovich

PHILADELPHIA, PENNSYLVANIA
Sophie's Yarns
918 Pine Street
Philadelphia, PA 19107
215-925-KNIT
Sophie's Yarns recently moved to a sunny, roomy shop with gorgeous yarns and books, all beautifully displayed. They host regular classes and knitting circles. I always feel welcome, even if I'm just browsing.   *Kitty Schmidt*

SAN FRANCISCO, CALIFORNIA
ImagiKnit
3897 18th Street
San Francisco, CA 94114
415-621-6642
www.imagiknit.com
A cozy, well-stocked, and very inviting shop. ImagiKnit is the kind of place that you want to visit just because the atmosphere is so

nice. One can get lost just handling the yarns, flipping through the books and patterns, or sitting in the back and working out the latest trouble spot with a friendly staff member.   *Michael Cooper*

SEATTLE, WASHINGTON
Hilltop Yarn
2224 Queen Anne Avenue North
Seattle, WA 98109
206-282-1332
www.hilltopyarn.com
Beautiful yarn, personal service, and expert instruction and advice can be found in this warm, elegantly restored Craftsman-style home in the Queen Anne shopping district.   *Jennifer Hill*

WASHINGTON, D.C., AREA
Knit and Stitch=Bliss
4706 Bethesda Avenue
Bethesda, MD 20814
301-652-7194
www.knitandstitch.com
A large yarn and needlepoint shop that carries hand-dyed and hand-painted yarns. The staff is sweet and enthusiastic, and they also donate yarns to worthy causes.

Michelle Strange

Springwater Fiber Workshop
808 North Fairfax Street
Alexandria, VA 22314-1703
703-549-3634
www.springwaterfiber.org
A nonprofit organization with an emphasis on natural fibers and

reasonably priced yarns, this small shop is crammed with colorful choices. It hosts a weekly spinning group, a knitting group, and a summer fiber camp for kids.

Michelle Strange

Woolwinders
404 King Farm Boulevard
Rockville, MD 20850
240-632-YARN
www.woolwinders.com
A new and wonderful shop, jam-packed with items and yarns I see nowhere else. The owner is incred-ibly welcoming to new knitters and has been very supportive of my Stitch 'n Bitch group.

Kristie Taylor

WICKFORD, RHODE ISLAND
And the Beadz Go On
14 Phillips Street
Wickford, RI 02852
401-268-3899
Set in an older storefront on the main street of a charming old port town, this store is expensive but on the cutting edge of yarn trends.

Lindsay Woodel

WOODMERE, OHIO
The Knitting Room
28450 Chagrin Boulevard
Woodmere, OH 44122
216-464-8450
The selection here is fabulous; you can find delicious yarn at any price, the women are wonderful and helpful, and the samples on display make you want to knit.

Marne Loveman

RESOURCES: YARN SUPPLIERS

Here are the names and addresses of the companies that sell the yarn featured in the patterns in this book.

Blue Sky Alpacas, Inc.
P.O. Box 387
St. Francis, MN 55070
888-460-8862
www.blueskyalpacas.com

Brown Sheep Yarn Company
100662 County Road 16
Mitchell, NE 69357
www.brownsheep.com

Classic Elite Yarns
300 Jackson Street
Lowell, MA 01854

Halcyon Yarn
12 School Street
Bath, ME 04530
800-341-0282
www.halcyonyarn.com

K1C2
2220 Eastman Avenue
Suite 106
Ventura, CA 93003
www.k1c2@ix.netcom.com

Knitting Fever, Inc.
(Distributes Jo Sharp,
    Gedifra, Noro, Katia)
35 Debevoise Avenue
Roosevelt, NY 11575
www.knittingfever.com

Karabella Yarns
1201 Broadway
New York, NY 10001
800-550-0898
www.karabellayarns.com

Koigu Wool Designs
RR#1
Williamsford, ON N0H 2V0
Canada
888-765-WOOL
www.koigu.com

Lion Brand Yarn
34 West 15th Street
New York, NY 10011
800-258-YARN
www.lionbrand.com

Muench Yarns, Inc.
(Distributes GGH)
285 Bel Marin Keys
Boulevard #8
Novato, CA 94949
www.muenchyarns.com

Patons
P.O. Box 40
Listowel, ON N4W 3H3
Canada
www.patonsyarns.com

Tahki • Stacy Charles, Inc.
8000 Cooper Avenue
Building 1
Glendale, NY 11385
800-338-YARN

Trendsetter Yarns
16745 Saticoy Street #101
Van Nuys, CA 91406
818-780-5497

Unique Kolours
(Distributes Mission Falls)
1428 Oak Lane
Downington, PA 19335
800-25-2DYE4
www.uniquekolours.com

Westminster Fibers
(Distributes Rowan)
4 Towndsend West, Suite 8
Nashua, NH 03063
www.knitrowan.com

ETC.

Artbeads
1-866-715-BEAD
www.artbeads.com

Cochenille Design Studio
P.O. Box 234276
Encinitas, CA 92023-4276
1-858-259-1698
www.cochenille.com

Reprodepot Fabrics
917 SW 152nd Street
Burien, WA 98166
www.reprodepotfabrics.com

credits

Special thanks to the following for allowing us the use of their locations: Alphabets, Rita Bobry at Downtown Yarns, Nelson Baretto at Ene Hair Salon, Inc., and Leshko's.

Fashion photography: John Dolan
Styling: Ellen Silverstein
Hair and makeup: Amy Schiappa

Cover
Cowgirl cover art: Design by Vickie Howell based on original art by Enoch Bolles
Author photo: Mark Mann
Hair and makeup: Wendy Brown

Back Cover
Fashion photography: John Dolan

PHOTO CREDITS: p. 2 Hulton/Getty Images; p. 12 (top) Hamburger Kunsthalle/bpk Foto: Elke Walford, (bottom) Chicago Historical Society (negative-DN-0069431); p. 13 (top) Library of Congress, Prints & Photographs Division, WWI Posters, (reproduction number, LC-USZC4-9645), (bottom) Janet Vicario; p. 46 Chicago Historical Society (negative-DN-0069140); p. 59 Chris Craymer/Getty Images; p. 72 Chicago Historical Society (negative-DN-0069345); p. 102 Bettmann/Corbis; p. 112 photo courtesy Cincinnati Museum Center. Still lifes and miscellaneous black-and-whites: Michael Fusco.

FASHION CREDITS: p. 123 Screaming Mimi's: leather jacket & parka, Ellen Silverstein: vintage coat; p. 125 McGinn: "opium dress"; p. 127 Urban Outfitters: sweaters; p. 129 (right) Screaming Mimi's: coat; p. 132 Screaming Mimi's: dresses; p. 133 (right) Screaming Mimi's: shirt; p. 137 H&M: denim skirt, Free People (Urban Outfitters Wholesale): tan sweater, Goorin: red cap, Girbaud: tan skirt; p. 141 Super Lucky Cat: skirt; p. 144 Goorin: hat, ABS: skirt; p. 146 Screaming Mimi's: shirt; p. 148 Living Doll: hat, Hue/Hotsocks: socks.